Social Change
and the Aged

Social Change and the Aged

**Recent Trends
in the United States**

Fred C. Pampel
The University of Iowa

LexingtonBooks
D.C. Heath and Company
Lexington, Massachusetts
Toronto

Library of Congress Cataloging in Publicaton Data

Pampel, Fred C
   Social change and the aged.
   Bibliography: p.
   Includes index.

   1. Aged—United States—Social conditions. 2. Aged—United
States—Economic conditions.
   I. Title.
   HQ1064.U5P27   305.2'6'0973   79-4752
   ISBN 0-669-02928-9

International Standard Book Number: 0-669-02928-9

Library of Congress Catalog Card Number: 79-4752

To Vicky

Contents

List of Figures

List of Tables

Preface

This book describes and analyzes changes in several indicators of the social conditions of the aged population in the United States over the last three decades. It focuses on changes in the position of the aged in postindustrial society rather than on the long-standing debate over the harmful effects of industrialization on the aged. The extent of changes in labor-force participation, income, living arrangements, financial satisfaction, education, occupational prestige, and health are described. In addition, the determinants of the changes are analyzed. Special attention is paid to the influence of changes in the compositional characteristics of the aged population and of changes in the process of aging on the position of the aged. In contrast to much previous research on aging, the analysis here examines aged females and nonwhites as well as the more commonly studied white males.

The approach is based on several assumptions about the social importance of age set forth in the work of Riley, Johnson, and Foner (1972) on the sociology of age stratification. They argue that age is a structural element of social organization—much like class, race, and sex—that forms a basis for structured social inequality. Age stratifies persons not only on the basis of physical or biological differences but also on the normative expectations for role performances and the allocation of rewards. The behavior of aging individuals, therefore, reflects this stratification and needs to be studied from a structural perspective. Furthermore, the sociology of age stratification argues that aging must be studied in the context of social change. The characteristics of age groups at any one time are affected by the processes of aging and cohort replacement. The effects of these processes on the social position of the aged can be separated only by comparison of data at several time points. Thus this research takes the perspective of the sociology of age stratification by focusing on the macro, structural-level determinants of individual behavior over a time span of thirty years.

This book can also be seen as part of the growing literature on social indicators (Land and Spillerman 1975). Early suggestions that social indicators measure the quality of life of the nation (U.S. Department of Health, Education, and Welfare 1969) have been replaced by a more broadly designed conception of social indicators as measures of social conditions that demonstrate some relationship to social change (Land 1975). It is hard to show that all the indicators studied here measure quality of life because there is often no consensus on what quality means. But this book does follow the suggestion of the more recent social-indicators literature in that it studies changes in the social conditions of one group—the aged.

A major contribution of this book will be to examine the effects of social change on the aged at both the individual and aggregate level of analysis. This will be done through the use of aggregate time-series data and individual-level consecutive cross-sectional surveys. The time-series data are based on variables measured as averages or summaries for the total aged population during a specified time period—in this case, one year. Thus the data are aggregated and summarize macrolevel characteristics of the aged. The second type of data measures characteristics of individuals at several time points by combining separate cross-sectional surveys that have identical measures of most variables. Although the same persons are not reinterviewed in the surveys, the consecutive random samples can be used to describe characteristics both of the total aged population and of individual aged persons at different time points. Both types of data are used to describe the trends in the position of the aged and to analyze causes of the trends.

The book is intended for an audience interested in stratification, demography, and social change, as well as in aging. Most of the issues treated, however, are analyzed using multivariate methods. The details of the text, therefore, are addressed primarily to researchers actively involved in multivariate quantitative analysis. I have attempted to present the substantive problems in the chapter introductions and the results in the chapter summaries in ways that can be understood by nonmethodologists. Of course, the crux of the book, and the basis of the conclusions, is in the detailed analysis contained in the text of the chapters.

Acknowledgments

My initial research on this topic was supported by grants from the National Science Foundation (#SOC76-15266) and the Department of Health, Education, and Welfare, Administration on Aging (#OHD/90-A-793). The final analysis and writing of the manuscript were supported by the Department of Sociology and the Graduate College at the University of Iowa, which also provided computer funds for the analysis. Summer support and computer funds for 1978 were provided by the Midwest Council for Social Research on Aging.

A large number of colleagues helped me in completing and improving the manuscript. I appreciate the help of Kenneth Land, Marcus Felson, Joan Huber, Robert Schoen, and John van Es in developing the problem and the approach to the research here. Several of my colleagues at the University of Iowa were helpful during later stages of the research. James Price, Robert Szafran, Jane Weiss, Charles Mueller, Hallowell Pope, Jay Teachman, and Karen Polonko commented on all or part of the manuscript. I greatly appreciate their assistance. I also benefited from presentation of some of the materials in the book at seminars of the Midwest Council for Social Research on Aging, on which I was a postdoctoral fellow from 1977 to 1978. Finally, I would like to thank my wife, Vicky, for her support of my work throughout the project.

The data were made available in part by the Inter-University Consortium for Political and Social Research and the University of Iowa Laboratory for Political Research and were collected by the Center for Political Studies of the Institute for Social Research, University of Michigan. Jim Grifhorst, John Kolp, and Chia-Hsing Lu of the Laboratory for Political Research assisted in creation of the data files used in the research. Neither the original sources or collectors of the data nor the Consortium bear any responsibility for the analyses or interpretations presented here.

1 Introduction

Problem

Growing old is a social problem. Older persons are disadvantaged relative to younger persons in their labor-force participation, income, family relationships, education, housing, health, personal contacts, and social participation. Although it is questionable whether the aged constitute a minority group, many minority-group characteristics describe the aged: old people are subject to economic disadvantage, negative stereotypes, and social discrimination. It remains to be seen whether a subculture or group consciousness develops (Rose 1965), but dissatisfaction with the position of the aged has been apparent for some time in the growth of protest-based organizations such as the Gray Panthers, and such publicity about the plight of older persons as the award winning book, *Why Survive: Being Old in America* (Butler 1975).

It has been commonly accepted that not only are the aged disadvantaged, but also that the disadvantage has increased in recent decades. Trends such as migration to urban areas, aging of the population, the decline in self-employment, inflation, mandatory retirement, and changes in the composition and functions of the family were thought to have brought social isolation, forced retirement, low income, and financial dissatisfaction to the aged. As Rosow (1965, p. 23) stated, "Changes in technology, the occupational system, urbanization, residential mobility, and the family have all been harmful to old people."

This idea has a long history in sociology. Theorists and researchers have argued that modernization or industrialization—and all the changes these concepts encompass—ended the favored position the aged enjoyed in preindustrial societies. For instance, Durkheim (1947) argued that in societies with mechanical solidarity, older persons were given prestige as the upholders of tradition; in societies based on organic solidarity, however, internal migration detaches persons from the influence of their original home and the influence of the aged. Similarly, Parsons (1954) felt that the isolation of the nuclear family and the bureaucratization and industrialization of the labor force were responsible for the increased separation of the elderly from family and work roles.

The view that twentieth-century social trends have had an adverse effect on aging persons in industrialized societies takes its most exaggerated form

1

in Burgess's *Aging in Western Society* (1960). Burgess contrasts ideal types of the aged in preindustrial societies with those in industrial societies. Aged persons in industrialized societies have lost the favored position they enjoyed in the "golden age" before industrialization. This one-sided view of the preindustrial aged has been criticized by historians (Laslett 1976; Stearns 1976; Fischer 1978). But Burgess's work is useful because he provides a systematic discussion of the societal-level changes in the twentieth century that are responsible for the reduced position of the aged. To summarize briefly, Burgess argues that extended longevity increased the risk of serious illness for older persons. The growth of large, formal work organizations with mandatory-retirement rules forced more older workers into retirement. Urbanization and reduction of the functions of the family increased the proportion of older persons living alone or in institutions. Finally, extended length of life along with forced retirement, low pensions, and isolation of the family increased the likelihood of inadequate income for elderly persons.

When such arguments are applied to societies changing from industrial to postindustrial societies (Bell 1973), the position of the aged is less clear. Theoretically, as the trends negatively affecting the status of the aged—such as bureaucratization and urbanization—continue, the social conditions of the aged should continue to deteriorate. Yet some have suggested that increased normative support for leisure and retirement in postindustrial societies, along with expansion of social-welfare and pension transfer payments, have counteracted the harmful effects of other trends (Atchley 1977; Hochschild 1973). Thus the relationship between industrialization and the position of the aged may be curvilinear (Palmore and Manton 1974).

Indeed, a number of recent studies indicate that the plight of the elderly may not be as serious as once thought; many of the negative characteristics of the aged said to result from social change are based on exaggerated stereotypes that apply to only a small minority of aged persons in contemporary American society (Maddox and Wiley 1976). For instance, the results of a Harris poll (1972) show that less than 10 percent of the aged sample said that they had serious problems with loneliness, boredom, not enough friends, not enough job opportunities, and insufficient medical care. When the non-aged were questioned, they greatly overestimated the percentage of older persons suffering from these problems (O'Gorman 1980). In the area of retirement, Schulz (1976) shows that only a small proportion of workers are forced to retire at the mandatory age specified by their employer—most prefer early retirement and, once retired, adjust well to their new situation (Streib and Schneider 1972). In the area of the family, Shanas (1979) has presented evidence that the aged are not isolated or alienated from their adult children. Rather, increases in income have allowed older persons to maintain desired separate residences, which previously they were unable to do (Michael, Fuchs, and Scott 1980). Finally, in the area of income, several researchers have noted that not only has the median income of the aged risen both in current dollars and in constant dollars, but also that income relative to that among the non-aged (Palmore 1976) and relative to the national average (Torda 1972) has also increased since the 1960s.

These arguments are not made to suggest that all the aged are well off—many groups, such as widows and minorities, face severe problems. It is also not to say that the aged and the non-aged have reached equality—in most ways the aged remain relatively deprived. The evidence does suggest, however, that in one postindustrial society, the United States, social trends have not continued to reduce the position of the aged, but have sometimes advanced it. Unfortunately, the evidence has simply described the broad outlines of the trends, perhaps with some post hoc explanations but without systematic analysis of the causes of the change. Rather than focusing on the position of the aged during the transition from preindustrial to industrial society—a topic that has received much attention in the literature—this book focuses on another question raised by the literature just cited: "What changes have occurred in the social position of the aged in postindustrial America, and what explains the changes?"

Objectives

The attempt to address this question involves several more specific objectives. First, I attempt to describe systematically trends in several indicators of the aged in more detail than has been done previously. The indicators to be studied are labor-force participation, income, living arrangements, financial satisfaction, and health. In describing the trends in these indicators, several new types of data—to be described shortly—will be used along with the more traditional time series used by others to describe social change.

Second, I attempt to test alternative explanations of the changes by setting up causal models predicting the indicators of the position of the aged. The models relate changes in the characteristics of society and the aged population to the indicators of the aged. I group the large number of hypotheses to be tested in the models into two broad categories based on the distinction between compositional and processual determinants of change. Briefly, compositional explanations focus on changes in the characteristics of persons brought about by cohort replacement, or on the entrance of new persons into the aged population as they grow old and the exit of other persons out of the aged population through death. The second explanation focuses on changes in the process by which background characteristics of aged persons determine the social indicators of the aged. Details of these explanations will be presented later in this chapter after more discussion of the means by which these objectives can be reached and the significance of the effort.

I will focus on changes in the position of the aged during the transition from an industrial society to a postindustrial society in the United States. A good deal of historical research has already examined the effects of the transition from an agricultural society to an industrial society by using a variety of literary, historical, and qualitative data (Achenbaum 1978; Fischer 1978). However, analysis of higher-quality, more systematic quantitative data on changes in recent decades has been less common. Hence, the focus of this book will be on trends since World War II, a period covering some major transitions in the economy, demography, and social structure of the country and one ideally suited for testing the effect of changes in postindustrial society.

In order to study changes over time, researchers typically must depend on data gathered by others for the early periods. I, too, will have to rely on such secondary data sources. The result is that it is often hard to obtain data on the desired variables over long periods of time, even periods as recent as the last three decades. Because of this problem, I am forced to limit the research to a small number of important indicators that have been measured by others over the relatively long time span. In fact, most of the analysis will be concerned with three of the most important changes: the decline of labor-force participation, the increase in income, and the rise in nonfamilial living arrangements. Also of concern, however, will be changes in financial satisfaction and in health. I make no claim to exhaust the indicators that should be measured, but prefer to focus on those that are adequately measured over a relatively long time span. Thus it is not possible to study other variables, such as adjustment to retirement, quality of family relationships, or economic need.

Despite limitations in the scope of the indicators, they do cover many of the most important social conditions of the aged. *Labor-force participation* measures involvement in the labor force either through being employed or actively searching for employment, and taps changes in retirement rates. *Income* measures the dollar value of family and personal income of older persons, although it does not include other aspects of economic welfare such as assets and in-kind benefits. *Living arrangements* measure whether persons share a household with one or more relatives, share a household with nonfamily members, or live alone. *Financial satisfaction* measures the subjective evaluation of income. *Health* measures the number of days in which older persons face restricted activity or bed disability. (More detailed discussion of the definition and measurement of each indicator will be presented in the substantive chapters.)

Higher levels of income, financial satisfaction, and health are often taken as improvements in the quality of life of persons. Higher levels of labor-force nonparticipation and nonfamilial living arrangements, however, have mixed connotations. Early theorists, such as Burgess (1960), considered these changes harmful. More recent evidence suggests that both retirement and independent living arrangements are desired by older persons (Schulz 1976; Shanas 1979). Thus these variables describe changes in many of the most important social conditions faced by the aged. Changes in levels of income and health among the aged can be measured both relative to the non-aged and as absolute values. However, most of the focus will be on changes in the characteristics of the aged rather than on changes in the characteristics of the non-aged.

Two types of data will be used to study changes in these indicators. First, I have gathered yearly time-series data for the years 1947-1978, or for all the years in that time span for which the data are available. These data are aggregated; that is, they are variables measured over the total population of older persons, and are therefore measured at the macro sociological level. Second, I have combined sets of cross-sectional surveys that measure nearly identical variables for different samples of persons from 1952 to 1978. These cross-sectional samples of the population, in contrast to the aggregate measures of the total population, measure individual or microlevel characteristics. The combination of the consecutive surveys allow individual analysis to be combined with time-series analysis. In particular, the University of Michigan election-year studies from 1952-1978 and the 1960 and 1970 *Public Use Samples* of the censuses of population include measures of the indicators listed that have been measured nearly identically over the time span and will be used in the analysis that follows.

Despite the inability to measure all the relevant variables over the total time span, the data to be used here substantially improve on previous studies of changes in the social conditions of the aged. The typical cross-sectional study has long been known to be inadequate to the goal of explaining both changes in the status of age groups and social change in general. It is often recommended that longitudinal studies be used instead to study the process of aging. However, for examining the compositional and processual explanations mentioned earlier, most longitudinal studies are inadequate. First, many cover only a relatively short time span, usually five years or less (Parnes, Nestel, and Andrisani 1973; Irelan 1972). Second, many sample from only a small number of cohorts, and shifts in composition across cohorts cannot be examined. Compositional changes in the sample may occur from mortality or dropout, but not from differential cohort experiences or replacement. Third, longitudinal studies are often unable to separate the effects of aging from the effects of time, since persons at the same age are not examined at different time points. This is crucial in examining the effect of processual changes over time compared with the compositional effects of age.

A more common treatment of the changes in the status of the aged has been to examine aggregate data for many countries at one point in time (Palmore and Manton 1973; Cowgill and Holmes 1972). Because it is often difficult to study one country over long periods of time, an alternative has been to examine countries currently at different stages of development. Assuming that the developing countries will reproduce the patterns already found in developed countries, researchers can gauge the effects of industrialization on the status of the aged. However, because the cultural contexts of the different countries will vary, the effects of industrialization on the aged also will vary. Since the method is a shorthand attempt to represent a dynamic model within one country, the method is not as useful as is studying actual changes over time within one country. In fact, the results are equivalent only under very restrictive conditions (Firebaugh 1978).

One approach of this study, then, will be to use time-series data over a thirty-year period in one country, the United States. This avoids the assumption that different countries will follow identical paths of development. In addition, however, it is important to examine U.S. time-series data in the context of causal models. Many time-series studies of the aged have been content merely to describe the trends (Palmore and Whittington 1971; Palmore 1976). Although this can be useful initially, it is necessary to relate trends in the status of the aged to other societal trends in order to understand the causes of change and to test more precisely the theoretical explanations that have been offered. Thus a major goal of this book will be to develop macrolevel models that explain changes in the social conditions of the aged.

Several weaknesses in aggregate time-series data, however, make it necessary also to analyze individual-level data. Because the time-series data are based on summary measures, much of the individual variation in characteristics of the aged population is lost. Furthermore, when years are the units of analysis, the number of available cases is limited (the time series for 1947-1978 provides only thirty-two cases). This limits the number of explanatory variables that can be used to explain changes in the indicators. As a result, the aggregate-level relationships do not always reflect the relationships at the individual level (Langbein and Lichtman 1978). In contrast, the second data set of consecutive cross-sectional surveys allows examination of individual relationships and can be used to supplement the time-series data. Also, in the consecutive cross-sectional surveys, the number of cases is increased by treatment of time as a variable and individuals as the unit of analysis.

In summary, there has been little study of the changes in social conditions of the aged in the United States in recent decades. The literature that does exist is primarily descriptive and methodologically limited. This book, then, describes in more detail than has heretofore been done the changes in the social conditions of the aged that have taken place, and tests alternative explanations of these changes by using both time series and consecutive cross-sectional surveys. In particular, the explanations to be tested involve the effect of compositional and processual changes on the current social position of the aged. The next section expands on the explanations.

**Explanations of Improvements in the Status
of the Aged**

The distinction mentioned earlier between compositional and processual changes is conceptually useful in organizing relevant literature on improvements in the status of the aged. The following discussion presents the broad outlines of the two arguments. In the substantive chapters to follow, attempts will be made to separate the causal effects of compositional and processual changes on the status of the aged. An overview of the arguments in this section will therefore provide a means of relating the treatments of the diverse indicators in later chapters. Since presentation of the detailed predictions concerning substantive topics must await the subsequent chapters, it will be necessary to make the more general distinction here between the dependent variable, or the indicator of the position of the aged, and the determinants of the indicators, or the independent variables (of course, in substantive analyses, variables may be independent in one context and dependent in another).

Compositional Changes and Age Stratification

Given a constant relationship between the determinants and the indicator of the aged, compositional effects involve changes in the distribution of the determinants within a population. With respect to the aged as a population, compositional changes occur from two sources. First, cohort change involves the replacement of older cohorts by newer cohorts. The newer cohorts will bring new characteristics into the aged population based on their unique historical experiences. As new cohorts with different experiences and characteristics replace older cohorts, the composition of the aged population changes. This argument is based on the assumption that age groups experience historical events differently, and that these experiences permanently affect characteristics of the cohorts. Second, characteristics of the aged population may change during old age (in contrast to fixed characteristics being brought into old age). For example, retirement levels, or the labor-force composition of the aged population, is a compositional change that occurs during old age rather than being a characteristic of cohorts (such as education) that is determined before old age.[1]

Compositional explanations have a long theoretical tradition in demography, where Ryder (1965) has used the term *demographic metabolism* to describe social change resulting partly from replacement of cohorts by others with different compositions. At the same time, the empirical concern of demographers with compositional effects is shown by the use of standardization techniques that allow comparisons across populations to be made by controlling for differences in composition, or by adjusting calculations on the assumption that the population compositions are identical (Kitagawa 1964; Althauser and Wigler 1972). Most recently, techniques of regression standardization have been used to compare status differences between males and females or between blacks and whites while standardizing for differences in background characteristics (Parcel 1979; Wolf and Fligstein 1979).

The treatment of compositional changes as an explanatory principle entered into the aging field from demography through the work of Riley, Johnson, and Foner (1972) on the sociology of age stratification. In this framework, persons are divided into age strata, where the strata are assigned different roles and allocated different rewards—in other words, a system of structured age inequality exists. The position of any age group at any one time is determined partly by the processes of cohort replacement and aging. Because the level of inequality of the position of one group depends on its compositional characteristics brought about by these processes (net of environmental changes outside the system of age stratification), it is necessary to examine the position of the aged in the context of social change and compositional change.

To be more specific, several changes in the composition of the aged population have been brought about by cohort replacement. One of the most detailed statements is provided by Cain's (1967) article, "Age Status and Generational Phenomena: The New Old People in Contemporary America" [see also Foner (1975) and Neugarten and Datan (1973) for similar arguments]. Cain argues that cohorts entering old age during the 1960s and after—those cohorts born after 1900—differ qualitatively from cohorts born before 1900 and reaching old age before the 1960s. The later-born cohorts entered adulthood after World War I, the watershed event that marks America's change from a rural, agricultural society to an urban, industrial one. Although the process of change is slow, the experiences of the later cohorts were different in the more urban environment. Later cohorts had higher education, more prestigious occupations, smaller families, higher rates of female labor-force participation, and more urban residents. As a result of all these changes, later cohorts were likely to maintain a higher standing of living than previous cohorts. These advantages developed during youth and middle age were brought with the cohorts into old age and improved the status of older persons during the 1960s and

1970s. This point is further supported by Uhlenberg (1977), who finds that during the decade of the 1960s, there was a 60-percent turnover in the population aged 65 and over, with much of the turnover involving replacement of rural, less educated persons by urban, more highly educated persons.

Consider more specifically some of the major changes that have occurred across cohorts entering old age during the last several decades. According to Cain (1967), persons born in the years 1885-1889 (aged 61 to 65 in 1950) completed a median of 8.4 years of school, compared with a median of 10.7 completed by persons born from 1910-1914 (aged 61 to 65 in 1975). This two-year increase in median years of school completed across the cohorts translates into more than a 100-percent increase in high-school graduates. Rather than being determined during old age, these cohort changes are determined primarily by historical changes in the size of the educational system when the cohorts are young. Once determined, however, educational increases across cohorts are brought into old age, thereby increasing the educational composition of the aged population and affecting other social characteristics of aged persons, such as labor-force participation and income.

Similar improvements in occupational status have occurred over time in the aged population as a result of cohort replacement. Over the century, there has been a shift in the occupational structure from low-status and agricultural occupations to higher-status, white-collar occupations. Later-born cohorts who enter the labor force during times when this upgrading of the occupation prestige structure is occurring have greater opportunities for mobility than earlier-born cohorts. The higher-prestige characteristics brought into old age by the new cohorts thus raise the occupational-status characteristics of the aged population. The census data to be analyzed later in the book show that the percentage of older persons in white-collar occupations increased from 28.9 to 35.5 from 1960 to 1970 (this refers to current occupations of workers and former occupations of persons not in the labor force). Conversely, the percentage of farm managers and laborers has declined from 15.1 to 9.3.

Related to cohort differences in education and occupation are differences in rural and urban residence. According to the Survey Research Center (SRC) data to be analyzed later, the percentage of rural residents in cohorts born after 1913 is 25 points lower than the percentage in cohorts born before 1890. There has been some recent trend in migration from urban to rural areas during old age (Fuguitt and Tordella 1980), but it is not large enough to mask the decline in rural residents brought into old age during the last several decades by cohort replacement.

For women, major changes have occurred across cohorts in labor-force participation. More recently born cohorts of women have had smaller fam-

ilies and more time during middle age for work outside the family. With expansion of female-labeled service jobs (Oppenheimer 1970), opportunities
for women workers have increased and the participation rate of females has
risen (see chapter 4 for a more detailed presentation of this reasoning).
Female cohorts that enter old age in more recent years are thus better
prepared financially for widowhood or retirement.

Finally, even controlling for education, occupational status, rural
residence, and labor-force participation of females, there may be other
cohort changes that are more difficult to measure but that may affect the
composition of the aged population. For example, it can be argued that
smaller cohorts obtain income advantages during their lifetime because they
face less competition for resources from persons their own age (Spaeth
1976; Easterlin 1978). The size of cohorts entering old age during the last
decade has risen, although the rate of increase has declined in recent years
(Uhlenberg 1977). These larger, more recent cohorts may be worse off
economically, net of other variables, than the smaller, earlier cohorts. As
another example, those cohorts who entered the labor market during the
Depression of the 1930s may have been handicapped in their later educational and occupational attainment compared to earlier cohorts that obtained a foothold in the labor market during the more prosperous years
before the Depression (Elder 1974). These Depression cohorts, born approximately 1910-1919, entered old age during the 1970s and may depress
income levels of the total aged population. Although such effects are not
likely to be large, they follow theoretically from the sociology of age
stratification.

To return to the original compositional argument, there have been
changes in the characteristics of cohorts entering old age that change the
composition of the aged population. The phrase "new old" refers to better-
educated, high-prestige, urban, and higher-participation new cohorts that
have entered old age during the late 1960s and 1970s, which are contrasted to
the less modern cohorts that entered old age during the 1950s and before.
The historical causes of these cohort differences are not the focus of this
book. But they will be treated as exogenous changes that will affect more recent changes in the labor-force, income, and family status of aged persons.

Processual Changes

Without changes in the characteristics of the aged population, environmental changes may still affect the way the compositional variables are
translated into indicators of the position of the aged. Where compositional
changes refer to changes internal to the aged population, processual
changes involve changes external to the system of age stratification. For example, even if educational levels had remained constant among the aged,

income levels might still have increased to the extent that the positive effect of education on income increased. Thus the process of status determination changes.

The crucial environmental change affecting the status of the aged is the transformation of America from an industrial to a postindustrial society. Postindustrial societies, according to Bell (1973), are characterized by a technology based on theoretical rather than applied knowledge; an economy oriented toward performance of services rather than production of goods; and a stratification system based on the preeminence of the professional class. Societies that have entered this stage (primarily the United States, but also some Scandinavian countries) seem to have an aged population of higher status than do industrialized countries; hence, a curvilinear relationship between industrialism and the status of the aged may exist (Palmore and Manton 1974; Cowgill 1974). There are several ways in which changes in a postindustrial society affect the status of the aged.

First, there have been major changes in the normative support for leisure. Hochschild (1975) notes that disengagement and activity theories, which emphasize the loss of identity and self-esteem upon retirement, were developed under the belief—common in industrial societies—that work is the primary focus of activity and source of prestige for men in the United States. In postindustrial society, normative support for leisure and retirement is much stronger and the psychological consequences of retirement are not so problematic. Thus the work ethic is not as ingrained in people as it once was, and many look forward to retirement as a deserved reward that will bring enjoyment of leisure rather than loss of meaning in life.[2]

Second, the continued growth of the economy has created an economic surplus that has permitted institutionalization of retirement-income programs sponsored by the government and private organizations. Although social security initially provided support for only a small part of the aged population (Fischer 1978), it has since changed to include a large proportion of the labor force (as well as spouses, survivors, and dependents) and has increased its benefits. The progress in private pension payments has been slower, since benefits are often not adjusted for inflation and many schemes have not been financially sound. Nonetheless, there has been improvement in the proportion of workers covered and in the size of average benefits. Schulz (1976) argues that the growth of pension programs reflects bargaining of unions and management at times when age increases were prohibited by governmental controls and unions thus focused on increases in nonwage benefits. Such programs are likely to develop in societies with strong unions and a fairly high standard of living for workers. Finally, other transfer programs have developed that involve benefits for the aged poor (Old Age Assistance, Supplemental Security Income) and in-kind benefits for housing, sickness, or food. All these programs have helped to improve the status of the aged.

A third change in the environment affecting the process of growing old in postindustrial America is the growth of public-interest groups supporting the aged. Calhoun (1978) argues that groups of gerontologists, educators, social workers, and social scientists have worked to institute a new, more positive image of the elderly. In order to encourage action on behalf of the aged, experts have presented the problems of the aged in terms of lack of social opportunities rather than in terms of biological or physical disability. Their efforts have been partly responsible for the view of old age as an exciting new stage of life that allows for personal growth and development. Other groups similarly have served the interests of the aged. Social security can be seen as an attempt by politicians to deal with the problems of aging that became apparent during the Depression; and pensions were supported ideologically by business, which wanted to control labor supply. Their efforts were thus also beneficial to the aged and helped to change the environment in which aging occurred.

These changes should have some major effects on changes in the determination of status of the aged in recent years. For example, the effect of occupational position on retirement may change; the growing popularity of retirement may have narrowed the differential retirement rates of high-status and low-status workers. In the area of income, the improved context of retirement may have reduced the loss of income experienced by retirees, so that retirees are better off financially than they were previously. As for financial satisfaction, it may be that persons with the same real income are more satisfied in more recent years because they are better adjusted to retirement.

In summary, one explanation is that the position of the aged in society has changed because the characteristics of older persons are different, whereas the other is that it has changed because older persons are treated differently. These two explanations, although not mutually exclusive, are analytically and conceptually separable. Researchers and theorists have tended to accept both explanations implicitly without explicitly distinguishing the separate components involved and comparing their relative influence. This book attempts to do just that in the following chapters by applying these general arguments to a number of specific indicators.

Data and Analysis: Overview

Although a detailed description of the variables to be analyzed must be postponed until later chapters, a brief overview of the data and methods to be used can be presented here. The first source of consecutive cross-sectional surveys is the University of Michigan Survey Research Center

(SRC) election-year surveys. Eleven SRC surveys are available for the following years: 1952, 1956, 1958, 1960, 1964, 1968, 1970, 1972, 1974, 1976, and 1978. Respondents for the surveys were chosen through modified, cluster-sampling procedures of the noninstitutionalized population.[3] Because noninstitutionalized persons are not included in the sample, some of the oldest and poorest aged persons are excluded. They make up only a small proportion of the aged population—less than 5 percent—but their exclusion makes necessary the use of other data that include institutionalized persons. After adjusting for panel respondents and oversampled blacks, the total weighted N is 17,883, of which there are 1,681 males and 2,633 females aged 60 and over.[4]

The second source of cross-sectional data is the 1960 and 1970 *Public Use Samples* (PUS) of the census of population. Although the census data cover a shorter time span, they have several advantages over the SRC data. The census PUS data are based on a random, 1-in-10,000 sample of the detailed questionnaire filled out by 5 percent of the population. The total number of persons in the 1960 sample is 18,002; for 1970 the number is 20,196. The number of males over age 60 in both years is 2,237, and the number of females is 2,849. The strictly random sampling of households and persons has statistical advantages over the cluster-sampling procedures used by the SRC surveys and includes institutionalized as well as noninstitutionalized persons. Further, the census bureau has developed procedures for replacing nonresponse data (Dualabs 1973; U.S. Bureau of the Census 1972). Finally, the census data have more detailed measures of occupation, hours and weeks worked, and income than do the SRC data.

The third source of data, the aggregate time series, is more difficult to describe because the source depends on the individual variable measured. However, most of the summary measures are based on figures gathered yearly by the census bureau from the Current Population Surveys. The results of these surveys, tabulated into summary measures before they are published by the government, must be used in the form in which they are presented. These summary measures are thus based on samples and are subject to some sampling errors.

Although the ages of persons to be included in the analysis will depend on the indicator, the lower age limit will be the late fifties. Age 65 has taken on significance as the point of entrance into old age, not so much because of any change in physical abilities as because of bureaucratic rules defining the age as appropriate for mandatory retirement and for obtaining pension and social-security benefits (Cain 1974). As society becomes more bureaucratized, the social meanings attributed to chronological age become more important. Given the significance of age 65, it will be useful to examine persons who have neared that age as well as persons who have passed it. Thus including persons in their late fifties and early sixties will provide a comparison with persons over age 65 without including too many middle-aged persons. In fact, for retirement or labor-force participation, it will be necessary to include persons in their late fifties since so many retire at this age; for income, it will be necessary to use a higher cutoff age in order to avoid overestimating the income of the aged population.

It might be desirable to compare the changes in the position of the aged with those changes for the non-aged, and in several instances I have done so. But to analyze persons at all stages of the life cycle is a task too great for one study. Variations on the analysis for young persons compared with middle-aged persons compared with old persons would be enormous, and the direct comparisons would be misleading. Hence there is little treatment of persons under age 55, and the focus is on the aged themselves.

For the time-series data, the age distinctions used must correspond to those used by the publications of the census bureau. Typically, all persons over age 65 are grouped together without finer age distinctions. Thus it is necessary to use the crude age distinctions with the time-series data.

The details of the analysis will vary depending on the indicator being studied and the type of model to be estimated. Detailed discussion of the estimation techniques for the time-series data is presented in chapter 2 and for the consecutive cross-sectional data in chapter 3. Normally, the models to be studied will be recursive and therefore can be estimated using the ordinary-least-squares techniques of multiple regression. For the cross-sectional models, where a number of variables are best treated as sets of categories, the regression results will be presented in the form of multiple-classification analysis (see chapter 3). The time-series results will be presented as partial coefficients with corrections for autocorrelation when necessary (see chapter 2).

Summary and Preview

This chapter has presented several arguments. The idea that social changes brought about by industrialization and urbanization are harmful to the aged must be reconsidered when applied to changes in postindustrial America since the midtwentieth century. Recent literature on the aged suggests that the problems they face are not as serious as suggested by the industrialization thesis. It is necessary to determine exactly what changes have occurred in postindustrial society and what their causes have been. No previous study has systematically described the changes in the position of the aged over the last three decades and attempted to test various explanations of the changes.

This study is a first attempt to describe changes in a large number of indicators and to analyze the causes of the changes in the indicators using two sources of data: aggregated yearly time-series data from archival sources, and consecutive cross-sectional survey data of individuals. These data will allow more precise description of the trends than has yet been presented. They will also allow tests for the influence of two sources of change in the position of the aged: compositional changes and processual changes. Although many of the explanations of changes in the position of the aged presented in the literature can be classified as either compositional or processual arguments, this is the first study to identify empirically the relative importance of the two components.

The indicators to be studied are limited to those variables that have been consistently measured by the data sources over the last several decades. The two most important variables to be considered are labor-force participation and income. Chapter 2 begins the analysis with examination of changes in the time-series measures of these two indicators. Analysis of the macrolevel indicators of labor-force participation and income will provide a structural overview of the changes from 1947 to 1976, which can be used to provide an initial starting point to consider changes in the individual-level indicators over a shorter time span.

Chapters 3 and 4 treat the labor-force participation of aged males and females using the individual-level consecutive cross-sectional surveys. In this analysis time is treated as a variable and its effects on labor-force participation are shown by the size of its regression coefficient. Chapter 3 in particular provides a detailed presentation of the strategy of analysis to be used with the consecutive cross-sectional surveys in later chapters.

Chapter 5 combines the analysis of time-series and cross-sectional data in considering one aspect of changes in income not considered in chapter 2—inequality in the distribution of income within the aged population. The time-series data are used to describe the trends, and the cross-sectional data are used to analyze the compositional and processual determinants of the trend.

Chapters 6, 7, and 8 use the cross-sectional data to examine changes in average income levels of the aged population (compared with the spread around the average considered in chapter 5 and the time-series data on the average considered in chapter 2). Chapter 6 is limited to white males and chapter 7 to white females. In chapter 8 changes in the income levels of whites and nonwhites and of males and females are compared.

Next, chapter 9 begins the analysis of indicators that have responded to changes in income. In chapter 9, family or nonfamily living arrangements are considered. In chapter 10, changes in financial satisfaction of the aged are studied. Finally, chapter 11 presents a note on changes in health levels and their relationship to the indicators studied previously. A summary and a review of the results are then presented in the final chapter.

Notes

1. Cohort effects usually refer to historical experiences affecting the current behavior of a cohort. In the case of retirement or changes that occur during old age, cohorts may differ as a result of age interacting with period; for instance, period changes increasing the probability of retirement will affect only those cohorts reaching retirement age. If period effects vary, there will be cohort differences resulting from reaching retirement age during different periods. Hence cohort differences for this second class of factors are a combination of age and period.

2. As a processual effect, changes in attachment to the work ethic are treated as an environmental or period change affecting persons at all age groups. Such changes might also be conceptualized as cohort changes if they result from differential socialization, the effects of which are permanent. However, period changes are likely to have stronger effects on the work norms of the aged than socialization that occurred fifty or more years earlier (Atchley and Seltzer 1976).

3. Because cluster sampling rather than strictly random sampling was used, standard errors will be underestimated and tests of significance must be used conservatively (Knoke and Hout 1974).

4. In combining the eleven surveys into one file, the data were weighted to adjust for use of panel respondents from 1956 to 1960 and from 1970 to 1976; for oversampling of blacks in 1964, 1968, and 1970; and for unequal sample sizes across surveys. Once adjustments for the panel respondents and oversampled blacks were made, the surveys were weighted to the harmonic mean of all samples, 1,625.71. This provides a weighted N of 17,883, compared with the unweighted N of 17,320. Because the weights equalized the number of adults across years, the sample sizes of aged persons from year to year will vary.

2 Trends and Causes of Aggregate Labor-Force Participation and Income of the Aged Population

The literature reviewed in chapter 1 suggested that in the last several decades the decline in social conditions brought about by industrialization has been reversed. Most of the prevous literature, however, has neither systematically described the changes in the aged population in yearly detail nor attempted to analyze the causes of the changes. This chapter, then, takes a first step in describing changes in two major indicators of the aged that are closely related to the quality of the life of the aged—labor-force participation and income. Second, the chapter makes a preliminary attempt to determine the causal effects of other structural, demographic, and economic changes on the two indicators. For example, the relative influences of occupational shifts from agricultural, self-employed work to work in large, bureaucratized organizations, and of the changes in public and private benefit levels on labor-force participation rates, can be considered. Similarly, the ability of increases in pension benefits to counteract loss of income from reduced labor-force participation can be examined.

These issues will be addressed using aggregate time-series data for the years from 1947 to 1976. As discussed in chapter 1, aggregate data hide much of the individual variation in the indicators and allow the use of only a small number of predictors. Yet there are several advantages of using such data as a starting point for the studies in this book. First, the time span for the time-series data is longer than for the consecutive cross-sectional survey data. Second, the focus of the time-series analysis is on the behavior of the aged as a group and therefore provides a structural, macro perspective from which the behavior of individuals to be studied later can be viewed. Some of the predictors to be examined in this chapter, such as national economic conditions or national expenditures for private and public pension programs, can best be measured at the aggregate level. Thus the next section describes the trends in labor-force participation and income; the section after that presents the macrolevel analysis of the causes of the trends.

Parts of this chapter appeared in Fred C. Pampel, "Changes in the Labor Force Participation and Income of the Aged in the United States," *Social Problems* 27, no. 2 (December 1979):125-142. Used with permission.

Trends in Labor-Force Participation and Income

The Current Population Survey, which provides the time-series data to be examined, measures labor-force participation rather than retirement. Labor-force participation is defined as involvement in the labor force, through either being currently employed or actively searching for employment, as a percentage of the noninstitutionalized population within the specified age range; nonparticipation refers to those not working and not having looked for work in sixty days. Retirement, by contrast, involves less than full-time, full-year employment and reception of income from a retirement pension earned from years of previous employment (Atchley 1976). For older men, most labor-nonparticipants are retired. As exceptions, some men out of the labor force and not receiving a pension may be planning to reenter rather than retire permanently; some aged men may be receiving retirement-pension benefits while they are in the labor force; and some men may have retired from full-time to part-time work while remaining in the labor force. In practice, however, the trend in labor-force partcipation will be closely related to the trend in retirement for older men—that is, the determinants will be the same for one as for the other. For older women the situation is more problematic, since women not in the labor force may be either housewives or retirees. These different types of labor-force nonparticipation will have to be considered in explaining the trend in participation. In any case, this section avoids the definitional problems of dealing with retirement and focuses on the labor-force participation of men and women aged 65 and over. Although many persons retire before age 65, the age groups used by the census bureau make it convenient to examine here only persons aged 65 and over. Labor-force participation before that age, along with other related measures of labor-force participation, will be considered with the Survey Research Center (SRC) and *Public Use Samples* (PUS) data.

Given this meaning of labor-force participation, the trends are straightforward (figure 2-1). For males, there is a steady decline from a rate of 47.8 percent in 1947 to 22.4 percent in 1974. For females, the participation rate at the older ages has fluctuated since 1947. The rate begins at 8.1 in 1947, increases to a high point of 10.8 in 1959, and declines to 8.2 in 1976. For men, the steady decline clearly indicates the important trend in retirement. But for women, the lack of change may mask changes in the proportion of nonparticipants who are housewives rather than retirees.

For income, the *Current Population Reports* (CPR) publish median income levels of persons aged 65 and over in several forms: individual personal income for males, individual personal income for females, family income, and primary individual income. The measures of personal income for males and females underestimate the income available to older persons

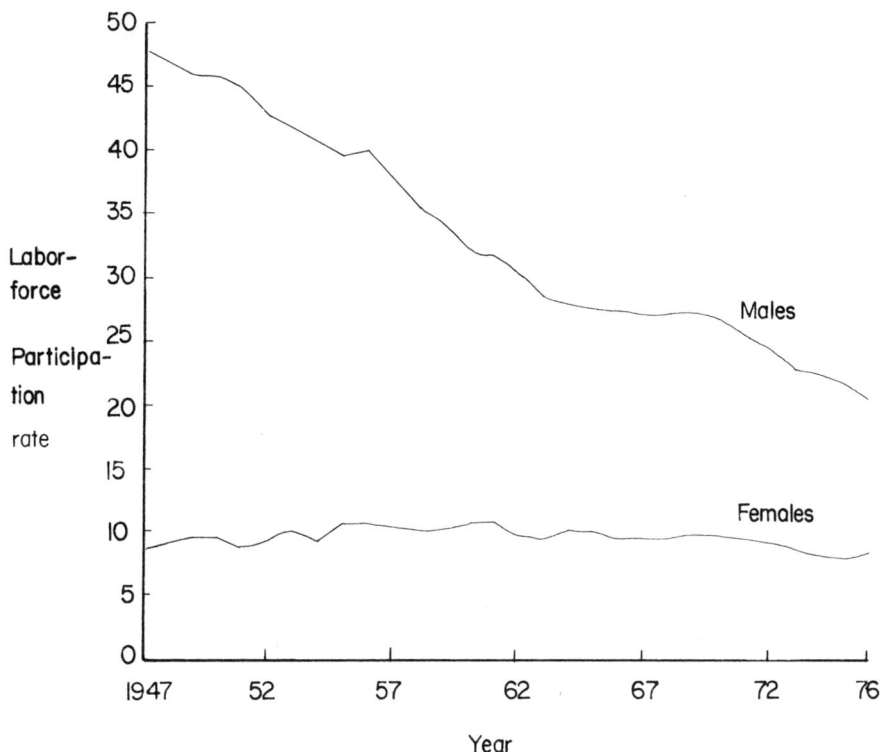

Source: Employment and Training Report of the President.
Figure 2-1. Trends over Time of the Labor-Force Participation Rate of
Males and Females Aged 65 and Over

who live with spouses or relatives but who have no income of their own. The
measure of family income is based on income of families headed by persons
65 and over; thus aged persons living with a younger head of household are
not included in the calculations. Moreover, the family and primary-
individual data do not distinguish between the incomes of females and
males. It is probably safest to look at all the measures, keeping in mind the
different meanings of each.

The CPR data, like all the income data in this book, also lack information on in-kind benefits and net worth. Moon (1977) estimates that benefits
such as Medicare, Medicaid, food stamps, and tax benefits are worth the
equivalent of 10 percent of income of the elderly. It is likely that these in-
kind transfers have increased over time at a faster rate among the aged than
among the non-aged. To the extent that this is true, improvements in the income of the aged will be underestimated, making it more difficult to accept

the hypothesis of higher levels of income among the aged over time. Similarly, wealth or assets not transferred into income are not included in the measures. Although the assets themselves are not spendable, and only a small proportion of income comes from liquidation of assets (Atchley 1976), accumulated net worth may reduce expenses and economic needs. Aged persons in particular have more time to accumulate housing, furniture, insurance, and savings that improve their economic welfare if not their income. Although it is likely that the wealth of the aged has increased over time, it is less clear whether the increases have been greater among the aged than among the non-aged. Hence it is not clear in what direction the omission of net worth biases comparisons across age groups.

The CPR present median income only for income recipients. By leaving out persons with no income, these figures overestimate actual personal income for aged men and women. I recomputed the percentile distribution of income for all age groups and all years by including persons without income and then using the new distribution to calculate the median. The family-income measures do not suffer from the same problem. However, these figures are missing for 1949 and 1953. I interpolated to obtain these values, which may reduce the fluctuation in the trend for the early periods.

Comparison of medians reflects changes only at the 50th percentile. Although these changes are theoretically important, they do not capture changes in the rest of the distribution. The problem with an alternative such as the index of net difference (Lieberson 1975) is that it is more sensitive to changes in the categories used by the Current Population Survey to classify income. Medians calculated here are not affected by creation of new categories at the upper income levels. The relationship between changes in median income of the aged and changes in the internal distribution of income among the aged is a topic that will be considered in a separate chapter.

Within these limitations, figure 2-2 presents the trends over time in current and constant dollars of the several measures of income of the aged. Despite higher income levels for families and males, and lower levels for unrelated individuals and females, the trend for all groups in current dollars is up. These increases are partly, but not completely, the result of inflation, since the trend in constant income is also up. The growth of income of the aged has especially accelerated since the mid-1960s.

To examine changes in relative income levels, figure 2-3 presents trends in the ratio of median income of males, families, and unrelated individuals 65 and over to the corresponding income of persons aged 25 to 64. The patterns here are less sharp than before. For families, the ratio declined from 1947 to 1966 and has increased since then, but has not yet returned to the high levels of the late 1940s. For unrelated individuals, the same pattern appears, except that current levels are as high as the peak in the late 1940s. For males, the decline from the late 1940s to the mid-1960s is not apparent;

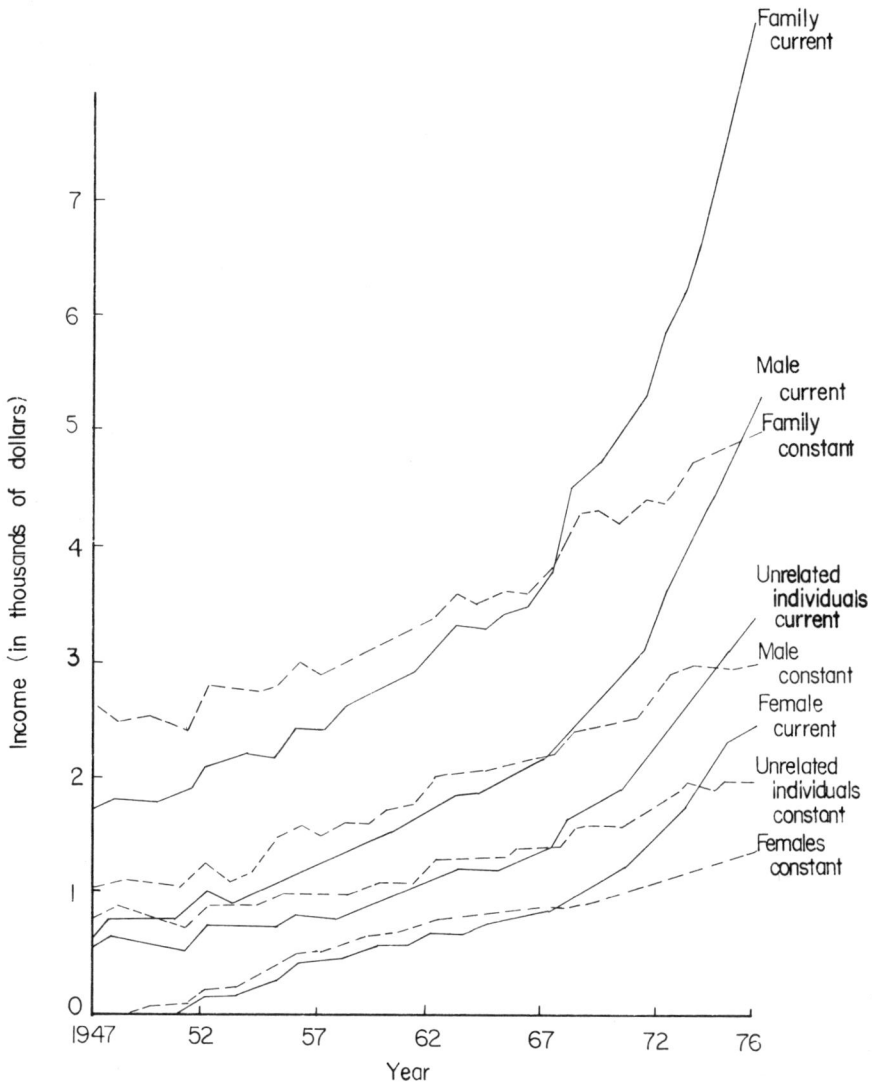

Figure 2-2. Trends over Time of Indicators of Current and Constant Income of the Aged (65 +)

rather, there has been a steady increase from the beginning of the time series. In any case, for all groups, there have been steady increases in relative income levels over the last ten years.

Depicting relative income of aged females is more difficult because the median income of females aged 25 to 64 was zero until 1960 (that is, over 50

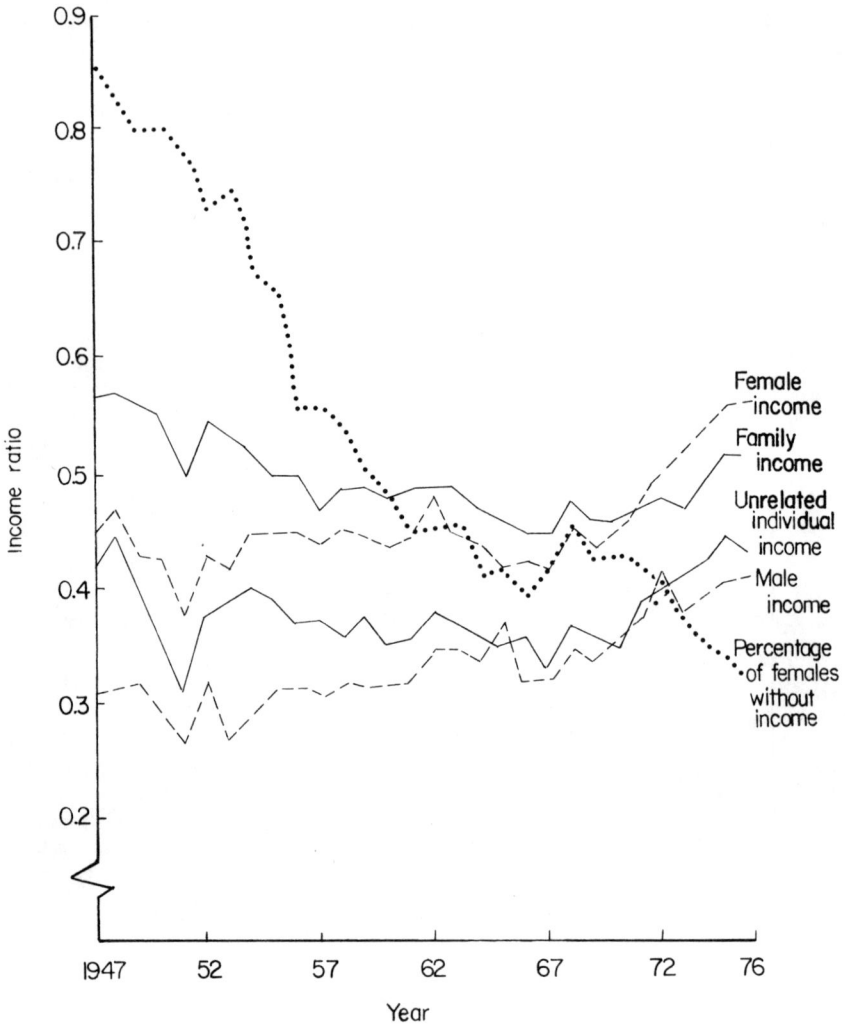

Figure 2-3. Trends over Time of Income of the Aged (65 +) over Income of
the Non-Aged (25-64)

percent had no personal income). Until that time, the ratio is either unde-
fined or zero. As an alternative, two other ratios are presented based on the
two components of median income of females: the first is the ratio of
percentage of aged females with no personal income to the percentage of
non-aged females with no income; the second is the ratio of median income
for aged females who received personal income to the median income of

non-aged females who received personal income. The trend for the ratio of females with no income shows a steady decline, indicating that the percentage of aged females with no income has declined faster than the percentage of non-aged females with no income. This change in personal income may result from an increase in older women who live alone and cannot depend on income of relatives. However, the ratio of median income of females who do receive income has also increased at a rate similar to the other ratios and reflects improvements in the position of the aged.

Determinants of the Trends

The previous section showed a decline in labor-force participation at the same time that there was an increase in absolute and relative income levels of the aged. This raises several questions about the causes of the changes. What role have increases in pension levels had on attracting persons into retirement in comparison with occupational changes that force persons into retirement? What effect has the decline in labor-force participation had on income? And have increases in pension benefits been able to counteract the loss of income that occurs with increased retirement?

The rest of this chapter will attempt to answer some of these questions through multivariate analysis of changes in labor-force participation and income. A theoretical discussion of the determinants of the trends will be followed by an analysis in which the cases are the twenty-eight years between 1947 and 1974 and the dependent variables are the sex-specific measures of labor-force participation and income. Regression analysis can be used to determine the effect of the independent variables, specified from the theoretical discussion, on the dependent variables.

Ordinary-least-squares (OLS) techniques will be used to estimate the equations under the typical error-term assumptions (Ostrom 1978). With time-series data, however, it is necessary to test for the existence of autocorrelation. In the event that the Durbin-Watson statistic does not allow acceptance of the null hypothesis of uncorrelated errors, the OLS estimates will be unbiased but inefficient and the standard errors will be underestimated. In such cases, the Cochran-Orcutt (CORC) procedure will be used to reestimate the equations. Briefly, this procedure assumes a first-order autoregressive process, estimates the first-order correlation between the errors, and uses generalized least squares to estimate the equation. (For a more detailed discussion of the techniques, see Kmenta 1971, pp. 287-289.) Thus for some of the following equations, the estimates will be from ordinary least squares, and for others from CORC techniques. The details of the tables and the variable measurement will be postponed to the analysis.

Male Labor-Force Participation

What explains the decline in male labor-force participation? The literature on work and retirement suggests that several factors have been important: long-term changes in the nature of work organizations and occupational characteristics, short-term changes in levels of retirement benefits, and fluctuations in the unemployment rate.

First, the shift from agricultural, self-employed work to industrialized, wage and salary work has affected the choices employees have concerning retirement (Sheppard 1976). With bureaucratization of work organizations, and the consequent emphasis on efficiency and productivity (Brennan, Taft, and Schupack 1967), employees are more likely to face mandatory-retirement rules based on chronological age, which limit the option to continue working (Friedman and Orbach 1974; Kasshau 1976).

Second, public and private pension systems have emerged in response to growth of an economic surplus (Atchley 1976) and the beginnings of retirement as an institutionalized role (Friedman and Orbach 1974). Theoretically, the availability of retirement income can increase retirement levels in two ways: it can have a "pull" effect, attracting workers to retirement, or it can have a "push" effect, requiring that workers retire at a specified age (Reno 1972; Palmore 1971). According to the pull argument, retirement income from pensions or other nonwork sources frees persons from work they may not find intrinsically rewarding. Although retirement income is seldom as high as preretirement wages, many persons feel that the sacrifice in wages is worth the gain in satisfaction that comes from increased leisure time (Bowen and Finegan 1969). In addition, public pensions often contain retirement-test provisions whereby benefits are reduced on the basis of earned income; continued work thus involves loss of potential retirement benefits (Boskin 1977).

It is difficult to separate the pull effects of pensions as an attraction to retirement from the push effects of mandatory-retirement provisions that go with pension programs (Reno 1972; Slavick 1966). Debate centers not on the extent of mandatory-retirement policies, but on the proportion of workers who are forced to retire despite their desire to continue working. The problem may stem from the subjective nature of the distinction between "willing" and "unwilling" mandatory retirement.[1] At the aggregate level, such distinctions are even more difficult to analyze empirically. In any case, although I am unable to separate empirically that proportion of the effect caused by push factors from that caused by pull factors, I hypothesize that growth of public and private pension benefits will reduce labor-force participation of aged males.[2]

A third determinant of the participation of aged males is the unemployment rate. Rosenblum (1975) has found that discouraged workers—those persons who drop out of the labor force after unsuccessful job searches—are most common at older ages. Older workers are less likely to become unemployed; but once they lose a job, they have more difficulty finding another (Riley and Foner 1968). Hence the higher the unemployment rate among the aged, the lower the participation. As a determinant of labor-force participation, unemployment may also capture changes in other variables, such as wages or hours worked related to the demand for workers.

The effect of these variables on participation of males aged 65 and over (MLFP65+) is shown in equations 1.1 and 1.2 in table 2-1. Percentage of the labor force employed in agriculture measures changes from home employment to organizational employment (Moore 1966). Pension and social-security benefits are measured as the ratio of average benefits to disposable income per capita for the total population. These two variables can be interpreted as replacement rates of retirement income relative to spendable income or the standard of living (Schulz 1976). Finally, the age- and sex-specific unemployment rate is included. The details of the measurement are presented in a footnote to table 2-1.

Table 2-1
Unstandardized Regression Coefficients and T-Ratios for Models of Labor-Force-Participation Rates of Aged Males and Females

(1.1) $\quad$ $\text{MLFP}_t^{65+} = \quad +34.62 + 3.00\%\text{AGLF}_t \quad - \quad 19.42\text{PENRR}_t \quad - \quad 23.57\text{SSRR}_t \quad - \quad 1.04\text{MUNR}_t^{65+}$
$\qquad\qquad\qquad\qquad (4.63)\ (23.27) \qquad\qquad (2.29) \qquad\qquad (2.20) \qquad\qquad (3.80)$

$\quad \bar{R}^2 = 0.982 \qquad\qquad \text{SEE} = 1.047 \qquad\qquad df = 22 \qquad\qquad \text{DW} = 1.270$

(1.2)[a] $\quad$ $\text{MLFP}_t^{65+} = \quad 20.64 + 2.71\%\text{AGLF}_t \quad + \quad 2.28\text{PENRR}_t \quad - \quad 16.60\text{SSRR}_t \quad - \quad 0.50\text{MUNR}_t^{65+}$
$\qquad\qquad\qquad\qquad (2.49)\ (11.38) \qquad\qquad (0.27) \qquad\qquad (1.37) \qquad\qquad (2.05)$

$\quad \bar{R}^2 = 0.980 \qquad\qquad \text{SEE} = 0.870 \qquad\qquad df = 21 \qquad\qquad \text{DW} = 1.718$

(1.3) $\quad$ $\text{FLFP}_t^{65+} = \quad -11.01 + 0.81\%\text{AGLF}_t \quad - \quad 3.12\text{CPEXB}_t \quad - \quad 5.14\text{CSSEXB}_t \quad + \quad 9.97\text{CWAGE}_t$
$\qquad\qquad\qquad\qquad (1.99)\ (3.98) \qquad\qquad (3.13) \qquad\qquad (5.54) \qquad\qquad (5.50)$

$\quad \bar{R}^2 = 0.628 \qquad\qquad \text{SEE} = 0.387 \qquad\qquad df = 22 \qquad\qquad \text{DW} = 2.123$

Note: Variables are defined as follows: MLFP^{65+} = monthly average of number of males aged 65 + in the civilian labor force as a percentage of the civilian, male non-institutionalized population aged 65 +; %AGLF = percentage of the civilian labor force employed in agricultural, hunting, or fishing industries; PENRR = expenditures of private pension and deferred profit-sharing plans per beneficiary as a proportion of national disposable income per capita; SSRR = expenditures of OASDHI, railroad, federal, state, and local retirement programs per beneficiary as a proportion of national disposable income per capita; MUNR65 + = monthly average of the number of unemployed males aged 65 + as a percentage of the male civilian labor force aged 65 +; FLFP65 + = monthly average of the number of females aged 65 + in the civilian labor force as a percentage of the female civilian noninstitutionalized population aged 65 +; CWAGE = average hourly wage in 1967 dollars for production and nonsupervisory workers on private payrolls; CPEXB = expenditures of private pensions and deferred profit-sharing plans in thousands of constant dollars per beneficiary; CSSEXB = expenditures of OASDHI, railroad, federal, state, and local retirement programs in thousands of constant dollars per beneficiary.
[a]CORC estimates.

Two versions of the MLFP65 + equation are presented—one with OLS estimates (equation 1.1), the other with CORC estimates (equation 1.2). For both equations, the table presents the unstandardized regression coefficients in parentheses.[3] The other information included is the r-squared adjusted for degrees of freedom, the standard error of estimate, the degrees of freedom, and the Durbin-Watson statistic to be evaluated at the .05 level with a two-tailed test. The years cover the period 1948-1974. Data on percentage employed in agriculture are not available for 1947, and years after 1974 are used to forecast later in this chapter.

The variance explained is high in both the OLS and CORC equations, but since the Durbin-Watson statistic in equation 1.1 is in the indeterminant range, I reestimated the equation with the CORC procedure. For all the variables, the metric coefficients are smaller in equation 1.2 than in equation 1.1 because the effects of autocorrelation are removed from the equation. Otherwise, the major difference is that the sign of the coefficient for pension benefits becomes positive and the t-ratio approaches 0 in equation 1.2.

The effects of pension and social-security benefits will be discussed first. The literature on retirement is not specific about how retirement benefits should be measured: as actual dollar benefits, as real dollar benefits, or as benefits relative to previous income levels. The choice has theoretical implications for the decision making of retirees; assuming they make rational decisions about the adequacy of retirement benefits, what metric do they use in their calculations? Are increases in retirement in current dollars sufficient to attract persons into retirement, or are increases in dollars relative to inflation or the standard of living necessary? Without entering the debate over the theoretical merits of different measures, I found that constant retirement-benefit replacement rates—where average pension or social-security benefits in constant dollars is the numerator and disposable income per capita in constant dollars is the denominator—better predict labor-force participation than do other measures of retirement income.[4] The replacement rate for pensions has declined from around 60 percent in the late 1940s to 43 percent in the 1970s, whereas the social-security-benefit replacement rate has increased during the same period from 43 to 50 percent. Levels of pension benefits, often determined in the 1940s and 1950s when a large number of programs were initiated (Schulz 1976), have not kept pace with the level of disposable income. As a consequence, the social-security-benefit replacement rate has consistently negative effects on participation, whereas the pension replacement rate has little or no effect on participation when adjustments are made for autocorrelation.[5]

The effect of percentage employed in agriculture (%AGLF), which is used as a measure of the shifts in the occupational structure, are positive and significant. The coefficients show that for a change of 1 percent in

%AGLF, there is close to a 3-percent change in MLFP65 + . Even given the effects of random error, the large coefficients appear to capture increases in mandatory-retirement rules among nonfarm workers as well as the proportion of nonfarm workers in the labor force. A more precise test of the effects of occupational change on labor-force participation, where some of the spuriousness can be reduced, can be done later with the consecutive cross-sectional data.

The effects of unemployment support the predictions. The discouraged-worker effect is shown by the unemployment coefficients: a 1-percent increase in unemployment leads to a decrease in labor-force participation of nearly the same size in equation 1.1 and of half the size in equation 1.2.[6]

Finally, I tested for a feedback relationship between participation and family income of aged males. Bowen and Finegan (1969) argue that the availability of nonwage, nonpension income of families decreases participation. It may thus be necessary to test for the effects of family income as a determinant of participation. However, since median income is also a function of labor-force participation, income and labor-force participation, under this argument, would affect each other simultaneously. Under these conditions, OLS estimates are no longer unbiased. In order to test for the effect of family income on the participation of aged males while controlling for the problem of simultaneity, I used two-stage least squares to estimate an equation that includes the variables in equation 1.1 and 1.2 as well as a family-income variable. The results show that family income is not significantly related to participation when controlling for pension and social-security-benefit replacement rates.

Female Labor-Force Participation

Predicting changes in female labor-force participation is problematic because there has been little change since 1947. Explanations have been offered for this, but testing these explanations with aggregate data is difficult and the analysis in this section must be considered especially tentative.

Participation of aged females has been argued to reflect two forces (Riley and Foner 1968). On the one hand, growth of female-labeled occupations in the service sector (Oppenheimer 1970) and higher wage rates (Cain 1966) have attracted middle-aged women into the labor force. On the other hand, forces increasing the retirement of men (such as retirement benefits and mandatory retirement) also increase the retirement of women (McEaddy 1975). Although more women are in the labor force at age 65, a higher proportion of them are retiring. These two trends—the upward trend in participation before retirement age and the downward trend after retirement age—are countervailing and result in a participation rate that has changed little in recent decades.

Based on this explanation, the model for aged females should include variables similar to those in the male model; but the size of the effects may differ. For example, in addition to decreasing participation through mandatory retirement, industrialization of the occupational structure may increase participation of older women by increasing demand for women to fill service and clerical occupations. In short, the effect of occupational change should be smaller for the women since it involves counterbalancing forces. Further, the effect of wage levels on participation should differ for men and women. Men, who have traditionally been strongly attached to the labor force, have been found to remain in the labor force despite decreases in wage rates (Bowen and Finegan 1969). Thus changes in wage levels were not included as predictors of participation of older men in the last section. Married women, however, may find it desirable to remain as homemakers when wages are low; when wages increase, they are likely to be attracted into the labor force. Thus the long-term increase in wages will increase the participation of women although it has little effect on the participation of men.

Testing for the counterbalancing forces using time-series data is difficult, since the forces are masked in the aggregation of the data; that is, the participation rate does not separate the increase in retireees from the decline in homemakers. It is likely that the small rise in participation from 1947 to 1959 reflects entrance of women into the labor force and that the decline in participation after 1959 reflects increases in retirement. Yet the changes are not large, and the analysis of them to follow is only a preliminary test of the theory.

Equation 1.3 presents the results of an equation that attempts to show the effects of the counterbalancing forces. The first variable, %AGLF, operates similarly for males and females. Its coefficient is positive, indicating that its effect in shifting workers into occupations where retirement levels are high is stronger than its effect in attracting new workers into nonagricultural, female-labeled occupations. For women, however, the size of the coefficient is smaller than for men, which may reflect the influence of the counterbalancing forces. Pension and social-security benefits are measured in constant dollars rather than as replacement rates, since the former measure better predicts the participation rate. It appears from this result that increases in pension benefits in constant dollars may induce aged females to retire, but that a stronger incentive—increase in replacement rates or pension benefits relative to increases in average income levels—is needed for men to retire. The variable most responsible for the increase in participation among older women is real wages. Although this variable was not important in keeping males in the labor force, its large positive effect in equation 1.3 provides some tentative support for the counterbalancing-forces argument.[7]

Male Personal Income

The results for male and female labor-force participation have shown the effect of increases in pension levels on the decline in participation at older ages. There is some evidence, then, that if it had not been for the ability to maintain a desired standard of living with pension benefits during retirement, the decline in participation might not have been as large as it was. This hypothesis can be further tested using median income levels as the dependent variable. Median income should increase in response to pension benefits despite the decline in participation.

The first determinant of changes in income levels to be considered is the growth of public and private pension benefits. Even with reduced participation, income of the aged can rise if pension and social-security benefits increase at a comparable rate. In fact, the effect of pension and social-security benefits on real income and relative income levels will show the extent to which retirement income of the aged has kept pace with inflation and with earnings of the non-aged.

Additionally, it is necessary to control for wage levels. Social-security benefits are the primary source of income of the elderly; but 43 percent of households headed by persons over age 65 obtain wage and salary income, and 21 percent of personal income comes from earnings (Schulz 1976). Although the effect is not likely to be as large as the effects of pension and social-security benefits, higher wages should increase the income of the aged.

Once pension and wage levels are held constant, the effect of labor-force participation is likely to emerge. In other words, the bivariate negative relationship between participation and income of aged males may be reversed once controls are used. With levels of wages and pensions held constant over time, the lower the participation rate, or the higher the retirement rate, the lower income would be. Thus if it were not for the drop in participation, the income of aged males might have increased even more than it did.

Finally, it may also be necessary to control for residual cohort changes that may account for long-term increases in income. As discussed in the first chapter, improved educational, occupational, and earnings characteristics of more recently born cohorts are likely to increase the income of the aged as cohort replacement occurs. According to Cain, the later-born cohorts, which entered adulthood after World War I, benefited more from growth of the educational system, urbanization, smaller families, structural mobility, and growth in the standard of living than did those born earlier. Thus Uhlenberg (1977) found that the largest improvement in cohorts entering old age occurred during the mid-1960s and early 1970s. Although the exact characteristics of the newer cohorts responsible for their improved status cannot easily be measured with aggregate data, the general process of cohort replacement should increase the income of the aged, especially in the last decade.

In testing the effect of these variables on male personal income, I have decided first to predict changes in income in constant dollars. Prediction of income in actual dollars is less useful since much of the increase will be the result of inflation and a higher standard of living for all age groups; this might cause spuriousness between the predictors and income changes. A further control for the higher standard of living in recent years is also to predict median income of the aged relative to that of the non-aged. The independent variables are labor-force participation, pension and social-security benefits, wage levels, and cohort characteristics. Pension and social-security benefits and wages are measured in thousands of constant (1967) dollars. These independent variables, however, differ from the dependent variable because they refer to the total population rather than to aged males. Pension and social-security benefits measure the average expenditure per beneficiary per year, and wages measure the average hourly wage for private nonsupervisory workers. Thus these variables must be interpreted as indicators of the relative size of the benefits and wages going to aged males.

The effects of retirement income on total personal income are shown in equation 2.1 (table 2-2).[8] An increase of $1,000 in social-security benefits increases total income of aged males by $1,144, and a $1,000 increase in private-pension benefits increases income by $596. The difference between the $1,000 increase in pensions and the $596 that reaches older males may indicate that large amounts of pension income go to persons under age 65 or to older females. The coefficient for social-security benefits, however, indicates some spuriousness, since $1,000 of social-security benefits is not easily transformed into $1,144 of income for aged males. This spuriousness may be related to the possibility of autocorrelation reflected in a Durbin-Watson statistic near the indeterminant range. The residuals for equation 2.1 show that income values for the 1967-1974 period are consistently underestimated (as might be expected given the accelerated growth in income during that period). Including a measure of real economic growth does not raise the adjusted r-squared or increase the Durbin-Watson statistic. The other possibility is that cohort improvements in education, health, occupational status, and income during the life cycle have increased the income of newer cohorts entering old age. It is difficult to quantify the lifetime educational, occupational, labor-market, health, and income experiences of cohorts; therefore, a proxy, based on the work of Cain (1967) and Uhlenberg (1977), is used to index cohort improvement. The proxy measures the percentage of the aged population that was born after 1900.[9]

Table 2-2
Unstandardized Regression Coefficients and _T_-Ratios for Models of Indicators of Personal Income Levels of Aged Males

(2.1)	$CMINC_t^{65+} =$	$-425.10 - 15.70MLFP_t^{65+} +$	$596.24CPEXB_t +$	$1143.90CSSEXB_t +$
		$(0.40) \quad (1.26)$	(3.58)	(5.80)
		$+404.13CWAGE_t + e_t$		
		(1.31)		
	$\bar{R}^2 = 0.979$	SEE = 88.405	$df = 23$	DW = 1.771
(2.2)	$CMINC_t^{65+} =$	$+1593.90 - 33.92MLFP_t^{65+} +$	$415.35CPEXB_t +$	$349.02CSSEXB_t$
		$(1.47) \quad (2.85)$	(2.75)	(1.18)
		$+227.49CWAGE_t +$	$8.288COH_t + e_t$	
		(0.87)	(3.23)	
	$\bar{R}^2 = 0.985$	SEE = 74.418	$df = 22$	DW = 2.074
(2.3)	$RMINC_t^{65+} =$	$0.352 - 0.002MLFP_t^{65+} +$	$0.044CPEXB_t +$	$0.133CSSEXB_t$
		$(1.70) \quad (0.90)$	(1.35)	(3.43)
		$-0.060CWAGE_t$		
		(0.99)		
	$\bar{R}^2 = 0.740$	SEE = 0.017	$df = 23$	DW = 2.203

Note: CMINC65 + = median total personal income in 1967 dollars of male, noninstitutionalized population aged 65 + ; C = prefix indicates constant (1967) dollars; COH = percentage of aged population (65 +) born after 1900; RMINC65 + = ratio of median personal income in 1967 dollars of male noninstitutionalized population aged 65 + to same for male noninstitutionalized population aged 25 to 64.

The effect of cohort in equation 2.2 is strong; it reduces the effects of the retirement income and wage variables, raises slightly the adjusted _r_-squared, and raises the Durbin-Watson statistic. Measured as it is, however, the cohort variable corresponds perhaps too closely to the behavior of the time series. Ideally, better measures of cohort characteristics at the aggregate level would provide more precise results; but without such measures, I present equations with and without the cohort proxy included. The adequacy of the equations, and the meaning of the cohort changes, can further be tested by forecasting the results of the two equations.

In both equations 2.1 and 2.2, the effect of labor-force participation on income is negative. In the first equation, the effect is not significant, but in the second equation it is. Thus despite the positive, individual-level relationship between income and labor-force participation, the addition of large numbers of retirees to the aged population has not caused a reduction in income, even controlling for wages and retirement benefits. In fact, the drop in labor-force participation and the increase in retirement would probably not have occurred if income levels of the aged population could not be maintained. This result shows that in the analysis of aggregate time-series data it is necessary to avoid the reverse of the ecological fallacy—making inferences about changes in the aged population from individual relationships.

Finally, equation 2.3 predicts the trend in personal-income levels of aged males relative to personal income of males aged 25-64. Again, the drop in labor-force participation does not significantly affect the ratio. Pension and social-security benefits do positively affect the ratio. The effect of wages on the ratio is negative, however, because wage increases would benefit younger males more than older males.

Income of Females, Families, and
Unrelated Individuals

The same variables argued to affect the personal income of aged males should also affect the income of aged females, unrelated individuals, and families. Thus pension and social-security benefits and wage levels will affect the income of these other groups as they affected male income. The major difference in predicting the other income measures is that the appropriate labor-force-participation measures need to be used. For female personal income, the female participation rate of those over age 65 should be used; for unrelated individuals and families the participation rates of both males and females should be used.

To begin, table 2-3 presents equations for three measures of aged-female income. The first equation predicts median income for all aged females. Because many aged females have no income (the median for 1947 and 1948 is 0, and the median does not rise above $500 until 1966), they must depend on the income of their spouses or families. Therefore, it is also useful to predict changes in a second measure—median income of aged females who have some personal income. A third measure is based on the income of aged females who have some personal income relative to that of non-aged females who have some income. The equations include labor-force participation, pension and social-security benefits, and wages in constant dollars. The effects of the percentage of aged females who are married and the cohort proxy were tested but found to be insignificant.

Constant social-security benefits are positively related to incomes of both all older females (equation 3.1) and older females with income (equation 3.2). The effects of constant pension benefits, however, are less reliable; the coefficient is negative in equation 3.1 and positive in equation 3.2. As was true for older men, decline of the participation rate has not translated into declining income; in fact, the coefficients are either negative or near 0. Similar results are shown for the income ratio (equation 3.3); the effects of social-security benefits are strong, whereas the effects of labor-force participation and pensions are weak. Constant wages, however, have

Table 2-3
Unstandardized Regression Coefficients and T-Ratios for Models of Indicators of Personal Income of Aged Females, Income of Families with an Aged Head, and Income of Aged Unrelated Individuals

$(3.1)^a$	$CFINC_t^{65+}$	$= -1542.9$ (6.67)	$- 13.61FLFP_t^{65+}$ (0.67)	$- 450.60CPEXB_t$ (2.25)	$+ 405.61CSSEXB_t$ (2.74)
		$+ 1052.5CWAGE_t$ (7.36)			
	$\bar{R}^2 = 0.989$	SEE = 46.26	$df = 21$	DW = 1.741	
$(3.2)^a$	$CWFINC_t^{65+}$	$=$ 63.34 (0.30)	$- 49.45FLFP_t^{65+}$ (2.69)	$+ 55.25CPEXB_t$ (0.30)	$+ 667.19CSSEXB_t$ (4.52)
		$+ 281.5CWAGE_t$ (2.00)			
	$\bar{R}^2 = 0.980$	SEE = 41.44	$df = 21$	DW = 2.210	
(3.3)	$RWFINC_t^{65+}$	$= 0.376$ (3.80)	$- 0.002FLFP_t^{65+}$ (0.21)	$+ 0.016CPEXB_t$ (0.26)	$+ 0.251CSSEXB_t$ (4.40)
		$- 0.097CWAGE_t$ (2.17)			
	$\bar{R}^2 = 0.632$	SEE = 0.021	$df = 22$	DW = 1.914	
$(3.4)^a$	$CFAMINC_t^{65+}$	$= -1126.1$ (0.70)	$+ 21.73MLFP_t^{65+}$ (1.04)	$- 159.18FLFP_t^{65+}$ (2.69)	$+ 537.20CPEXB_t$ (1.20)
		$+ 894.13CSSEXB_t$ (2.12)	$+ 1623.6CWAGE$ (2.59)		
	$\bar{R}^2 = 0.976$	SEE = 130.10	$df = 21$	DW = 1.745	
(3.5)	$CUNRINC_t^{65+}$	$= -220.4$ (0.32)	$+ 0.01MLFP_t^{65+}$ (0.00)	$- 61.38FLFP_t^{65+}$ (2.41)	$+ 279.16CPEXB_t$ (1.95)
		$+ 625.73CSSEXB_t$ (3.73)	$+ 474.55CWAGE_t$ (1.95)		
	$\bar{R}^2 = 0.975$	SEE = 58.14	$df = 22$	DW = 2.067	

Note: CFINC65+ = median personal income in 1967 dollars of the female noninstitutionalized population aged 65+; CWFINC65+ = median personal income in 1967 dollars of income recipients in the female noninstitutionalized population aged 65+; RWFINC65+ = ratio of median personal income of income recipients in the female noninstitutionalized population aged 65+ to the same for income recipients in the female noninstitutionalized population; aged 25 to 64. CFAMINC65+ = median family income in 1967 dollars of families headed by persons aged 65+; CUNRINC65+ = median income in 1967 dollars of unrelated individuals aged 65+ in the noninstitutionalized population.
[a]CORC estimates.

a negative effect on the income ratio but positive effects on absolute income. This again supports the interpretation that wage increases, net of social-security-benefit increases, reduce the relative income levels of the aged.

To complete the model, equations 3.4 and 3.5 predict income of aged families and unrelated individuals. The independent variables include the three income measures—pension benefits, social-security benefits, and wages—as well as the labor-force participation of aged males and females. The income variables all have positive, significant effects. In contrast to the results for male personal income, labor-force participation of aged males has a positive but insignificant effect on income of families and unrelated individuals. Female participation has negative effects for both families and unrelated individuals. Net of changes in all other factors, the decrease in male participation has had little effect on income, and the recent and smaller decrease in female participation has not reduced income.

In summary, the results for female income and for the incomes of families and of unrelated individuals reinforce the findings for personal income of aged males. Improvements in retirement benefits—primarily social-security benefits and secondarily private pension benefits—have had a large influence on improvements in absolute and relative levels of median income. Although it is no surprise that higher retirement benefits lead to higher income, the size of the increase in benefits is perhaps more unexpected. These benefits partly account for more than a 100-percent increase in income of the aged. Even more surprising are the negative relationships between measures of participation and income. Contrary to the arguments of Burgess, macrolevel changes in the proportion of the aged population not working have not reduced the aggregate measures of income over time even though such an effect occurs at the individual level. However, these results must be taken as preliminary until the individual-level data can be examined.

Forecasts

The goal of this chapter is primarily to explain past trends rather than to predict future trends. However, ex post forecasting with time-series data provides a further test of the estimates and model specification. Ex post forecasts use observed post-sample values for the dependent variable. Table 2-4 presents the observed 1975 and 1976 values for the dependent variables with the predicted values and the percentage difference between the two.[10]

Most of the forecasts are within a 5-percent error. The female-participation equation underestimates the actual value, possibly resulting from increasing commitment of older women to work. Among the male-income equations, the one including the cohort proxy overestimates the observed value. This supports Uhlenberg's (1977) contention that improvement of cohorts entering old age has slowed. Yet some other variable, perhaps welfare or other transfer programs, is responsible for observed values of RMINC65+ and CFAMINC that are well above the estimated values.

Table 2-4

Conditional (ex Post) Forecasts of the 1975 and 1976 Observed Values of Indicators of Labor-Force Participation and Income of the Aged

		1975			1976		
Equation		Observed	Forecast	Percent Error	Observed	Forecast	Percent Error
(1.1)	MLFP65+	21.7	20.8	4.1	20.3	20.6	−1.5
(1.2)	MLFP65+	21.7	21.2	2.3	20.3	20.6	−1.5
(1.3)	FLFP65+	8.3	7.9	4.8	8.2	7.9	3.6
(2.1)	CMINC65+	3,050	2,995	1.8	3,081	3,083	−0.1
(2.2)	CMINC65+	3,050	3,097	−1.5	3,081	3,199	−3.8
(2.3)	RMINC65+	0.445	0.412	7.4	0.429	0.419	2.3
(3.1)	CFINC65+	1,500	1,376	8.3	1,521	1,448	4.8
(3.2)	CWFINC65+	1,641	1,595	2.8	1,650	1,644	0.4
(3.3)	RWFINC65+	0.560	0.512	8.6	0.559	0.522	6.6
(3.4)	CFAMINC65+	4,998	4,740	5.2	5,115	4,826	5.7
(3.5)	CUNRINC65+	2,054	1,980	3.6	2,050	2,033	0.7

Note: Percent Error = (Observed − Forecast/Observed)*100.

Summary

The first part of this chapter described the trends in the aggregate indicators of labor-force participation and income of aged males and females. The participation rate of males aged 65 and over has declined from 47.8 percent in 1947 to 22.4 percent in 1974. In contrast, the female participation rate has changed little from the 8.1 rate in 1947. During the same period, all measures of the median income of the aged, in both current and constant dollars, increased. The increases were largest for family income and personal income of aged males, but were also apparent for income of unrelated individuals and aged females. The time series for income of the aged measured relative to increases in the income of the non-aged began with a decline during the 1950s but ended with increases during the 1960s and 1970s.

An increase in income at the same time that labor-force participation has declined (at least for males) suggests that changes in retirement benefits have affected both indicators. In fact, regression analysis of the male labor-force-participation rate shows positive effects from average social-security benefit payments (average benefit payments from private pension programs are smaller and less consistently related to participation of females). Changes in male participation are also shown to respond to a decline in the percentage of the labor force employed in agricultural, self-employed occupations and to short-term fluctuations in the unemployment rate.

It can be argued that the lack of change in female participation reflects the counterbalancing changes of entrance of women into the labor force during middle age, on the one hand, and higher retirement probabilities during old age on the other. Since the aggregate data masks the separate components of these changes, the model of participation must be considered tentative. The regression results do show, however, that higher wage levels have attracted women into the labor force while higher retirement benefits have reduced participation.

Not surprisingly, increases in pension and social-security benefits and in wages play a major role in accounting for increases in income among the aged. What is more surprising is that controlling for these variables, decreases in labor-force participation have not lowered the median income of the aged population. If aggregate participation rates have any effects, they are in the opposite direction. It is likely that retirement would be less common if retired persons could not maintain aggregate income levels of the aged population.

The results show that the growth of public and private transfer programs, improvement of cohorts reaching old age, and entrance of women into the labor force at younger ages have countered the harmful effects argued to result from urbanization and bureaucratization of the labor force. Based on the trends in relative income levels, the historical turning point for increases in the status of the aged may be as recent as twenty years ago. For the 1960s and 1970s, however, the results here suggest that stereotypes of worsening plight of the aged are exaggerated.

The macrolevel perspective of this analysis provides a picture of the trends without reference to changes at the individual level. Although this is useful in identifying some of the structural forces affecting the aged, the individual-level relationships must also be examined. For instance, the effect of the percentage employed in agricultural occupations must be seen as a proxy for a large number of social-structural changes affecting participation of aged men and women. The negative effect of participation on income is puzzling. And the lack of change in female participation must be investigated with data that allows differentiation of older female retirees and homemakers. All these relationships will be examined in the next chapters using individual-level data.

Notes

1. Bowen and Finegan (1969) use results from Social Security Administration studies in 1951 and 1963 to show that the percentage of noninstitutionalized males forced to retire increased from 11 to 21 percent during that time. Yet Schulz (1976) finds that less than 10 percent of

workers who face mandatory retirement by age 65 are forced to retire against their wishes. The different conclusions may be the result of changes from negative attitudes toward retirement in the 1950s (when the data on which Bowen and Finegan base their calculations were gathered) to more positive attitudes in the late 1960s (when the data on which Schulz bases his conclusions were gathered). Thus, considering all persons retiring with pensions, there may be a change from a situation in which forced retirees were most common to one in which willing retirees are most common. Again, however, it is difficult to separate these motivations in practice. A worker's negative attitude toward retirement may change to willing acceptance when he realizes there is no other choice.

2. I use pension and social-security benefits, rather than pension or social-security coverage, as determinants. The latter variables include persons of all ages who will not retire for years to come. Pension and social-security benefits, however, go only to those who actually retire and are therefore more appropriate.

3. There is some debate over the meaning of significance tests when the data—as is the case here—include the total population (Berk 1977). I do, however, present the t-ratios for convenience of interpretation, while recognizing that there is no other population or universe. In addition, there has been some experimentation with alternative measures and specifications of the equations, which further suggests that the t-ratios should be interpreted with caution.

4. Disposable income per capita includes income from transfers, interest, and dividends; it excludes income used for tax payments. It does include money that is saved as well as that going toward consumer expenditures.

5. I also tested for the existence of a threshold—the level at which the replacement rate is high enough that large numbers of persons withdraw from the labor force. However, inclusion of a quadratic term showed no curvilinearity in the relationships of the pension and social-security replacement rates to labor-force participation. A threshold level may exist, but not in the range of the independent variables for this time period.

6. Other measures of the effect of unemployment were tried in the equation with similar results. Use of unemployment of males aged 55 to 64, average number of weeks unemployed for persons of all ages, and the unemployment rate lagged one or two years supported the discouraged worker effect. I present the results for the unemployment rate of males aged 65 and over to keep the age groups consistent throughout the model. In addition, the correlation between the age-specific unemployment rates and participation rates may be artificially increased by the common component in the ratio variables. My concern is with the ratios themselves rather than with the components, which makes the problem of spurious correlation less

serious. Nonetheless, using a Pearsonian formula (Fuguitt and Lieberson 1974) and assuming that the correlation between the components is 0 gives a correlation of $-.01$. Thus only a small part of the relationship is the result of common components.

7. A measure of wage levels calculated separately for males and females is not available. Wage levels for females are no doubt lower, and the effect of females' wages on female participation may differ from the estimates.

8. The two-stage least-squares estimates (corresponding to the estimates for male labor-force participation) are nearly identical to the OLS estimates in equation 2.1.

9. Alternative measures of cohort were less successful. For example, cohort succession can be measured by a time variable beginning in 1947, which would indicate constant and continuous improvement throughout the time period. A similar time variable beginning in 1965 could also be used. The measure used in table 2-2 increases at a much faster rate and assumes no change before 1965, but does not assume an identical improvement each year. Rather, improvement depends on the size of the cohort entering old age. In addition, the percentage of the population over age 65 was included as a measure of age-structure changes. Growth of the relative size of the aged population may increase ability to control resources (Easterlin 1978). However, the percentage over age 65 was not significantly related to income with controls for labor-force participation and for pension and social-security benefits.

10. The only missing variable for these years is pension expenditures per beneficiary for 1976. That time series will be replaced by another in the next few years. To deal with the missing year, I regressed pension expenditures per beneficiary on time and time squared and used that equation to predict the 1976 value.

Appendix 2A:
Sources of Time-Series
Data

%AGLF, MLFP65+, FLFP65+, MUNR65+, HOURS, CWAGE: U.S. Department of Labor, *Handbook of Labor Statistics.*

PEXB, SSEXB, PENRR, SSRR: U.S. Bureau of the Census, *Historical Statistics*, 1970, and *Statistical Abstract*, various years.

CGNPOP, consumer price index, disposable income: U.S. Department of Commerce, *Economic Report of the President.*

%FMAR65+: U.S. Bureau of the Census, *Current Population Reports*, Series P-20, various years.

MINC65+, RMINC65+, FINC65+, WFINC65+, RWFINC65+, FAMINC65+, UNRINC65+: U.S. Bureau of the Census, *Current Population Reports*, Series P-60, various years.

3 Compositional and Processual Effects on Changes in the Labor-Force Participation of Aged Males

In contrast to the macrolevel data of the previous chapter, the microlevel data to be analyzed in this chapter make it possible to distinguish between compositional and processual determinants of changes in labor-force participation. Given the cross-sectional relationships between participation and the characteristics of individuals, compositional effects involve changes in the distribution of those characteristics within the aged population. In particular, changes in the occupational and financial characteristics of cohorts reaching retirement age may reduce participation. Processual effects, which result from period-specific environmental changes, involve changes over time in the process or probability of participation for persons in the same occupational or financial situation.

For example, shifts in the proportion of rural residents, agricultural workers, and self-employed workers in the aged population are compositional changes that should reduce participation. The probability of retirement for these persons is lower than it is for urban residents, nonagricultural workers, and wage and salary employees (Bowen and Finegan 1969). The compositional shifts thus increase the proportion of the population in positions where the probability of retirement is high. Similarly, assuming that a certain level of real nonwage income is necessary for retirees to maintain an adequate standard of living (Barfield and Morgan 1969), expansion of the proportion of the population with retirement income above that level will reduce participation. Expansion of social-security and pension systems to cover new groups of workers and increases in the size of the benefits among the covered workers can thus be seen as compositional changes that reduce participation.

Even if there were no changes in the occupational or financial composition of the aged population, the processual argument would predict decreases in participation. Growth of normative support for retirement or expansion of mandatory-retirement rules within occupations, for example, may have increased the probability of retirement for all persons in the aged population. In empirical terms, the effect on labor-force participation of background characteristics such as age or occupation will change over time in ways that reduce participation in the aged population.

To be more precise, three patterns of processual change may have occurred in recent decades. The first pattern predicts that increases in the

41

probability of retirement have occurred equally for all groups in the aged population. Given differences in retirement probabilities between, say, college graduates and noncollege graduates, this type of processual change would increase the probability of both groups equally and would thus maintain their relative position. The second pattern predicts that the processual changes will affect some groups differently than others. Specifically, there may be a convergence of the effects of the background characteristics on the probability of retirement; that is, differences in probabilities between groups may become smaller. As an example, compare retirement levels of professionals and blue-collar workers. In early periods, retirement may have been less attractive to professionals, who receive more intrinsic reward from their work. In later periods, the growing popularity of retirement may have made the prospect of retirement equally attractive to both professionals and blue-collar workers. The third pattern predicts that background differences in retirement will become more important over time. Levels of retirement may have increased little among low-retirement-level occupational groups, but may have further increased among high-retirement-level blue-collar occupations. In summary, all three patterns are consistent with the increase in retirement over time, but specify a different form in which the process changes.

The objective of this chapter is to identify the relative influence of compositional and processual effects on the participation and retirement of older males. This will involve determining how background variables such as age, education, occupation, and nonwork income affect income and how the distribution of these variables within the aged population has changed. Further, changes or lack of changes in the way these background variables affect participation will be studied. If processual effects are found, the direction of the changes—toward convergence, divergence, or equality—can be determined. These analyses will provide a more detailed description of the changing patterns of retirement than has been presented before and will explore some of the underlying components of the changing patterns.

The last chapter was not able to address the differences between compositional and processual effects or attain the objectives set forth in the last paragraph. Time-series studies such as were done in chapter 2 assume that the effects of variables such as percentage in agricultural occupations or average social-security benefits are constant over time; therefore, the studies focus only on compositional effects. This assumption is shown in the work of Bowen and Finegan (1969), who estimate the effects of several independent variables on the labor-force participation of older men in 1960. Then, assuming these effects are constant, they calculated the percentage change in labor-force participation owing to compositional changes in the independent variables over a twenty-year time period. Changes in the process of, or the effects of the background variables on, labor-force participation are not considered. Other studies have been no more successful in separating these effects. Longitudinal studies (Streib and Schneider 1972; Irelan 1972; Parnes, Nestel, and Andrisani 1973), for instance, cover relatively small age groups over short time periods and cannot be used to compare compositional characteristics across time periods or cohorts. In other words, processual but not compositional effects are considered.

To avoid the problems of longitudinal and time-series studies, I will use data from consecutive cross-sectional surveys, which allow (1) examination of the trends over time in retirement and participation while adjusting for compositional changes and (2) examination of changes over time in the net effects of the determinants of retirement and participation (that is, processual effects). Both the Survey Research Center (SRC) and census surveys discussed earlier will be used in the analysis. These data are superior to longitudinal data in their coverage of many cohorts and time periods and superior to time-series data in their measurement of individual-level characteristics. Thus occupational and retirement-income characteristics of the total aged population measured in the last chapter can be measured as individual characteristics in this chapter.

The SRC data to be analyzed measure retirement, whereas the census data measure labor-force nonparticipation and participation. Although the terms used by the SRC and census surveys are different, the practical meaning of the different terms is identical. In this chapter, then, I will use retirement and nonparticipation—or nonretirement and participation—interchangeably.

Research Strategy

I take retirement to be a function of time and a number of compositional control variables: respondent's age, race, rural residence, family membership, nonwage income, education, occupation, self-employment, and union membership. A first group of four variables measures demographic background characteristics; previous literature suggests that being old, black, an urban resident, and single will reduce the likelihood of participation and increase that of retirement (Bowen and Finegan 1969).[1]

There is a second group of variables involving educational and occupational characteristics. The effects of these variables on retirement are likely to be related to taste for work (Bowen and Finegan 1969) and retirement desires. Education is best taken as a measure of taste for work; that is, those with more education are likely to have more rewarding jobs and to have been socialized to value the intrinsic satisfaction of their work. Similarly, persons in higher-prestige occupations are likely to remain in the labor force longer since they find their jobs more rewarding. Taking account of education and occupation, self-employed workers further are likely to remain in the labor force since they have total control over their age of retirement; wage and salary workers with the same education and occupation may be subject to forced retirement despite their enjoyment of work. Finally, union membership is likely to indicate participation in private pension programs as well as employment in large organizations with mandatory-retirement rules, both of which should increase retirement levels.

Retirement income is perhaps the most important factor in the model and is the hardest to measure. Theoretically, persons with the highest potential retirement income should be the most likely to retire (controlling for the other variables). But since potential retirement income is difficult to measure, researchers have examined the effect of nonwork income: the greater the nonwork income, the greater the probability of retirement (Bowen and Finegan 1969).

When the independent variable, retirement/nonretirement, is regressed on time and these control variables, the sizes of the compositional and processual effects are easily determined. The trend in retirement levels is shown by the size of the regression coefficients for the time categories without any other control variables. The net trend in retirement levels, controlling for compositional changes, is shown by the partial regression coefficients of time net of the compositional variables. This net trend describes the change in retirement levels that would occur if there were no changes in the composition of the aged population (as measured by the control variables). The difference between the gross and net trends in retirement shows the influence of compositional changes. If there is no difference between the gross and net effects of time, this would indicate that compositional changes have not contributed to changes in retirement levels. If the net effects of time are not significant, compositional changes would completely explain the increase in retirement.

If the net effects of time are significant—if there have been changes in the process of retirement—further tests can be made to determine the pattern of the processual changes. The regression model that includes the additive effects of time assumes that changes in the probability or process of retirement affect all groups in the aged population equally. In order to determine whether the change in the process has affected some groups differently than others, it is necessary to test for interaction of time with retirement and the control variables. Significant interaction would show that the effect of time on retirement differs for subgroups of the aged population. Changes in the probability of retirement would thus depend on the demographic or status characteristics of the persons in the sample. If significant interaction does exist, the effect of the control variables on retirement levels can be examined for different time periods. Changes in the size and direction of the effects of the control variables will indicate whether there is convergence or divergence in the processual changes.

Data and Analysis

Respondents from both the SRC and the census data who are in their late fifties or older—the ages at which retirement becomes common—will be included in the analysis. As mentioned earlier, the census data cover a shorter time span, but provide a strictly random sample that includes institutionalized persons and a large number of cases for each time point. The census data also contain more detailed occupational and income measures than do the SRC data. For both data sets, the separate surveys are combined into one file where time measures year of survey. This provides eleven time values for the SRC data and two for the census data.

The theoretically specified models in this chapter—as well as those in the chapters to follow—are recursive and can therefore be estimated using the ordinary-least-squares (OLS) techniques of multivariate regression. The results of these estimates are sometimes presented in the form of traditonal multiple-partial-regression coefficients. More often, however, I have found it useful to present the results in the form of multiple-classification analysis (MCA). In muliple-classification analysis, an analysis-of-covariance framework is used where independent variables are treated either as a set of categories or as a covariate (Andrews et al. 1974). Treatment of an independent variable as a set of categories allows for nonlinear relationships with the dependent variable or for inclusion of ordinal and nominal independent variables. Linearly related independent variables can be treated as covariates. The MCA estimates are identical to those of dummy-variable regression, but for ease of interpretation the coefficients are presented in a different format. The coefficients for the categorical variables or factors are presented as gross and net deviations from the grand mean of the dependent variable. The gross deviations of each category added to the grand mean show the category means of a variable. The net deviations added to the grand mean show the category means adjusting or controlling for the other variables in the model. The covariates are presented as unstandardized regression coefficients.

Additionally, the gross and net deviations for a factor are typically accompanied by eta and beta coefficients. The eta coefficient is equivalent to the multiple-correlation coefficient when the dummy variables corresponding to the categories of the independent variable are regressed on the dependent variable. The beta coefficient can be seen as the multiple partial coefficient when controlling for other factors and covariates in the equation. These can be used as an overall summary of the strength of the relationship; they cannot, however, be interpreted as regression coefficients since they do not reflect a linear relationship.

The use of this type of analysis will allow time, which will be treated as a factor with categories distinguishing year of survey, to be nonlinearly related to retirement levels. The gross deviations for each time category added to the grand mean will show the percentage of persons retired in each year. The net deviations added to the grand mean will show the yearly means when the values for the other independent variables are held constant. Differences in the gross and net deviations will therefore show the size of the compositional and processual effects. The difference between the eta and beta for time will also show the strength of the time effects with and without the compositional controls. Other variables such as age or education, which are related nonlinearly to retirement levels, will also be treated as factors; and the coefficients will be presented in the form of gross and net deviations. Variables that are linearly related will be treated as covariates and reported as unstandardized regression coefficients.

In the multiple-class analysis to follow, the dependent variable will be qualitatively measured as "retired" or "not retired" ("not in the labor force" or "in the labor force"). When retirement is coded 1 and nonretirement 0, the gross and net deviations added to the grand mean can be interpreted as the conditional probability of retirement for persons in any one category. (To reduce the use of decimals, the probabilities in the tables to follow will be treated as percentages rather than as proportions.) Use of regression techniques (such as MCA) with a dummy dependent variable, however, may lead to heteroscedasticity and predicted values above 1 or below 0. This problem is most serious when the split on the dependent variable includes one group with less than 20 percent of the cases (Knoke 1976). But since I will be examining older persons only, the split on retired/not retired will be well between 20 and 80 percent.

As a final summary of the relative size of compositional and processual effects, regression-standardization techniques can be used. These techniques take the gross differences in mean retirement levels across the time periods and decompose the difference into four components: (1) differences in the means of the independent variables; (2) differences in the regression coefficients of the independent variables; (3) differences in the regression intercept or constant; and (4) the combination of components (1) and (2) (Althauser and Wigler 1972; Iams and Thornton 1973). The size of the compositional effects on changes in retirement is summarized by the first component while the size of the processual changes is summarized by the second and third components. The results of the decomposition can therefore provide a brief summary of the more detailed MCA results.

Results: SRC Additive Model

The models to follow can actually be estimated with several variations on the dependent variable. The SRC surveys use the following categories to measure employment status of adult men: employed, unemployed, and retired. The retired category is a residual grouping equivalent to nonparticipation. (Disabled persons are also included in this category.) However, since unemployment frequently leads to retirement at the older ages, it may also be useful to include unemployed persons with the retired nonparticipants. This creates another dependent variable measuring nonemployment rather than nonparticipation. The MCA results of the analysis of covariance for both these dependent variables are presented in table 3-1. Retirement (or nonparticipation) and nonemployment are coded 1; participation and employment are coded 0.

The other variables are measured as follows. Age is coded into four-year categories in order to correspond to the four-year gap between many of the surveys. The age categories were subdivided in order to separate retirement before and after age 65. Education is divided into seven categories based on years of schooling completed. Family status is measured by a dummy variable for married persons and by the number of persons in the respondent's household.[2] The covariates are all measured as dummy variables, with values of 1 given to union members, rural residents, or black respondents.

Occupation is measured only in the seven categories used in 1952: professional, managers, clerical and sales workers, skilled blue-collar workers, protective service workers (such as police), unskilled blue-collar and service workers, and farmers and farm workers. More detailed categories that distinguish self-employed workers from others are available for the years after 1952 and will be examined shortly.

Finally, there is no measure of retirement income available for the surveys. Examination of the effect of this variable on retirement will have to be postponed until analysis of the census data.

The trend in retirement is shown in table 3-1 by the gross deviations for time.[3] The increase in the percentage of aged males who are retired is 31 percent from the low value of 29 percent in 1952. With some fluctuations in 1958 and 1972, the trend is otherwise steadily upward. The gross trend for not employed also shows a similar pattern. The net deviations of time controlling for the compositional variables are nearly identical to the gross deviations. This finding, along with the lack of differences between the eta and beta coefficients, indicates that the compositional variables explain little of the increase over time in retirement. Instead, the results show major processual changes that have increased the probability of retirement for all persons in the aged population.

To illustrate the extent of the changes in retirement, consider the age differences in retirement shown in table 3-1. In 1952, only 9 percent of persons aged 61 to 64 were retired ($48 - 22 - 17 = 9$), whereas 54 percent of persons aged 69 to 72 were retired. In 1978, 41 percent of persons 61-64 were retired, whereas 86 percent of persons aged 69 to 72 were retired. This indicates major changes in the probability of retirement.

Table 3-1
Multiple-Classification Analysis of Retirement and Nonemployment: SRC Males Aged 57 and Over

Independent Variables	N	Retired Gross	Retired Net	Not Employed Gross	Not Employed Net
Time					
1952	157	−19	−17	−18	−16
1956	163	−15	−14	−15	−15
1958	191	−3	−2	−3	−3
1960	181	−6	−6	−7	−7
1964	179	−2	−1	−1	−1
1968	192	1	2	3	4
1970	196	3	4	2	3
1972	165	9	8	9	8
1974	172	6	4	6	4
1976	171	12	9	12	9
1978	152	12	15	9	12
		0.19	0.18*	0.18	0.17*
Age					
57-60	446	−37	−36	−36	−35
61-64	431	−22	−22	−22	−21
65-68	326	10	10	10	10
69-72	294	24	23	24	23
73-76	199	36	36	36	35
77+	223	38	36	38	35
		0.58	0.56*	0.57	0.55*
Education					
0-7	542	10	4	.11	4
8	439	2	1	1	1
9-11	323	−5	−2	−6	−3
12	190	−6	−2	−6	−2
12+ tech.	126	−1	1	−1	1
13-15	132	−9	1	−8	1
16+	167	−13	−11	−12	−10
		0.15	0.08*	0.15	0.08*
Occupation					
Professional	147	−9	−2	−9	−2
Manager	346	−5	−1	−6	−2
Clerical-sales	178	−9	−6	−9	−5
Skilled blue collar	682	6	5	7	6
Protective service	36	−13	−10	−14	−12
Unskilled service	246	−1	1	1	4
Farm	284	3	−8	2	−9
		0.12*	0.10*	0.13	0.11*
Covariates					
Married			−7.7*		−8.2*
Household size			−0.4		−0.4
Union member			−2.8		−4.0
Rural resident			−1.3		−1.3
Black			−6.7		−7.9**
R^2			0.393		0.382
Grand mean			48		49
N			1,918		1,919
df			1,885		1,885

Note: Coefficients are measured in percentages, or the probability of retirement or nonparticipation multiplied by 100.

*$p < .01$

**$.01 < p < .05$

After age and time, the variable most closely associated with retirement is occupation. Retirement is highest among blue-collar workers and low-status workers. Farmers have the lowest retirement rate of all, as expected, but professional and managers are near the average (protective service workers have low retirement levels, but the category N is small). Net of occupation, union membership does not significantly affect retirement.

More information on these relationships can be obtained from more detailed measures of occupation and industry for the years 1956-1978. Table 3-2 presents the gross and net effects for occupation and industry separately. Because the two variables are so closely related, it was not possible to include them in the same model. The net coefficients indicate deviations from the mean, controlling for all the other variables included in table 3-1 (excluding the 1952 category). The net occupational results show that self-employed managers, craftsmen, and farm managers have low retirement levels. Otherwise, the blue-collar occupations show higher retirement levels than do white-collar occupations. The pattern is similar for the effects of industry, where retirement levels are low in service, white-collar industries and high in manufacturing and transportation industries. Nonetheless, the controls for the detailed occupational and industry characteristics do not explain the net trend in retirement levels.

SRC Results: Interaction Model

The previous results show that controlling for the compositional variables in table 3-1 did little to explain the upward trend in retirement levels. The additive effects of time thus assume that the probability of retirement for each group in the population has increased equally. The next step is to see whether the coefficients change over time—in other words, whether there is an interaction of retirement, time, and the independent variables. In order to do this, the model in table 3-1 was estimated for separate time periods. Because of the small number of cases, and the difficulty in interpretation, estimation of separate models for each year was rejected. Instead, I separated the surveys into three groups: one for the years 1952-1960, one for the years 1964-1970, and one for 1972-1978.[4]

The first step in testing for interaction effects is to determine whether a model alowing the effects of the variables to differ over time explains significantly more variance than a model that limits the effects of time to be additive. To test this hypothesis, an additive model (with all the variables in table 3-1 except that only three time categories are used) and an interactive model was estimated. The interactive model includes multiplicative interaction terms (the dummy variables for time period multiplied by the other independent variables). Significant interaction terms would indicate that the

Table 3-2
Multiple-Classification Analysis of Retirement of Detailed Occupation and Income Categories: SRC Males Aged 57 and Over, 1956-1978

Occupation	N	Retired		Industry	N	Retired	
		Gross	Net			Gross	Net
Professional	133	-9	-2	Agriculture	265	0	-9
Self-employed manager	133	-15	-9	Mining	155	9	9
Manager	157	2	6	Manufacturing	457	8	8
Clerical	90	-1	1	Transportation	138	15	12
Sales	71	-23	-17	Retail	58	-14	-4
Self-employed craft	44	-1	-9	Wholesale	109	-16	-10
Foremen	54	-0	2	Business finance	111	-14	-13
Craft	307	11	9	Personal service	81	-22	-17
Operatives	267	5	5	Professional service	89	-20	-10
Protective service	30	-14	-12	Government	136	4	4
Service	95	-1	0				
Farm laborer	30	2	-6				
Laborer	109	2	6				
Farm manager	241	1	-10				
		0.17	0.15			0.23	0.20
R^2		0.408				0.434	
Grand mean		49				47	
N		1,762				1,599	
df		1,723				1,564	

Note: The effects of occupation and industry are estimated separately with controls for time, age, education, and covariates. Coefficients are multiplied by 100.
*$p < .01$
**$.01 < p < .05$

effects of the independent variables differ across time periods. Overall, the additional variance explained by the multiplicative interaction terms is significant using the standard formula for the F-test: at 44 and 1,850 degrees of freedom the F-value of 2.11 is significant at .01 and provides justification for separate models.

The MCA results of the models for the three time groups are presented in table 3-3. Except for time, the variables in the model are the same as those in table 3-1. Because of the large number of coefficients here, it is important to keep the objectives of the analysis clear: have the effects of the independent variables on retirement changed over time?[5] Consider the effects of education first. The beta in the first time period is significant, but those in the second and third periods are smaller and not significant. In short, the effect of education on retirement has become smaller over time. This supports the convergence argument—that education's effects on retirement are declining. For example, the mean retirement level for persons with less than a grammar-school education in the first period is 43, whereas the level for college graduates was 15; there is a difference of 28 percentage points between the most educated and the least educated. In the last period, the mean retirement levels for the least and most educated are 59 and 47 respectively—a difference of 12 percent. The declining gap thus indicates that the trend in retirement is larger for highly educated persons.

In contrast to the changing effects for education, the effects of occupation appear to be increasing over time. In the first time period, the beta for occupation is not significant while for the last two time periods, the beta increases and becomes significant. There is a good deal of fluctuation in the category deviations over time, especially given the small Ns for some of the categories; and a consistent pattern of the changes is hard to determine.

The models described in table 3-3 can be further analyzed in a way that will better summarize the large number of coefficients. This can be done by decomposing the changes in the mean retirement levels across the three time periods into the components caused by compositional and processual change. Specifically, the size of the compositional components is calculated by subtracting the means of independent variables in the second period from the means in the first period and multiplying the result by the regression coefficients for the variables in the second period. This shows the change in retirement levels that would occur from the first to the second period as a result of changes in the means of the independent variables when the coefficients across periods are assumed to be the same.

Changes in retirement levels because of changes in the coefficients are calculated by subtracting the coefficients for the independent variables in the second period from the coefficients in the first period and multiplying the result by the means of the variables in the second period. This shows the change in retirement levels resulting from changes in the regression coeffi-

Table 3-3
Multiple-Classification Analysis of Retirement for Separate Time Periods: SRC Males Aged 57 and Over

Independent Variables	1952-1960			1964-1970			1972-1978		
	N	Gross	Net	N	Gross	Net	N	Gross	Net
Age									
57-60	162	-30	-27	146	-37	-38	138	-44	-43
61-64	161	-26	-25	119	-22	-22	151	-18	-18
65-67	109	1	1	94	14	15	123	14	14
70-72	108	22	19	84	29	30	102	22	20
73-76	76	43	42	59	35	33	63	32	31
77+	76	43	39	65	34	35	82	37	35
		0.60	0.56*		0.59	0.60*		0.59	0.58*
Education									
1-7	239	13	6	167	10	1	136	10	2
8	200	0	4	115	1	-4	124	12	2
9-11	114	-12	-6	97	-5	-3	112	2	2
12	39	-20	-13	54	1	14	97	-11	-4
12 + tech.	25	-6	-9	36	-6	3	65	-3	2
13-15	32	-10	5	44	-16	-5	56	-7	3
16	43	-15	-22	53	-6	-3	70	-20	-10
		0.23	0.17*		0.15	0.10		0.22	0.08

Occupation									
Professional	45	−7	7	41	−5	3	61	−17	−9
Manager	111	2	6	124	−6	−4	111	−10	−5
Clerical sales	64	−13	−5	55	−15	−15	59	−0	4
Skilled-semiskilled	207	1	1	199	9	10	276	6	6
Protective service	16	2	1	4	−49	−59	16	−18	−11
Unskilled service	115	−1	−3	70	−2	1	60	9	8
Farm	133	5	−5	73	5	−9	78	3	−14
		0.10	0.09		0.18	0.20*		0.18	0.16*
Covariates									
Married			−8.5**			−6.7			−10.5**
Household size			−4.1			5.4			0.2
Union			−0.9			−5.0			−0.7
Rural			−1.4			0.3			−1.4
Black			−9.3			−8.0			−4.2
R^2			0.401			0.400			0.395
Grand mean			37			49			57
df			668			543			637
N			691			566			660

Note: F-test for increment to explained variance accounted for by the time-independent variable multiplicative terms is 2.11, significant at .01 with 44 and 1,850 degrees of freedom. Coefficients are multiplied by 100.

*p < .01

**.01 < p < .05

cients when the means (or compositional characteristics) are assumed to be constant. Thus the interactive effects of time on the relationship between the independent variables are reflected in this component.

Processual effects are also shown by the third component of the regression standardization: the difference between the regression intercept or constant. This difference shows the change in the percentage of retirement resulting from the additive effects of time; the interactive effects of time are shown by the second component. Both the additive and interactive time effects, however, are interpreted here as processual effects.

Finally, the fourth component multiplies the differences between the means for the two time periods by the differences between the coefficients of the independent variables. This component reflects the interaction of processual and compositional effects.[6]

The regression-standardization calculations will be done using the unstandardized regression coefficients from the results of a dummy-variable regression analysis that corresponds to the MCA results presented in table 3-3. Since the MCA and regression results differ only in format of presentation, the regression-standardization results will reflect the relationships shown in table 3-3.

The decomposition is presented in table 3-4. The negative difference in percentage retired from the first time-period to the second shows an increase of 11 percent. The effect of differences in the means across the independent variables on the change in retirement is small. If the means in period 2 were identical to those of period 1, retirement levels in period 2 would be 1.3 percentage points lower. The effects of changes in the regression coefficients relating the independent variables to retirement are much larger than the compositional effects. The negative effect of the changing regression coefficients indicates that if the coefficients were identical in the two periods, retirement would be 41 percentage points lower in period 2. The effect of the changing coefficients is overstated, however, because it is balanced by a large positive effect resulting from differences in the intercepts. Added together, the differences in the coefficients and intercepts show processual changes of 11.77 percentage points.

In the comparison of period 2 with period 3, most of the effects are smaller than in the previous comparison—the major changes in the process of retirement appear to have already occurred. The compositional effects are again modest. The effect of differences in the coefficients is also small, primarily because of counterbalancing effects of occupation and family. The positive effect on retirement levels of household size becomes smaller in period 3: if the effect of household size in period 3 were as large as in period 2, retirement levels in the last period would be higher. Similarly, the negative effect of marital status becomes stronger in period 3; if the coefficient in period 3 were as weak as in period 2, retirement levels would be

Table 3-4
Regression-Standardization Decomposition of Changes in Percentage Retired: SRC Males Aged 57 and Over

Independent Variables	1952-1960 versus 1964-1970 Change in Percentage Retired Owing to Different:			1964-1970 versus 1972-1978 Change in Percentage Retired Owing to Different:		
	Means	Coefficients	Interaction	Means	Coefficients	Interaction
Age	0.64	-11.52	-0.29	-2.30	-2.81	0.23
Education	-0.56	-6.62	2.50	0.44	1.13	-1.12
Occupation	-1.72	-3.50	0.84	-0.11	-11.98	-0.01
Marital-household size	0.31	-19.69	-1.08	-0.03	12.66	0.14
Covariates	0.03	0.07	0.00	-0.10	-0.46	-0.04
Total	-1.30	-41.26	1.97	-2.10	-1.46	-0.80
Difference in intercepts		29.49			-4.48	
Difference in percentage retired		-11.09			-8.85	

Note: Calculations are made from means and unstandardized regression coefficients corresponding to the MCA results in table 3-3.

higher. In the other direction, the stronger effects of occupation on retirement have increased retirement levels in later periods. Finally, the differences in intercepts shows that the additive effects of time would increase the retirement rates of persons in period 3. Thus both additive and interactive processual effects are important, but compositional effects are small.

In summary, the SRC data show that changes in the characteristics of the aged population had little or no effect on increases in retirement levels over time. Rather, processual changes have occurred, which increase the probability of retirement for aged persons regardless of their background characteristics. There is some evidence that differences in retirement levels for persons of different educational attainment have become smaller. Overall, however, the trend toward increased retirement levels has affected all groups similarly.

Census PUS Results

The major weakness of the previous analysis is that a measure of retirement income is not available, the result of which may be to reduce the importance of compositional effects. To test further for the effects of compositional and processual changes for a shorter time span, but with better variable measurement, I turn to the 1960 and 1970 census *Public Use Sample* (PUS) data (table 3-5).

Several differences between variable measurement in table 3-5 and that in the previous SRC tables exist. Former occupation is available in the census data only for persons who have worked within the last ten years. Since all persons without occupational measures are out of the labor force, it would provide little information to include them in the analysis. Hence, table 3-5 includes men over age 55 who have worked sometime in the last ten years. The result of this deletion of cases is to reduce the mean level of nonparticipation and to focus on more recent retirees.

The measurement of the dependent variables for the data sets differs as well. Whereas the SRC surveys allow the respondents to identify their own labor-force status as employed, unemployed, or retired, the census data are based on classifications made by the census bureau. The basic difference is that in the census data persons currently without a job must have actively looked for a job within the last sixty days of the survey in order to be classified as unemployed. This is not likely to lead to estimates of participation that differ greatly from the SRC estimates. Finally, the PUS data allow one additional dependent variable to be examined—"not employed full time" and "employed full time." To the extent that retirement involves reduction of full-time work without complete withdrawal from the labor force, those men not working full time can be grouped with those not in the labor force.

Table 3-5
Multiple-Classification Analysis of Labor-Force Nonparticipation, Nonemployment, and Less-Than-Full-Time Employment: PUS Males Aged 55 and Over

Independent Variables	N	Not in Labor Force		Not Employed		Not Full Time	
		Gross	Net	Gross	Net	Gross	Net
Age							
55-59	856	−24	−15	−23	−14	−25	−14
60-64	662	−12	−6	−12	−6	−12	−5
65-69	477	22	13	21	12	23	13
70-74	314	35	20	34	18	34	17
75-79	155	29	15	28	14	31	15
80+	75	35	24	38	27	37	23
		0.51	0.29*	0.49	0.28*	0.50	0.27*
Education							
0-7	802	0.10	7	12	8	14	9
8	603	0.01	0	1	0	2	1
9-11	392	−0.03	−1	−4	−1	−5	−2
12	363	−0.08	−4	−9	−5	−12	−7
13-15	179	−0.08	−6	−9	−7	−13	−9
16+	200	0.16	−14	−18	−15	−20	−16
		0.18	0.12*	0.20	0.14*	0.23	0.16*
Constant dollars nonwork income							
None	1,076	−24	−17	−24	−17	−25	−18
$1-499	284	−10	−6	−10	−7	−13	−9
$500-999	204	5	1	6	2	11	6
$1,000-1,499	222	22	13	23	14	26	15
$1,500-2,499	351	29	18	29	18	31	21
$2,500+	402	32	26	30	25	30	26
		0.52	0.36*	0.49	0.35*	0.51	0.37*
Occupation							
Professional	204	−12	−7	−12	−6	−14	−6
Manager	302	−4	0	−5	0	−8	−4
Sales	173	−8	−10	−9	−10	−10	−10
Clerical	162	2	1	1	0	0	1
Craft	563	1	3	2	4	2	4
Operative	411	4	3	4	3	3	3
Laborer	190	2	1	6	4	11	8
Service-private household	271	4	−1	3	−2	5	−1
Farm manager	201	2	1	0	−1	1	−4
Farm laborer	62	11	−0	10	−2	18	4
		0.11	0.08*	0.11	0.08*	0.15	0.10*
Class							
Private	1,644	0	0	1	1	1	0
Public	309	2	4	0	3	−1	2
Self	586	−2	−3	−3	−4	−1	0
		0.02	0.05**	0.03	0.04	0.01	0.01

Table 3-5 *(continued)*

Independent Variables	N	Not in Labor Force		Not Employed		Not Full Time	
		Gross	Net	Gross	Net	Gross	Net
Covariates							
Time			4.4*		3.5**		2.9
Married			−5.1*		−4.7*		−6.8*
Household size			−1.6		−1.7		−1.5
Black			−0.1		0.9		5.9**
Rural			3.0		3.0		4.1**
R^2			0.378		0.357		0.381
Grand mean			33		35		42
N			2,539		2,539		2,539
df			2,507		2,507		2,507

Note: Coefficients are multiplied by 100.
*$p < .01$
**$.01 < p < .05$

Table 3-5 contains a measure of income from nonwork sources for the calendar year previous to the survey.[7] Following Bowen and Finegan (1969), this measure is intended to show the positive effect of income from assets, rents, or retirement programs on the probability of retirement. However, there is simultaneity bias here since many males may have nonwork income because they are retired; others who are currently working could have higher levels of nonwork income if they were to retire. Without any measure of potential retirement benefits, however, nonwork income will have to serve as a proxy. The weaknesses of this measure are clear, but the direction of the bias makes the analysis of nonwork income useful. The effect of nonwork income on retirement will be overestimated because it will contain the simultaneous effect of retirement on nonwork income. When the compositional effects of nonwork income are overestimated, it provides a more severe test of the influence of processual effects. If processual effects remain when compositional changes in the overstated measure of nonwork income are included, the processual effects will have been proved to be strong. Hence, the measure biases the results in favor of the compositional argument.

The other census measures in table 3-5 are similar to those for the SRC data, with some minor modifications. Age is grouped into five-year (instead of four-year) categories for the census data to correspond to the ten-year gap between surveys. Hence, the analysis is for men aged 55 and over rather than 57 and over. Education is measured in six categories and differs from the SRC data only in the lack of information on technical training after high school. The occupational categories are more detailed than those for SRC data. In particular, measures of self-employment and public employment are included among the covariates for the census models.

In table 3-5, the effect of nonwork income on participation, employment, and non-full-time work are all stronger than any other variable in the model. Nonetheless, even with controls for changes in nonwork income, the effects of time—represented as a dummy variable—are significant for participation and employment. The effect of time shows that participation levels are 4.4 percent higher in 1970 than in 1960 and that employment levels are 3.5 percent higher in 1970 than in 1960. Even given the limited time span, and controls for the compositional variables, significant processual effects exist. The exception to this is that there has not been a significant increase in full-time work net of the control variables. For the other dependent variables, however, the results offer further evidence of the processual effects.

The next step in the analysis is to determine whether the effects of time, as assumed in the previous model, are additive or whether they interact with the independent and dependent variables. Tests for interaction of not in the labor force, time, and the independent variables show that interactive processual effects do indeed exist. The F-test for additional variance explained by the interaction terms is significant at .05.

Rather than presenting the detailed coefficients for the separate models of each time point, it will be more to the point to look at the regression-standardization decomposition of the differences across the two time points. This analysis will summarize the differences in the coefficients across time as well as differences in the means of the independent and dependent variables. The decomposition for changes in labor-force participation is presented in table 3-6. The change in labor-force participation over the ten years is 7.17. There is a change of almost 3 percentage points in labor-force participation owing to changes in the means of the independent variables. This compositional effect is almost completely the result of increases in nonwork income between 1960 and 1970: if there had been no increase in nonwork income, nonparticipation would have been 3.43 percentage points lower. This effect is overshadowed by the size of the effects caused by differences in the regression coefficients and intercepts. The negative sign for the component owing to changes in the coefficients indicates that if there had been no change in the coefficients, retirement levels would have been 8 percent lower. Thus changes in the process have favored increasing retirement. Finally, the difference in the intercepts is positive. When both the additive and interactive effects of time are combined, the total size of the processual effects are moderated but are still larger than the compositional effects.

Table 3-6
Regression-Standardization Decomposition of Changes in Percentage Not in the Labor Force: PUS Males Aged 55 and Over

Independent Variables	Change from 1960 to 1970 Owing to Different:		
	Means	Coefficients	Interaction
Age	−0.58	−4.68	0.15
Education	1.16	−2.04	1.18
Nonwork income	−3.43	0.99	−0.13
Occupation and class of worker	0.30	−1.17	−0.70
Covariates	−0.28	−1.56	−0.12
Total	−2.83	−8.46	0.38
Difference in intercepts		3.75	
Difference in percentage not in labor force		−7.17	

Summary and Discussion

Although there are weaknesses in the measurement of retirement income in this analysis, the results show that compositional changes explain little of the upward trend in retirement. Rather, processual effects, which have increased the probability of retirement of workers, are more important in explaining changes in retirement levels.

There are several important substantive implications of these results. First, theories that suggest that retirement has increased because more persons work in bureaucratic, wage and salary occupations rather than in agricultural and self-employed occupations find little support when tested with the individual-level data for the years from 1952. In fact, occupational changes may have worked in the opposite direction—to limit retirement rather than increase it. High-status workers are less likely to retire than low-status workers (except for farmers). Thus, shifts into higher-prestige occupations, which would lower retirement, balance shifts from agricultural occupations into nonagricultural occupations, which increase retirement. Even more surprising is the evidence that increases in the amount of nonwork income available for retirees has not explained the increase in retirement. It is often argued (as in chapter 2) that because of the growth of retirement income, many more people can afford to retire. Yet the results show that this compositional effect is minor—that retirement would have increased even if nonwork income had not increased at all.

The retirement process has changed so that a person in 1978 with the same occupation and nonwork income as someone in 1952 has as much as a 30-percent higher probability of retirement. This indicates a major change in the way in which persons make retirement decisions. The change in the decision-making process is likely to be the result of one of two factors. First, the desire for the benefits of retirement—or, in economic terms, the demand for the leisure time—may have increased so that persons with the same level of nonwork income or the same status job are much more likely to retire. In other words, there has been a normative change in the meaning of retirement. Second, mandatory-retirement rules may have increased within certain occupations, forcing more persons to retire regardless of occupation or financial situation.

There is no way to evaluate these two explanations with the data analyzed in this chapter. However, a recent article by Schulz (1976) suggests that increased popularity of retirement rather than increased forced retirement is responsible for the change. Schulz finds from a survey of new social-security beneficiaries that 46 percent of workers are not subject to mandatory-retirement rules and that 40 percent retired before the mandatory age or willingly at that age. That leaves 14 percent who are unwillingly forced out of work. Hence the increase in retirement net of compositional changes appears to result from increased demand for the benefits of retirement.

This change in demand for the benefits of retirement has affected differentials of retirement. Traditionally, there have been gaps between retirement levels of persons with low education and those with high education, and between persons in high-prestige and low-prestige occupations. As retirement becomes more popular among all groups in the aged population, this gap has become slightly smaller. Although not all the differences have declined, and although the increase in retirement has occurred among all groups, the trend seems to have increased slightly more quickly among traditionally low-retirement-level, high-status persons. The emerging pattern of retirement thus shows convergence.

The major changes in the process of retirement occurred from the 1950s to the 1960s (see tables 3-3 and 3-4), but changes slowed only slightly during the 1970s. Some observers suggest that the boom in retirement will slow during the 1980s because of inflation and income problems of retired persons and because of weaknesses in the social-security system (Jaffe 1971; Walker 1976). But according to the results presented in this chapter, much of the recent increase in retirement occurred independent of inflation and retirement income. A decline in benefits during the 1980s will therefore not guarantee a decline in retirement unless major structural changes in the process of retirement occur (Barfield and Morgan 1978). A slight indication of such a change is shown by the results in table 3-4, but major change is not yet apparent and may not come easily.

As a final note to this chapter, a comparison of the time-series results in chapter 2 with the cross-sectional results in this chapter needs to be made.

The results in chapter 2 indicated major compositional effects from occupational change and retirement income, whereas the results in this chapter did not. It appears that the time-series results, while reflecting causal relationships, overemphasized the strength of these relationships. Much of the relationship between the variables at the aggregate level reflects processual changes in the demand for retirement. This further indicates the need to supplement the more common time-series analysis of social change with individual-level analysis.

Notes

1. No attempt will be made here to separate age, period, and cohort effects. I would argue that cohort has little substantive, theoretical import, net of age and period, for the labor-force status of males (Kreps and Clark 1975). Cohorts differ in levels of retirement because they reach retirement age during different time periods. Reaching retirement age during periods of expanded pension programs will foster higher retirement levels among certain cohorts; but it is the combination of age and period that contributes to retirement, not the historical experiences of the cohorts. In this sense, cohort is not distinguishable from the combination of age and period and will not be treated as an independent variable.

2. The number of persons in the respondent's family would be more appropriate, but only the household measure is available. Further, for the SRC data, only adults in the household are counted. In some years, this is further limited to politically eligible adults. Persons living in group quarters are given a household-size value of 1. For the PUS data, persons of all ages and eligibility are counted.

3. The sum of the category Ns may differ slightly from the total N because of rounding error in the fractional weighting of cases.

4. A problem created by this procedure is that if the time categories are included within the groups, the models would not be directly comparable and regression-standardization techniques would be inappropriate. Fortunately, comparison of models including the within-group time categories and excluding the time categories are nearly identical. Hence, the deletion of the time effects in the models does not greatly affect the results.

5. Another way to state the question is: are the effects of time on retirement different for groups in the population? Each question involves the interaction of three variables—time, retirement, and an independent variable.

6. The formula for the standardization is as follows:

$$\overline{Y}_1 - \overline{Y}_2 = (C_1 - C_2) + \Sigma \ X_2(b_1 - b_2) + \Sigma \ b_2(\overline{X}_1 - \overline{X}_2) + \Sigma \ (b_1 - b_2)(\overline{X}_1 - \overline{X}_2)$$

where $\overline{Y}$ refers to the means of the dependent variables, C to the constants, $\overline{X}$ to the means of the independent variables, and b to the regression coefficients.

7. Because the measures of income refer to the previous year and labor-force status to the week previous to the April survey, the strength of the relationship will be underestimated.

4

Cohort Change and Retirement among Aged Females

The analysis of male labor-force participation showed some discrepancy between the macro, time-series results and the micro, cross-sectional survey results. In particular, the effects of variables measuring occupational change and retirement benefits on labor-force participation were overestimated in the time-series analysis; the compositional effects of these variables in the individual-level analysis were overshadowed by more general processual increases in the probability of retirement. Since changes in occupational structure and retirement benefits were also found (in chapter 2) to affect female participation, it is important to validate the relationships further with the individual-level data. Moreover, because the aggregate measure of female labor-force participation did not show changes in the relative proportions of housewives and retirees, the results in chapter 2 were considered tentative. This chapter thus provides a more detailed test of the theoretical explanations of participation of females at the older ages using the consecutive cross-sectional surveys.

To review the theoretical arguments: because of the counterbalancing effects of increasing participation of women during middle age and of retirement during old age, the labor-force-participation rates of females aged 65 and over have changed little over the last thirty years. This argument focuses on the characteristics that cohorts bring into old age and on the subsequent behavior of those cohorts during old age. On the demand side, the expansion of female-labeled service and clerical occupations (Oppenheimer 1970) and higher wage rates for female workers (Cain 1966) attracted large numbers of married, middle-aged women into the labor force. On the supply side, life-cycle changes have freed many middle-aged women from household and child-rearing duties that previously might have limited their participation. With time available, these women were especially attracted to work and the additional income because expected levels of standard of living were high (Sheppard 1976) and family expenses during the stage of the life-cycle when the wife was middle aged were high. Thus recent cohorts of women have brought higher levels of participation—as well as higher education, fewer children, and more urban residents—into old age. Given the increase in participation of women entering old age, forces increasing the probability of retirement among men would also increase retirement levels among women. Improvements of public and private pension programs for women workers and for spouses (McEaddy 1975), along with increased retirement levels among husbands (Palmore 1965; Sherman, 1974), have reduced participation during the older ages.

Most studies of changes in participation of aged women over time have been limited to published census data (as in chapter 2), which does not distinguish between retirees and housewives at the older ages. If the counterbalancing-forces argument is correct, it is necessary to demonstrate first that cohort changes in labor-force participation have reduced the proportion of housewives that enter old age. Second, it will be necessary to demonstrate that, controlling for cohort change in labor-force participation, the probability of retirement among older women has increased. Third, given an increase in the probability of retirement, the role of compositional and processual effects in explaining the increase needs to be examined. By separating the analysis of housewives from that of workers and retirees, and by examining labor-force participation before as well as after age 65, these objectives can be reached. The following discussion and analysis, therefore, will deal with two dependent variables: long-term nonparticipation (or being a housewife) and short-term non-participation (or being retired). The first variable is relevant to all women and compares housewives with workers or retirees. The second variable applies only to those with recent labor-force participation and compares employed women with retired workers.[1]

Changes in Long-Term Nonparticipation

The first step in testing these arguments is to determine the effect of cohort membership on the probability of being a housewife. The assumption of the counterbalancing-forces theory is that unique historical experiences of cohorts involve a combination of age and period events; cohorts at different ages are likely to experience historical changes differently. More recent cohorts are likely to have reached middle age—the time at which decisions to reenter the labor force have often been made—during periods where the opportunities for female workers were improving. According to Cain (1967), the environment faced by women reaching adulthood in the 1920s (those born after 1900) was more modern than the environment of earlier-born cohorts. As a consequence, the later-born cohorts had a higher probability of working. Other cohort-specific events are also important. Women in cohorts that were young or middle aged during World War II were most likely to work. This work experience, not gained by cohorts reaching old age in the 1950s, led to greater participation after the war (Bowen and Finegan 1969). In summary, more recent cohorts should have higher probabilities of having been in the labor force than earlier cohorts (Farkas 1977).

The effects of cohort on the probability of being a housewife should be examined net of cohort-related changes in education and rural residence. For instance, women with higher levels of education have been found to be more likely to be in the labor force than less educated women, presumably because they have more opportunity to work in high-status jobs where the psychic and monetary rewards are greatest. Further, unmarried, female urban residents have higher participation levels than rural residents (Sherman 1974).

Given these determinants of participation, the compositional arguments can be applied. According to the counterbalancing-forces argument, an increase over time in the proportion of women in the labor force entering old age is the result of different cohort experiences before old age. Thus, controls for cohort membership, or for cohort composition within the aged population, should reduce the effects of time on nonparticipation. Further, cohort increases in educational levels and residence should also reduce the effects of time on long-term participation. Finally, given the increases over time in female heads of households resulting from increases in divorce and widowhood, controls for family status may explain some of the increase in participation over time.

Note that with controls for cohort, age need not be included as a predictor of being a housewife. Age is unlikely to be of importance in determining the probability of long-term participation of women during old age. Those who are housewives at age 65 are likely to remain housewives for the rest of their lives. Those who have already entered the labor force by middle age or who are in the labor force at age 65 are likely to remain until retirement. Thus age variation in the probability of being a housewife for women in their midfifties or older should be small. Exclusion of age also has statistical advantages, since use of age with cohort and time creates estimation problems.

Processual Changes

The second task is to identify processual changes. For women, the processual argument must take a different form than for men. If increases over time are a result of cohort and other compositional changes, it may be that the process of work has changed across cohorts rather than across years; that is, the relationship between the independent variables and participation will differ across cohorts. In particular, as the demand for workers becomes stronger for more recent cohorts, or as the attractiveness of work increases, background differences will become less important. In other words, in the new cohorts, convergence in the determinants of participation, such as education or residence may occur.

Differences in Family Status

A third task is to examine in detail the influence of family status on nonparticipation. In contrast to men, unmarried women are more likely to work than married women. Despite great increases in participation of married women in recent decades, they still work less often than unmarried women who have no other source of income in the family. In fact, the difference between women who head their own households and those who do not is important enough to suggest interaction with other dependent variables in determining status. The effects of variables such as cohort, education, or residence may differ for heads of households and nonheads of households. For example, educational, residential, or cohort differences are likely to be less important determinants of nonparticipation for heads of households who have less choice over participation than nonheads of households.

Let me summarize the hypotheses to be tested concerning changes in the probability of being a housewife during old age. First, compositional changes are predicted to explain the decline in the proportion of housewives in old age. The most important compositional variable is likely to be cohort membership, although other cohort-related variables such as education may also help explain the trend over time. Second, processual effects are predicted to show up in differences across cohorts; background variables may be less important in predicting participation in the labor force in more recent cohorts. Third, family status is likely to have both compositional and processual effects. Compositionally, increases in the proportion of women who are heads of households may have reduced the prevalence of homemakers in the aged population. Processually, the determinants of labor-force participation may differ between heads of households and nonheads.

Changes in Retirement Levels

Retirement can be studied only for women who enter old age while in the labor force. Changes in retirement must therefore be considered while holding constant changes in the proportion of workers, as opposed to homemakers, entering old age. This can be done by excluding homemakers from the analysis and examining changes in the probability of retirement for those who have been in the labor force. Naturally, a model predicting retirement among female workers will differ greatly from a model predicting the probability of being a housewife. Thus the relationships specified in this section will differ greatly from those specified in the last section.

According to the counterbalancing-forces argument, the trends in retirement should be similar for men and women once adjustments are made for the changing proportion of housewives. For male retirement, there were independent processual changes increasing retirement probabilities above and beyond compositional changes. Although compositional effects have just been argued to reduce the proportion of homemakers, compositional effects are not predicted to greatly affect the retirement of women. Rather, as was the case for men, processual effects should be larger. Further, as was the case for men, age is used as a predictor of retirement rather than the cohort measure predicted to affect being a housewife. Retirement results from persons reaching the appropriate age during time periods in which conditions are conducive to leaving the labor force. Cohort characteristics brought into old age are less important than age and period characteristics combined. Thus cohort predicts being a housewife, but age predicts retirement of women.

There are, however, likely to be two major differences in the retirement levels of women compared to those of men. First, the effect of the background variables on retirement is likely to be smaller among women than among men. The literature on retirement of women suggests that women are more likely to retire than are men with the same background characteristics. It is not clear whether this results from weaker attachments of women to the labor force or from expectations of others such as employers, family members, or friends that women should retire early. Yet previous studies have not found important occupational or educational differences in retirement rates of women (Palmore 1965). Age is also likely to be related differently for females since women are likely to retire earlier than men.

The second major difference between men and women concerns the effect of family status on retirement. For one thing, married women are more likely to retire, whereas the opposite is true for men. This difference may have implications for the effects of compositional changes. Increases in the proportion of unmarried women, heads of households, or primary individuals in the aged population would increase nonretirement over time. Further, the process of retirement may differ for heads of households and nonheads; those women who are married may retire earlier because their husbands do or because they can better afford to retire. In short, it may be necessary to consider interactions among household status, retirement, and the other independent variables.

Methods and Data

Except for some variable measurement, the data and methods will be the same as in the previous chapter on male retirement; thus I will focus here on those variables that require special measurement for females. Measuring labor-force status is more complicated with females since the definition of housewife is not commonly agreed on. The SRC data allows the respondent to identify her labor-force status as employed, unemployed, retired, or housewife. Those who say they are employed, unemployed, or retired are asked for their current or former occupation (retired housewives are then grouped with housewives). Thus the distinction is left up to the respondent, especially insofar as it involves deciding whether a woman is retired or a housewife.

The census data do not make distinctions among persons out of the labor force. What they do present is a distinction between those who have worked in the last ten years, those who have worked before the last ten years, and those who have never worked. Information on former occupation can be obtained for those persons who have worked in the last ten years. Those who have never worked can clearly be classified as homemakers; those who have worked in the last ten years can clearly be classified as retired. The ambiguous category—those who have worked but not for at least ten years—may refer to persons who have been retired for more than ten years or to current homemakers who worked when they were much younger but have not been in the labor force in a long time. Some experimentation with alternative measures of the dependent variable will be necessary.

SRC Results

As an initial comparison of the trend in labor-force status, we can examine the percentages of women in each of the employment-status categories (employed, unemployed, retired, housewife) over the twenty-six-year period. For the total sample of women aged 57 and over, the percentage of women employed increases by only 2 percentage points from 1952 to 1978 (table 4-1). Since the percentage unemployed is small and shows no pattern over time, the percentage employed must be affected by the percentage retired and the percentage homemaking. The percentage retired has increased by 29 points while the percentage of homemakers has declined by 31 points.

The trends are slightly different when analyzed separately for women who are heads of households and women who are not. Since women who are not household heads have been able to depend partially on the income of their spouses or other relatives, they have been less likely to enter the labor force than heads of households who often must depend completely on their own resources. In table 4-1, the percentage employed has declined for household heads while it has increased for nonheads. For household heads, the increase in retirees has been larger than the decline of housewives—overall employment has therefore dropped. For nonheads of

Table 4-1
Trends in Employment Status by Household Headship: SRC Females Aged 57 and Over

Employment Status	*Year* 1952	1956	1958	1960	1964	1968	1970	1972	1974	1976	1978
Total											
Employed	18	19	22	20	19	24	23	19	20	18	20
Unemployed	2	0	3	0	2	2	2	1	2	0	3
Retired	8	7	10	18	26	20	23	25	32	37	37
Housewives	71	74	65	62	53	54	52	55	46	45	40
N	203	183	191	209	247	245	267	272	265	290	242
Household heads											
Employed	26	25	25	18	24	29	25	21	18	19	19
Unemployed	3	1	5	0	2	3	2	2	4	0	4
Retired	14	9	14	31	35	28	32	32	42	42	45
Housewives	56	65	56	51	38	40	41	45	35	38	30
N	100	92	85	103	124	145	156	141	153	164	125
Nonhousehold heads											
Employed	9	12	20	20	14	17	21	17	22	15	22
Unemployed	1	0	1	0	1	0	2	0	1	0	1
Retired	3	4	7	6	16	9	9	17	17	30	27
Housewives	87	84	73	75	68	74	68	65	60	55	49
N	102	90	104	105	123	100	110	130	111	120	117

household, the decline of housewives has been larger than the increase in retirement—overall employment has been larger than the increase in retirement—overall employment has therefore increased. In 1978 the percentage employed is similar for the two groups (19 percent compared to 22 percent). Yet housewives are more common among nonheads and retirees more common among heads of households.

Changes in Levels of Housewives

The next step is to identify the determinants of being a housewife (or identifying oneself as a housewife) and the trend over time controlling for these determinants. As discussed, being a housewife is taken as a function of time, cohort, education, rural residence, race, household size, and household position (head, wife of head, or other family member). The results are presented separately for heads and nonheads of households.

Household Heads. The multiple-classification analysis (MCA) results predicting being a housewife for heads of household are presented in the first half of table 4-2. Since these women are not married, none are typical housewives; rather, the term refers to those who do not work, are not retired, and have little labor-force experience. First, consider the gross deviations (from the grand mean of 43 percent). There is a clear decline in housewives over time. The gross effects of cohort similarly show that later-born persons are less likely to be housewives than earlier-born persons. Because persons in the newer cohorts will reach old age during the later time points, the gross trends for time and cohort will be closely related.

To disentangle the effects of cohort and time, deviations for several different models of long-term nonparticipation are presented. The net coefficients labeled one show the effects of time with control for all the variables except for cohort. The effects of time in this model remain significant (with a beta of 0.15) when compositional changes in education and the covariates are controlled. However, the second model includes controls for cohort as well as the other variables. The net deviations for this model (labeled net 2) show a strong trend for cohort, but the effects of time are reduced and the direction of the relationship reversed. More recent cohorts are much less likely to be housewives. However, within the cohorts, the effects of time show that the probability of being a housewife has grown in recent years—just the opposite of the prediction. Since the effect of time is not strongly significant, and since the reversal of the direction of the relationship to being a housewife makes little theoretical sense, the findings suggest that cohort membership best explains the decrease over time.

Other variables in the model are significant but explain little of the trend

Table 4-2

Multiple-Classification Analysis of Self-Identification as a Housewife for Heads and Nonheads of Households: SRC Females Aged 57 and Over

			Household Heads					Not Household Heads	
				Net Deviations					Net Deviations
	N	Gross	(1)	(2)	(3)	N	Gross	(1)	(2)
Time									
1952	99	13	8	−10	2	102	19	17	4
1956	92	22	15	2	−4	86	16	14	3
1958	79	11	9	−6	−4	99	4	5	−3
1960	101	9	10	−4	−3	105	7	7	0
1964	124	−5	−5	−11	−12	123	0	−1	−4
1968	144	−3	−2	−2	−1	100	6	7	9
1970	155	−3	−3	0	−2	110	0	−1	4
1972	140	2	2	9	8	130	−3	−3	3
1974	153	−8	−8	2	1	110	−9	−7	0
1976	162	−5	−1	10	8	118	−13	−14	−5
1978	123	−14	−11	2	−1	116	−18	−16	−8
		0.19	0.15*	0.13**	0.11**		0.23	0.21*	0.10
Cohort									
Before 1880	88	30		29	31	42	9		13
1881-1884	71	15		17	10	35	20		14
1885-1888	114	28		27	27	68	22		22
1889-1892	148	12		12	11	94	12		10
1893-1896	226	0		3	4	150	10		10
1897-1900	171	0		−1	−1	156	3		4
1901-1904	150	−5		−5	−2	156	−2		−2
1905-1908	153	−11		−11	−10	147	−5		−6
1909-1912	133	−21		−21	−17	168	−10		−14
1913-1916	77	−31		−33	−29	100	−13		−11
After 1917	42	−28		−27	−20	82	−19		−12
		0.34		0.34*	0.30*		0.23		0.23*
Education									
0-7	330	13	17	14	13	258	7	9	8
8	286	8	6	5	3	248	4	2	2
9-11	250	−1	−3	−2	−2	208	2	2	2
12	166	5	4	5	4	182	−5	−4	−4
12 + tech	114	−20	−21	−16	−15	109	−15	−13	−11
11-13	120	−14	−13	−14	−10	107	4	2	2
16+	107	−29	−30	−26	−21	87	−14	−15	−15
		0.27	0.29*	0.24*	0.21*		0.16	0.16*	0.14*
Marital[a]									
Single	129	−28			−26				
Separated	80	−33			−21				
Divorced	41	−23			−15				
Widowed	1,018	7			5				
					0.23*				
Covariates									
Black		−32.7*	28.9*	31.1*			−31.8*	−32.4*
Rural		7.2*	4.5	2.3			9.3	8.8*

Table 4-2 *(continued)*

	N	Gross	Net Deviations (1)	(2)	(3)	N	Gross	Net Deviations (1)	(2)
			Household Heads					*Not Household Heads*	
Household size			1.6	2.7	2.6			1.6	1.8
Not wife								−22.7*	−27.7*
R^2			0.140	0.204	0.251			0.135	0.155
Grand mean			43	43	43			68	68
df			1,351	1,340	1,235			1,177	1,166
N			1,371	1,371	1,268			1,198	1,198

Note: Coefficients are multiplied by 100.
*$p < .01$
**$.01 < p < .05$
[a]Results based on data for 1956 and after.

over time or the effect of cohort. The results show that highly educated women are less likely to be homemakers and that black women are less likely to be homemakers than are white women. As a final control, marital status is added to the model (net deviations 3). However, since the 1952 data distinguish only married from nonmarried women, cases for that year were deleted. The deviations show that widowed women are much more likely to be housewives than single, separated, or divorced women. The differences between the groups are striking. It is not surprising that widows are less likely to enter the labor force than are single women of other statuses, because of old age, insurance, or lack of work experience.

Nonheads of Households. The second half of table 4-2 presents the model for nonheads of households. The variables in the model are nearly identical to those in the model for heads of households except that marital status is excluded, since nearly all nonheads are married. The pattern of the gross and net effects for the time and cohort are similar for nonheads and heads of households: the gross effects of time and cohort are strong and negative, whereas the net effects of time are reduced to insignificance by controls for cohort. Although the probability of being a housewife begins at a higher level for nonheads of households (the grand mean is 68), cohort changes nonetheless explain much of the decline in the probability over time.

For the other variables, both education and race are significantly related to being a homemaker for nonheads, as they are for the heads of households. Rural residence, however, is significant only for the nonheads. For those who head their own households, work is common in both rural and urban settings. But for nonheads or wives work is much less common in rural areas than in urban areas. Finally, those nonheads who are not married to the head are much less likely to identify themselves as housewives than are spouses of the head. It is difficult to determine whether this results from previous work histories of the nonwives or from their unwillingness to identify themselves as housewives when they are not married to the household heads. Some of the respondents may interpret the term *housewife* as applicable only to the wife of the head; those female respondents who are parents, siblings, in-laws, or other relatives of the head may identify themselves as retired, reserving the term *housewife* for the wife.

In comparing the results of heads and nonheads of households, table 4-2 shows that the effects of cohort are stronger for the heads of households. The social change that occurs from replacement of cohorts is greater for the heads of households. Participation of older women has become acceptable for both groups, but the greater change has occurred among those that have the most need for their own source of income—women who head their own households.

Since the net effects of time are not significant, tests for processual effects of the interactive effects of time are not appropriate. It is more useful to test for changes in the process across cohorts or to test for the interaction of cohort, being a housewife, and other independent variables. Indeed, such tests for interaction are significant. Without presenting the more detailed tables, the results can be summarized as follows. For both heads and nonheads of households, the effects of education become less important in determining nonparticipation in newer cohorts than in later cohorts. This supports the convergence hypotheses: as participation becomes more common, traditional differences between the less and more educated decline. Thus the increase in participation in the newer cohorts has especially affected low-participation groups.

In summary, these results support the first half of the counterbalancing-forces argument. There has indeed been a decline in the proportion of housewives entering old age as a result of cohort replacement; thus compositional changes completely explain the trend over time. The effects of cohort have been especially strong for heads of households compared to nonheads of households. Other variables, such as education, are related to being a housewife but explain little of the change over time; in fact, the evidence suggests that background variables have become less important predictors of participation in newer cohorts than in earlier cohorts.

Changes in Levels of Retirement

It is necessary to examine changes in retirement when controlling for the decline in the proportion of housewives. This can be done by examining the probability of retirement when housewives are excluded. For women who are in the labor force during old age, the counterbalancing-forces argument predicts that changes in retirement for women should be similar to the changes that have occurred for men. A model predicting retirement for women who have recently worked is presented in table 4-3. The major difference in the variables in this table compared to those in table 4-2 is that

Table 4-3
Multiple-Classification Analysis of Retirement: SRC Females Aged 57 and Over

Independent Variables	N	Gross	Net		Independent Variables	N	Gross	Net
Time					Occupation			
1952	55	−24	−22		Professional	181	6	10
1956	44	−27	−16		Manager	104	−5	−8
1958	57	−28	−21		Clerical sales	301	−2	2
1960	75	−4	−1		Skilled-semiskilled	167	3	4
1964	110	4	2		Unskilled-service	328	−1	−6
1968	104	−9	−10		Farm	32	−2	−8
1970	124	−3	−2				0.07	0.13*
1972	115	4	4					
1974	140	8	8		Covariates			
1976	145	15	13		Black			6.2
1978	143	11	6		Rural			−2.6
		0.25	0.20*		Household size			−1.0
					Union			−11.5**
Age								
57-60	295	−37	−35		R^2			0.417
61-64	236	−22	−21		Grand mean			50
65-68	184	15	16		N			1,112
69-72	144	25	24		df			1,078
73-76	112	37	34					
77+	142	38	36					
		0.60	0.57*					

Education			
0-7	197	6	6
8	202	-3	1
9-11	198	7	6
12	148	-4	-1
12 + tech	127	-7	-3
13-15	110	-5	-10
16	129	0	-6
		0.10	0.10**
Family relationship			
Head	747	5	0
Head's wife	296	-13	0
Other	69	7	3
		0.16	0.02

*$p < .01$
**$.01 < p < .05$

age is used rather than cohort. Otherwise, the controls for education, family, race, residence, and time are similar to those in the model for housewives.

Tests for interaction of retirement, the independent variables, time, and household status were performed. The additional variance explained by the interactive models was not significant; hence the model in table 4-3 allows for additive effects of time and household status. Once a person is in the labor force, the processes of retirement do not differ greatly across households or time groups.

The gross effects of time on retirement show that, controlling for the proportion of housewives in the aged female population, there is a large increase in the incidence of retirement—35 percentage points over twenty-six years. This trend is only partially explained by compositional changes—the net effects of time are weaker than the gross effects, but the decline is still apparent.

The effects of the other variables on retirement of women are similar to the effects found for men. Age has the strongest effect, whereas retirement and occupation have smaller effects. The gross effects of education and occupation on retirement of women are smaller than the same effects for men, based on the size of the eta coefficients. The size of the beta coefficients, however, are similar across the two groups. Focusing on the net coefficients, we find little evidence that background characteristics are less important for women than for men. In most ways, in fact, the trends and characteristics of retirees are similar across sexes.

Census PUS Results

The census data does not have a great deal of information that can add to the SRC results for women. One of the problems is that no distinction is made between housewives and retirees; both groups are combined in the category "not in the labor force." An alternative is to construct a measure of being a housewife from a question on the number of years since last worked asked of women not currently employed. This question distinguishes among women who have never worked, who have not worked in the last ten years, and who have worked in the last ten years. Those who have never worked can clearly be classified as housewives. Yet there may also be some housewives in the category of those who have worked but not in ten years. Use of the never-worked classification to identify housewives would exclude those women who had some attachment to the labor force over ten years ago but who have spent most of their lives as homemakers. The alternative is to include all women who have not worked in the last ten years as housewives. This alternative has the problem of classifying older retirees, who have been out of the labor force for more than ten years, as housewives. These problems indicate the difficulty of operationalizing the concept of housewife without some kind of self-identification of the respondent. In order to use the most conservative proxy for housewives and to avoid counting retirees as housewives, I will analyze changes in the percentage of older females who have never worked.[2]

The effects of cohort and time on these two dependent variables are presented in table 4-4. The net effects of these variables are based on controls for cohort, education, marital status, family status, race, residence, and household size.[3] Separate results are presented for heads and nonheads of households. To avoid presentation of a great deal of information that essentially replicates previous results, only the coefficients for variables reflecting compositional and processual changes are shown (that is, the effects of cohort and time).

For the dependent variable measuring never having worked, there is a decline in housewives across cohorts. Net of other variables, 60 percent of the oldest cohort never worked, whereas only 9 percent of persons in the

Table 4-4
Multiple-Classification Analysis of the Effects of Cohort and Time on Never Having Worked for Heads and Nonheads of Households: PUS Females Aged 55 and Over

	Heads of Households			Nonheads of Households		
	N	Gross	Net	N	Gross	Net
Birth Cohort						
Before 1881	43	42	39	108	15	20
1881-1885	100	18	15	149	14	18
1886-1890	172	14	11	227	10	11
1891-1895	223	3	2	334	8	8
1896-1900	265	-3	-3	432	1	1
1901-1905	222	-9	-8	566	-4	-5
1906-1910	125	-14	-12	299	-6	-8
After 1910	142	-15	-12	404	-12	-13
		0.32	0.28*		0.19	0.22*
Covariates						
Time			2.3			2.9
R^2			0.176			0.092
Grand mean			21			27
N			1,292			2,519
df			1,266			2,495

Note: Control variables include education, marital status, family status, race, residence, and household size. Coefficients are multiplied by 100.
*$p < .01$
**$.01 < p < .05$

newest cohort (born after 1911) never worked. There is a gap in the percentage never having worked between women born before and after 1900. According to Cain (1967) this reflects the entrance of the later-born women into the labor force after World War I, when urbanization and modernization increased opportunities for participation. Once controls for cohorts and the other variables are included, time does not have a significant effect on never having worked. As with the SRC data, trends for heads of households are larger than for nonheads of households.

I now consider only those women who have worked in the last ten years, so that current participants can be compared with recent retirees. Because the census does not obtain information on former occupation for those who have been out of the labor force for ten years, it is necessary to exclude older retirees from the sample. Tests for interaction of the dependent variables—not in the labor force and not working full time—with household headship and the other independent variables are not significant. Hence the model is additive with respect to time as well as household status (table 4-5).

In contrast to the results for the SRC data, these figures include data on nonwork income. The effects of the variable are strong and reduce the importance of education, occupation, and age both on participation in the labor force and on full-time work. In fact, with controls for these variables, the effect of time is not significant for either dependent variable.

The size of the beta for many of the variables in table 4-5 are similar to the comparable betas for men, at least in relative size. The major difference is that the net effects of time are not as strong for women as they are for men, at least for this ten-year time span.

Summary and Discussion

A counterbalancing-forces argument has been used to explain the lack of change in participation of older women in the face of increasing participation at other ages. The argument suggests that cohort replacement has brought a higher proportion of female workers into old age, but that higher retirement rates during old age—similar to the increases for men—have balanced the entrance of persons into old age. Although the argument is hardly original, and follows from work on labor-force participation of women at younger ages (Oppenheimer 1970), it has not been validated empirically with appropriate data. This chapter has been able to test the explanation systematically through the use of consecutive cross-sectional survey data, where distinctions are made between older women who are housewives and those who are retirees. With data covering many time points, independent trends in the probability of being a housewife and the probability of retiring were considered.

Table 4-5

Multiple-Classification Analysis of Labor-Force Nonparticipation and Less-Than-Full-Time Employment: PUS Females Aged 55 and Over Who Have Worked in the Last Ten Years

		Not in Labor Force		Not Full Time	
	N	Gross	Net	Gross	Net
Age					
55-59	570	−17	−11	−13	−7
60-64	401	−5	−2	−7	−4
65-69	279	15	7	14	6
70-74	168	27	17	23	13
75-79	64	20	14	23	17
80+	35	36	30	29	23
		0.34	0.22*	0.29	0.17*
Education					
0-7	331	8	6	9	6
8	329	2	0	2	−1
9-11	266	−1	0	−3	−1
12+	323	−4	−3	−5	−2
13-15	144	−8	−5	−5	−1
16+	124	−6	−5	−6	−5
		0.11	0.08	0.11	0.07
Constant Non-work income					
None	737	−16	−14	−16	−15
1	175	−7	−4	−2	1
2	178	18	12	18	13
3	168	17	13	14	11
4	141	25	21	22	21
5	118	29	31	28	33
		0.37	0.32*	0.34	0.33*
Occupation					
Professional	200	−8	−5	−4	−1
Manager	90	−4	−2	−12	−10
Sales	149	4	2	4	2
Clerical	325	−3	−1	−9	−6
Craft	24	−4	0	−4	−1
Operative	255	0	−3	2	−1
Laborer	11	23	14	10	4
Service-private household	431	5	3	8	7
Farm manager	14	−5	−15	−18	−29
Farm laborer	18	26	22	24	18
		0.11	0.09	0.15	0.13*
Family relationship					
Head	627	−1	−7	−2	−8
Wife	659	2	9	4	11
Other	164	0	−4	−3	−7
Sec Ind	67	−11	−20	−11	−21
		.05	.18	.08	.21

Table 4-5 *(continued)*

		Not in Labor Force		Not Full Time	
	N	Gross	Net	Gross	Net
Covariates					
Self-employed			−1.4		5.2
Private			2.8		6.0
Black			−1.1		1.3
Rural			2.9		1.5
Time			−1.2		−3.1
R^2			0.217		0.204
Grand mean			41		54
N			1,517		1,517
df			1,484		1,484

Note: Coefficients multiplied by 100.

*$p < .01$

**$.01 < p < .05$

The first step was to present a cohort analysis of the probability of being a housewife (compared to being in the labor force or being retired) to test the argument that the participation rates of women entering old age have changed. Indeed, the analysis showed major decreases in the prevalence of housewives across cohorts: the average percentage of housewives for women born before 1900 (who reached old age before the 1960s) is 64 percent, whereas the average for women born in 1900 or after is 44 percent. The replacement of older cohorts with a high proportion of housewives by newer cohorts with a lower proportion of housewives explains the trend over time in the proportion of housewives for the total aged population. This is one example, then, of compositional changes in the aged population that account for change over time. Changes in the behavior of women at younger ages greatly affect characteristics during old age.

The cohort analysis is limited to the use of proxy variables measuring year of birth rather than the actual experiences of cohorts. The pattern of the coefficients for the cohort proxies suggest that historical changes in the opportunities for work are being tapped. Cohorts entering the labor force after the 1920s, when female-labeled service occupations began to expand, faced increased demand for female workers. Later-born cohorts were also more likely to work during World War II and to use this experience for later participation (Bowen and Finegan 1969). Finally, the decline in the number of children born to women in later cohorts made it possible for more women to enter the labor force (Cain 1967). Other variables, however, such as urbanization and higher education of women, were found in the analysis to explain little of the cohort differences in participation.

Given the decline in the proportion of housewives, the pattern of retirement has increased over time. The pattern found for women is similar to that found for men. There are some cross-sectional differences in the determinants of retirement—the effects of the background variables are sometimes smaller for women—but the trend over time is similar. Thus, female retirement patterns show increases in retirement for all groups independent of compositional changes. Because husbands and wives often retire together, it is not surprising that the trends over time have been similar across the sexes.

It is likely that these changes in participation and retirement among women have led to improvements in the conditions under which older women live. Some experience in the labor force as well as their own retirement benefits should be especially important for women who head their own households. In fact, participation rates are much higher for heads of households, and cohort changes in participation have been much larger for heads of households. The likely effect of these changes on income is an increase in income, which is the topic that will be considered in the following chapters.

Notes

1. Conceptually, it is at times difficult to distinguish between housewives and retired women. Some housewives may at times enter and reenter the labor force for short periods, and it is not clear which of these women should be considered housewives once they withdraw from the labor force. It would not be useful to specify minimum numbers of years of work, or the reception of some form of pension, as requirements for retirement since the number of years or levels of pensions chosen would be arbitrary. The analysis to follow will therefore depend on self-identification of the respondents as housewives or retirees.

2. Analysis of changes in "not worked in ten years" indicates that changes in levels of housewives are confused with changes in levels of retirees in the measure. For instance, the effects of time net of cohort are much larger for those who have not worked in ten years than they are for those who have never worked or for the SRC data. This suggests that the net trend in retirement is reflected in the results for those who have not worked in ten years.

3. A measure of family income brought in by family members other than the respondent, which is calculated from total family income minus person's income, is also included in the equation. Those women with the highest level of other family income are less likely to have worked, net of other factors (Sweet 1973). This is not the most appropriate measure, however, because it is based on current economic situation rather than on

lifetime economic situation. Widows in particular might have little current other family income but may have not worked when they were younger and married because other family income was higher. In fact, the results show a small effect for women who are still married but show no effect for those who are not. Because of the limitations of the measure, the results are not presented in the table.

5

Changes in Income Inequality within the Aged Population

Chapter 2 showed that the median income of the aged has steadily increased over the last several decades, whether income is measured in current dollars, constant dollars, or dollars relative to the income of persons aged 25-64. An equally important characteristic of the income distribution of the aged population that has received less attention is the dispersion or variability around the average. The median rather than the mean is commonly used as a measure of central tendency for income in order to limit the influence of a small number of highly skewed, positive income values. Yet by describing the income of cases at the 50th percentile, the median does not capture all the changes that occur in other parts of the distribution (Lieberson 1975). It is possible for the median income to rise while the distribution becomes less skewed and more peaked. Conversely, the median income may rise while the distribution becomes more skewed and less peaked. Or, finally, the shape of the income distribution may remain constant while the median rises.

Increases in income inequality within the aged population would indicate that increases in median income have benefited the more advantaged groups in the aged population—white males, workers, family members, and the highly educated. If income inequality declines, groups that have traditionally faced the most serious income problems—widows, retirees, minorities, and the very old—are likely to have benefited more from the increases in income. Thus changes in the well-being of the aged population depend on who is receiving the income and on changing levels of inequality.

The objective of this chapter is to describe changes in inequality of the income distribution among aged persons in the United States from 1947 to 1974. This time-series analysis is intended to supplement the time-series findings of chapter 2 and to provide a more precise picture of trends in income distribution among the aged. The data to be used to describe the trends in income inequality, then, will be from the same yearly *Current Population Reports* (CPR) used to calculate the median-income figures studied earlier.[1]

In addition to the description of the time series, this chapter will attempt to explain partially the trends by analyzing the 1960 and 1970 census data. While the ten-year gap between the censuses does not cover the twenty-eight-year period described by the time series, the individual-level nature of the data will allow examination of compositional and processual effects on inequality among the aged population. In particular, the effect of increased levels of retired persons and unrelated individuals on inequality can be determined. Because appropriate tables presenting the income of the aged disaggregated by labor-force status or family are not available from the CPR data, similar analyses cannot be done for all the years. The Survey Research Center (SRC) data, because of the small number of aged persons in each survey year, are also not appropriate for separating compositional and processual effects.

For both types of data, inequality will be measured by changes in the Gini and Theil indexes of inequality and in the proportion of income that goes to aged persons in each quintile of the income distribution.

Explanations and Predictions

The distinction made earlier between compositional and processual effects can be applied to inequality. Compositional changes involve shifts of the population into groups with relatively high or low levels of inequality. For instance, increases in the proportion of unrelated individuals may increase the numbers of low-income persons and therefore increase inequality. Processual changes involve changes in the distribution of income between and within the population groups. Holding compositional changes constant, inequality may still change if the income distribution changes in favor of unrelated individuals in general or in favor of low-income unrelated individuals in particular. The following sections review more systematically the types of compositional and processual changes that may affect inequality within the total aged population.

Compositional Changes

First, the increase in unrelated individuals and in female-headed households, whose income is lower than that of families and male-headed households, may increase inequality. For the total population, Kuznets (1974) has argued that income inequality has remained constant in the face of increasing transfer payments because of compositional shifts in the population away from younger, male-headed households and toward older, female-headed households. Since similar shifts have occurred within the aged population, inequality may have increased or any decline in inequality may have been masked.

The second major shift in the composition of the aged population that is likely to affect inequality is the change in the proportion of retired persons. However, it is not clear whether the change in retirement levels has increased or decreased inequality within the aged population. If inequality is higher in the retired aged population than in the working aged population, then increases in retirement will increase inequality. If, on the other hand, inequality is lower in the retired population than in the working-aged population, increases in retirement levels will reduce inequality. Whether or not income inequality is higher in the retired or working population will depend, of course, on the distribution of retirement benefits compared to the distribution of wages and salaries. On the one hand, retirement benefits would seem to be more equally distributed than wages because social-security benefits are partly based on a welfare strategy whereby retirees with the lowest previous wages get a larger percentage return on their wage contributions. On the other hand, equality may be lower among retirees than among workers because some receive benefits from private pensions while others receive none. Even if social-security benefits redistribute income, huge differences in private pension benefits will create greater equality among the retired population (Orbach 1979). In any case, this is an empirical question that needs to be tested.

Processual Changes

Controlling for compositional changes in the aged population, such as the increases in retired persons and in unrelated individuals, inequality may still change if the process of income distribution in the aged population changes (Danziger and Plotnick 1977). This may occur in one of two ways. First, using the distinction between family members and unrelated individuals as an example, inequality may decline if income is redistributed to the more deprived group—unrelated individuals. In other words, income inequality *between* family members and unrelated individuals may be reduced. If income is redistributed to family members, who are less deprived, income inequality between the groups should increase. Thus the effect of transfer payments on reducing income inequality will depend on which group receives a disproportionate share of the benefits. A similar argument may be applied to work-status differences. If income is redistributed to the lower-income retired population, inequality between workers and retirees should decline. If wage increases have outpaced retirement benefits, income will be redistributed in favor of the workers and inequality will be increased.

A second type of processual change in inequality may occur when income *within* subgroups of the aged population is redistributed. Among unrelated individuals, for instance, income may be redistributed to lower-income persons, thereby reducing income inequality within the group and within the aged population as a total. Or income may be further distributed to high-income persons, which will increase inequality within the population of unrelated individuals. Similar changes may occur among retired persons, working persons, or family members. In contrast to changes in between-group inequality defined in the previous paragraph, this second type of inequality is referred to as within-group inequality.

In summary, this chapter will attempt to answer several questions. First, what has been the trend in income inequality within the total aged population? Second, how do levels of inequality among retired aged or aged unrelated individuals compare to levels among working aged or aged family members? Third, given the differentials in inequality across these groups, how have shifts in their prevalence in the aged population affected income inequality? Fourth, how has the process of income redistribution affected inequality, both between and within labor-force-status and family-status groups in the aged population?

Data and Methods

The data to be used in describing trends in income inequality within the aged population come from published figures of the Current Population Survey (CPS).[2] These data are presented for two measures of income of the aged: (1) income of families headed by persons aged 65 and over and (2) income of persons aged 65 and over. Further, family income is presented separately for persons in families and for unrelated individuals (one-person families); and personal income is presented separately for males and females.[3] Since the income needs of families are greater than those of individuals, and since the process of income determination of males and females differs greatly, separate analysis of families and individuals or of males and females is warranted. This provides four measures of changes in income inequality.

Although the topic was discussed in chapter 2, it is important to mention the weaknesses in these measures of income. The measure of family income is limited to families headed by persons age 65 and over; aged persons living in families headed by persons under age 65 are not included in the measure. Personal income, although it includes aged persons in younger families, does not control for family status. As a result, the inequality of personal income may be overstated because individuals with no personal income may differ in levels of income they can share with their family members.[4] Further, neither measure of family or personal income includes institutionalized persons. A more important problem with all the measures, however, is that they do not include those components of economic welfare, such as in-kind benefits or assets, that do not transfer into dollar income (Moon 1977). As a result, the level of income inequality could decline while inequalities in wealth or assets remain constant. Similarly, income inequality could increase while higher in-kind, nonmonetary benefits maintain the relative economic standing of low-income aged persons. In general, it is likely that there have been changes in nonincome aspects of economic welfare that have both increased and decreased inequality among the aged population. Although substantial growth in nonmonetary transfer programs has benefited the low-income aged (Moon 1977), increases in accumulated wealth are likely to have been greater among the high-income aged. Although there is no reason to believe that these factors completely balance one another when measuring current income, there are no reliable time series on assets or in-kind benefits of the aged that can be analyzed in place of income. Thus it is necessary to use the best indicator of economic welfare available—income.

The published income distributions include the proportion of families of persons in specified income categories. In order to adjust for inflation and the rising standard of living, the census bureau has periodically changed the income categories it uses. Since such changes can affect the measurement of inequality, it is necessary to note when they occur (see appendix 5A). Comparison of the absolute levels of the inequality measures across the years in which the changes have occurred should be avoided, since it is difficult to apportion change resulting from changing categories from that caused by changing inequality.[5] Rather, changes in the levels of the inequality measures within the periods set off by category changes will provide a more reliable index of the trends.[6]

Two measures of inequality will be used. The first, the Gini index, is based on the cumulative proportion of income that goes to each cumulative proportion of the aged population. In terms of a graph that plots the cumulative proportion of the population on the x axis against the cumulative proportion of income on the y axis, the Gini index is the proportion of the total area below the diagonal that lies between the diagonal and the plotted Lorenz curve (Shryock and Siegel 1975).[7] The lower the Gini index, the more equal the distribution and the closer the Lorenz curve to the diagonal line of perfect equality. However, since the Gini index has been shown to be most sensitive to changes in the middle of the income distribution, I will also present the proportion of income that goes to each quintile of the aged population. This will provide more information on the income of the persons at the high and low extremes of the distribution as well as those in the middle. Second, Theil's information-based measure of inequality will also be calculated. The information-based index, or I, has the advantage of allowing decomposition of total inequality into between-group and within-group inequality. For a description of the formula and explanation of the decomposition techniques, see Theil (1967) or Theil (1972).[8]

The indexes and quintile distributions were calculated as follows. To obtain the amount of income owned by members of each income category, the proportion of the population in each category was multiplied by the geometric mean of the income limits of that category (for the open-ended category, the midpoint is estimated as 4/3 times the lower limit) (Treas and Walther 1978). The cumulative proportions of population and income were then calculated and substituted into the standard formula for the Gini index (Shryock and Siegel, 1975) and the Theil (1967) index. Similarly, interpolation was used to determine the proportion of income owned by each quintile of the aged population.

Trends in Inequality

Table 5-1 presents the Gini indexes and the quintile distributions of income for families and unrelated individuals.[9] Graphs of the changes over time in the Gini index are presented for families in figure 5-1 and for unrelated individuals in figure 5-2. Changes in categories used to measure income are shown by the horizontal lines in table 5-1 and by vertical lines in figures 5-1 and 5-2.

For family income, figure 5-1 indicates a decline in inequality that has been steady for the entire time span. The quintile distribution of income for families, shown in table 5-1, indicates that the greatest increase in income has occurred in the poorest fifth of the aged population. In terms of percentage increase from 1947 to 1974, the income owned by the poorest fifth has tripled. Further, the greatest loss occurred among the highest fifth of the income distribution. Even if complete equality is not in sight, there has been some redistribution of family income over the last thirty years.

The results for unrelated individuals show more fluctuation in the Gini index than do the results for families. A major jump occurs from 1962 to 1963, which is no doubt primarily the result of changes in income categories. Allowing for this jump, however, the Gini index shows considerable decline before and after 1963. The quintile distribution of income for unrelated individuals demonstrates that the largest improvement in income has occurred among the second quintile, followed by the first quintile. Further, the loss of income among the highest quintile is large. In sum, inequality among unrelated individuals is greater than among families; but it has also declined over time.

Table 5-2 presents the same calculations as does table 5-1, only for the personal income of males and females (figures 5-3 and 5-4 plot the changes). Compared to family income, the Gini indexes for personal income are higher, which would be expected because persons who have no personal income of their own will share the income of family members. Over time, the index for females declines by 0.227 (35 percent), and the index for males declines by 0.338 (43 percent).

Table 5-1
Gini Ratios and Quintile Distribution of Income for Families Headed by Persons Aged 65 and Over and Unrelated Individuals Aged 65 and Over

Year	Families: Gini Ratio	Quintile Percentage of Income					Unrelated Individuals: Gini Ratio	Quintile Percentage of Income				
		Low	2	3	4	High		Low	2	3	4	5
1947	0.517	1.9	7.1	13.5	29.8	47.6	0.674	0.5	0.5	12.3	19.2	67.5
1948	0.492	2.1	7.8	14.3	24.4	51.5	0.591	0.5	0.4	15.6	19.5	60.2
1949												
1950	0.518	1.5	7.1	13.8	23.7	53.9	0.631	0.5	1.2	15.9	18.0	64.4
1951	0.514	2.1	7.1	13.6	23.7	53.5	0.616	0.5	0.5	16.7	19.6	62.6
1952	0.489	2.5	8.0	14.3	23.5	51.7	0.567	0.4	8.3	12.2	19.7	59.4
1953												
1954	0.496	2.4	8.1	13.7	23.3	52.5	0.574	0.4	7.7	12.3	19.6	60.1
1955	0.475	3.0	8.5	13.8	24.0	50.7	0.567	0.4	8.8	11.6	19.9	59.4
1956	0.468	3.5	8.3	14.3	23.6	50.3	0.502	0.4	11.3	12.9	22.5	52.9
1957	0.450	3.9	8.8	14.5	23.9	48.9	0.523	0.4	10.6	12.4	21.3	55.4
1958	0.443	4.1	9.2	14.5	23.5	48.6	0.523	0.4	10.6	12.9	20.6	55.5
1959	0.449	4.1	9.1	14.0	23.4	49.4	0.525	1.4	9.5	13.1	19.8	56.2
1960	0.452	4.2	9.2	13.7	22.7	50.2	0.492	3.1	9.3	13.5	20.0	53.9
1961	0.455	4.3	8.9	13.8	22.2	50.1	0.486	3.6	9.0	13.9	20.1	52.3
1962	0.437	4.9	9.3	14.1	22.5	49.2	0.470	4.9	8.9	13.8	19.4	53.0
1963	0.460	4.1	8.9	14.0	22.3	50.8	0.580	0.4	4.0	15.5	22.1	58.1
1964	0.462	4.3	9.0	13.6	21.9	51.2	0.608	0.3	4.2	13.3	20.5	61.6
1965	0.444	4.6	9.4	14.2	22.2	49.5	0.565	0.4	5.7	14.6	22.2	57.1
1966	0.440	4.8	9.2	14.3	22.8	48.9	0.540	0.3	9.0	13.7	20.6	56.4
1967	0.448	4.6	9.1	13.9	22.6	49.8	0.554	0.3	8.4	13.3	20.2	57.7
1968	0.420	5.1	9.8	14.0	22.7	47.6	0.513	1.1	9.8	13.7	20.6	54.7
1969	0.430	4.8	9.6	14.5	22.8	48.3	0.507	2.3	9.3	13.5	20.0	54.9
1970	0.426	5.1	9.7	14.3	22.4	48.4	0.473	3.3	10.2	13.8	20.5	59.2
1971	0.411	5.4	10.3	14.6	22.3	47.4	0.458	4.2	10.2	13.8	20.5	51.2
1972	0.406	5.7	10.1	14.8	22.1	47.3	0.432	4.8	10.8	14.5	20.8	49.1
1973	0.401	6.0	10.3	14.5	22.4	46.8	0.413	5.6	11.0	14.7	20.9	47.8
1974	0.379	6.4	10.7	15.3	22.9	44.7	0.395	6.5	11.2	14.3	20.8	47.2
Δ[a]	-0.138	4.5	3.6	1.8	-6.9	-2.9	-0.279	6.0	10.7	2.0	1.6	-20.3

[a]Calculated from 1974 value minus 1947 value.

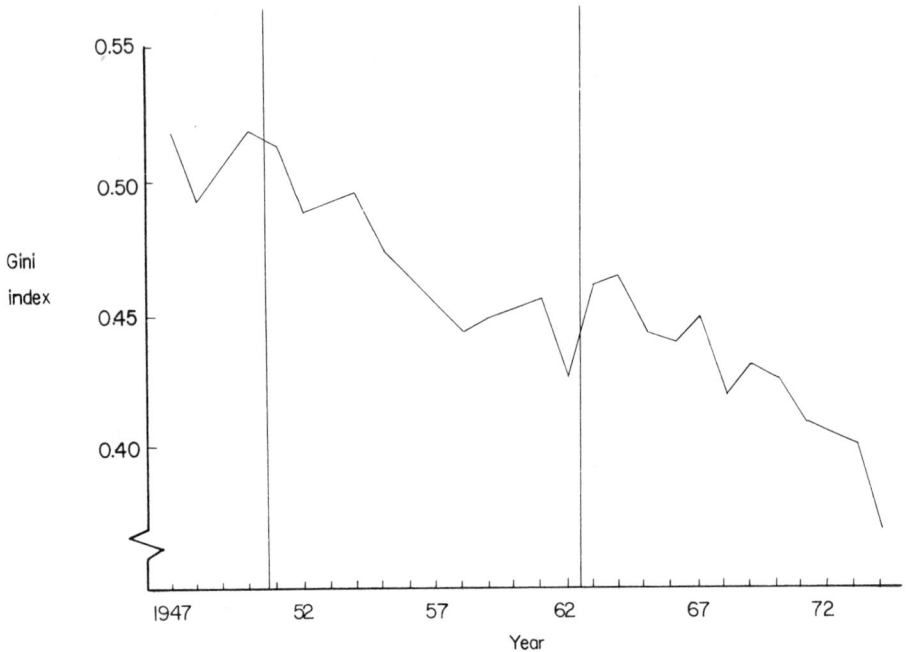

Figure 5-1. Trends in Gini Index for Income of Aged Families in the
United States, 1947-1974

Although the Gini indexes drop for males and females, the quintile in
which the most change occurs is different for each sex. For males there was
improvement in the three lowest quintiles, whereas for females the most
change occurred in the middle three quintiles. This might indicate that the
poorest widows are not benefiting from income increases as much as are
persons in the higher parts of the distribution. It might also be the result of
the presence of a large number of married women who do not have any of
their own income but depend on the income of their spouses; in terms of
personal income, their share would increase little, although in terms of
family income they would benefit more.

In summary, the income of families, unrelated individuals, males, and
females shows declining inequality over the last several decades. For family
income and personal income of males, the greatest increase in percentage of
owned income has occurred among the lowest quintile of the income
distribution, whereas for income of unrelated individuals and females, the
largest gains have been made by the middle quintiles.

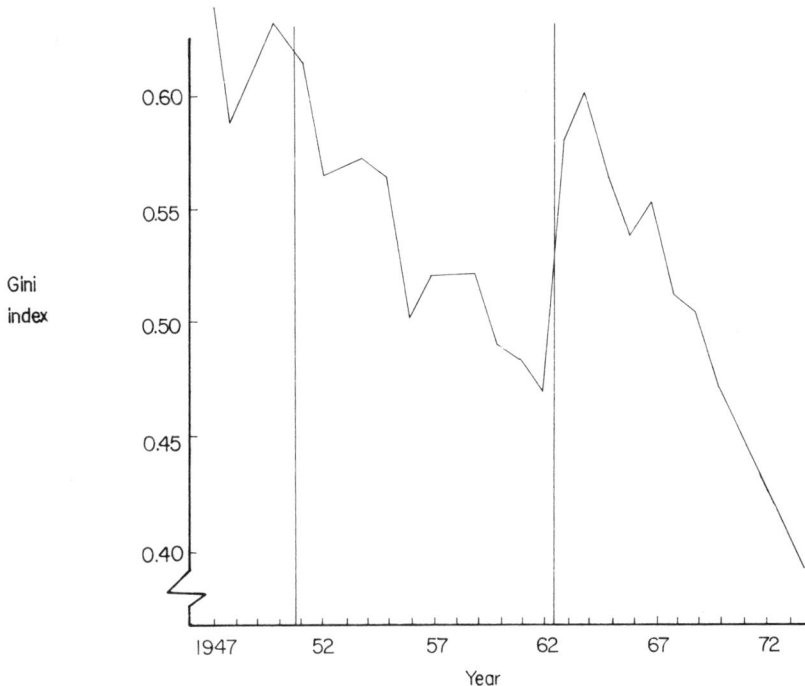

Figure 5-2. Trends in Gini Index for Income of Primary Individuals Aged 65 + in the United States, 1947-1974

Retirement and Declining Inequality

In order to determine the effects of changes in retirement levels on changes in inequality, and to compare income inequality among working aged and among nonworking aged, I turn to cross-sectional data from the 1960 and 1970 census data. By using the census-data files, cross-tabulations not available from the published reports can be analyzed. In particular, I obtained the income distribution for males and females in the labor force and not in the labor force in both 1960 and 1970.[10] Income is measured both as total family income and as total personal income, collapsed into twelve categories similar to those used by the CPS studies. With these income distributions, I calculated the Theil measure of income inequality rather than the Gini index because the Theil measure allows decomposition of total inequality into between-group and within-group inequality.

Table 5-3 presents the Theil information-based index for a variety of groups. First, inequality was calculated separately for males and females,

Table 5-2
Gini Ratios and Quintile Distribution of Personal Income of Males and Females Aged 65 and Over

| | Males: | | | | | | Females: | | | | | |
| | Gini Ratio | Quintile Percentage of Income | | | | | Gini Ratio | Quintile Percentage of Income | | | | |
Year		Low	2	3	4	High		Low	2	3	4	High
1947	0.810	1.1	1.1	1.1	9.5	87.1	0.651	0.3	1.2	10.7	23.2	64.6
1948	0.760	1.3	1.3	1.3	17.2	78.9	0.601	0.3	4.3	11.8	23.5	60.0
1949	0.756	1.3	1.3	1.3	17.6	78.4	0.626	0.3	2.8	11.3	23.1	62.5
1950	0.776	1.2	1.2	1.2	16.0	80.5	0.629	0.3	3.3	10.8	22.6	62.9
1951	0.768	1.2	1.2	1.2	17.3	79.1	0.612	0.3	4.4	10.7	22.4	62.2
1952	0.753	0.8	0.8	0.8	21.3	76.2	0.587	0.2	6.8	10.8	22.2	60.0
1953	0.767	0.8	0.8	0.8	20.5	77.1	0.621	0.2	5.2	10.2	21.3	63.0
1954	0.732	0.8	0.8	1.3	23.9	73.3	0.597	0.2	6.1	10.9	21.8	60.9
1955	0.716	0.7	0.8	4.0	23.5	70.9	0.583	0.4	6.8	11.7	20.4	60.6
1956	0.670	0.7	0.7	10.1	21.6	67.0	0.555	1.6	6.8	12.5	20.8	58.4
1957	0.686	0.6	0.6	10.0	19.9	68.8	0.526	2.2	7.3	12.9	21.6	55.9
1958	0.642	0.6	0.6	13.7	21.2	63.9	0.504	2.6	8.4	13.3	22.0	53.8
1959	0.636	0.5	0.5	16.1	20.1	62.8	0.524	2.9	8.0	12.3	20.1	56.9
1960	0.642	0.5	0.5	14.6	19.6	64.8	0.520	3.1	8.1	12.3	20.0	56.5
1961	0.605	0.5	2.2	15.7	21.2	60.5	0.537	3.0	7.8	11.9	19.3	58.0
1962	0.589	0.4	4.2	14.2	22.0	59.2	0.487	3.7	8.7	13.3	20.5	53.8
1963	0.602	0.4	4.5	13.4	20.8	60.9	0.491	3.9	8.7	13.2	19.5	54.7
1964	0.600	0.4	6.1	11.9	20.1	61.6	0.520	3.6	8.0	12.4	18.8	51.3
1965	0.576	0.4	7.5	11.6	20.8	59.7	0.474	4.4	8.9	13.2	20.5	53.0
1966	0.571	0.3	7.4	12.9	20.7	58.8	0.482	4.4	8.6	12.9	20.1	53.9
1967	0.594	0.3	6.6	12.2	19.6	61.3	0.492	4.3	8.2	12.6	19.8	55.1
1968	0.566	0.3	7.4	13.0	20.7	58.6	0.466	4.5	8.9	13.6	21.4	51.3
1969	0.563	0.2	7.4	13.1	20.7	58.5	0.475	4.3	8.9	13.5	20.3	53.0
1970	0.550	0.4	7.9	13.6	20.7	57.5	0.464	4.6	8.8	13.9	20.5	52.2
1971	0.535	0.8	8.3	13.8	20.9	56.1	0.450	5.0	9.4	13.8	20.6	51.3
1972	0.523	1.2	8.6	13.8	21.6	54.8	0.442	5.1	9.7	14.1	20.5	50.6
1973	0.499	1.7	8.9	14.9	22.0	52.6	0.446	5.1	9.6	13.6	20.5	51.2
1974	0.472	0.2	10.2	14.9	21.9	50.9	0.424	5.4	10.1	14.3	21.5	48.7
Δ	-0.338	-0.9	9.1	13.8	12.4	-36.2	-0.227	5.1	8.9	3.6	-1.7	-15.9

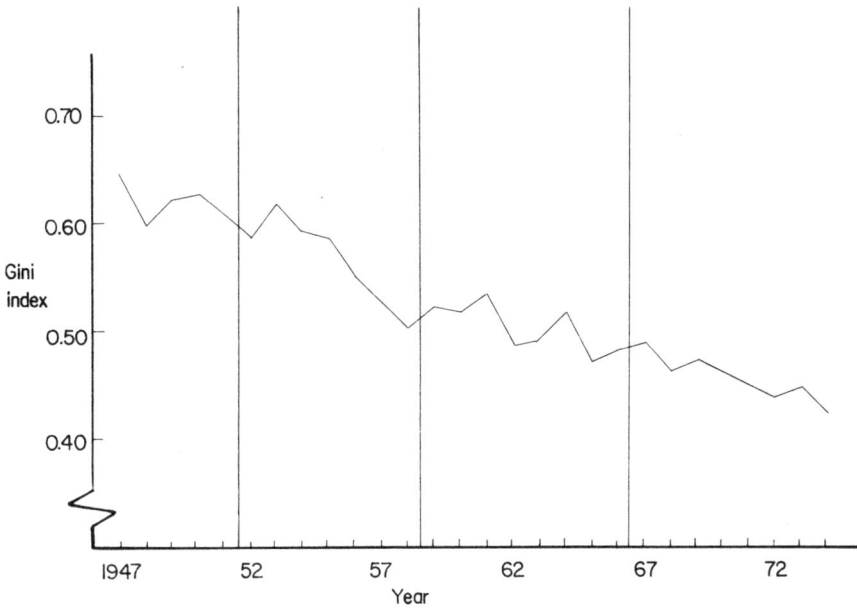

Figure 5-3. Trends in Gini Index for Personal Income of Males Aged 65 and Over, United States, 1947-1974

for family income and personal income, and for 1960 and 1970 data. Within these larger categories, the index is calculated for labor-force participants and nonparticipants. The category sample sizes are also presented below the inequality measures for the separate groups. For example, total male inequality for family income declines from 0.479 in 1960 to 0.445 in 1970. A similar decline is apparent from 1960 personal income of aged males (0.658 to 0.550), family income of aged females (0.601 to 0.519), and personal income of aged females (1.054 to 0.748). The data here show a decline in inequality consistent with the previous findings.

The second question to be addressed concerns the levels of inequality among participants compared to nonparticipants. For all the comparisons in table 5-3, inequality is higher for nonparticipants. For male family income in 1960, the Theil index for participants is 0.386 compared to an index of 0.466 for nonparticipants. The same relationship holds for 1970 personal or family income and for females. This supports the argument that transfer payments are distributed less equally to retired persons than are wages and salaries to working persons.

How do these differentials affect the trend in total inequality? For women there is little or no effect because the proportion of nonparticipants changed little. For men, inequality would have been lower in 1970 had it not

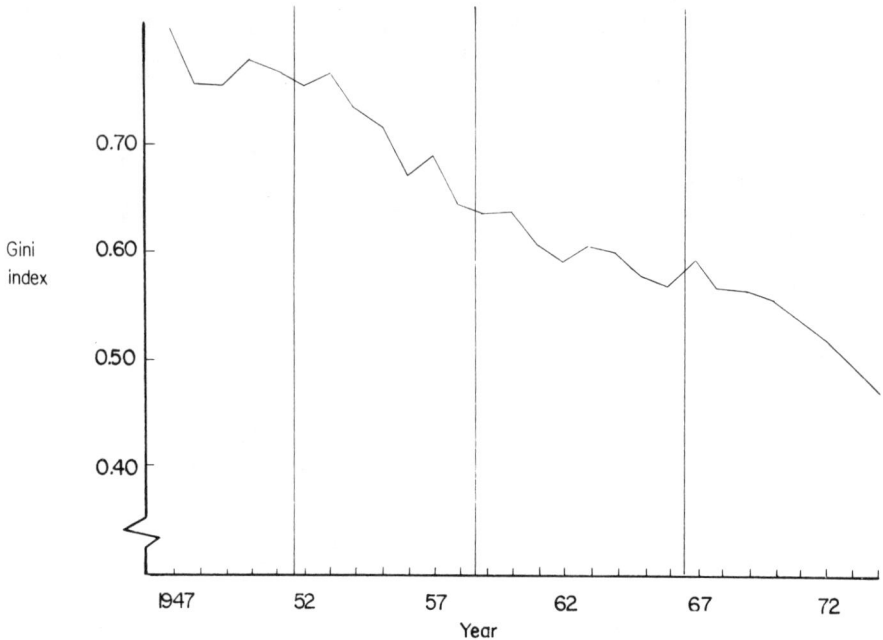

Figure 5-4. Trends in Gini Index for Personal Income of Females Aged 65
and Over, United States, 1947-1974

been for increases in the proportion of the retired population. A standardized inequality index shows what the 1970 index would have been if the
distribution of nonparticipating males in 1970 was the same as in 1960.[11]
The standardized indexes are somewhat smaller than the unstandardized
ones, indicating that increasing retirement has contributed modestly to inequality.

What has been more important, and explains the drop in inequality
despite the growth of the retired population, is the change in the process of
income distribution. As discussed, processual changes involve changes in
both between-group inequality and within-group inequality. The results in
table 5-3 show that inequality between labor-force participants and nonparticipants is less than inequality within these groups. Yet levels of
between-group inequality have declined and partially explain the decline in
total inequality. For instance, between-group inequality accounts for 10
percent of the total inequality of male personal income in 1960; for 1970,
the figure is 8.5 percent. Similar declines in the percentage of total inequality owing to between-group inequality are apparent for females and for personal income. Note that between-group inequality is less important for

Table 5-3
Decomposition by Labor-Force Status of Information-Based Measures of Inequality: PUS Males and Females Aged 65 and Over

	Family Income		Personal Income	
	1960	1970	1960	1970
Males				
Total inequality	0.479	0.445	0.658	0.550
Between-group inequality	0.049	0.038	0.179	0.099
(Percentage of total)	10.2%	8.5%	27.2%	18.0%
Within-group inequality	0.430	0.407	0.479	0.451
In labor force	0.386	0.311	0.470	0.373
N	(204)	(203)	(204)	(203)
Percentage	29.8	24.1	29.8	24.1
Not in labor force	0.466	0.462	0.493	0.514
N	(480)	(639)	(480)	(639)
Percentage	70.2	75.9	70.2	75.9
Standardized		0.437		0.544
Females				
Total inequality	0.601	0.519	1.054	0.748
Between-group inequality	0.001	0.002	0.123	0.046
(Percentage of total)	0.2%	0.4%	11.7%	6.2%
Within-group inequality	0.600	0.517	0.931	0.702
In labor force	0.386	0.351	0.357	0.307
N	(95)	(117)	(95)	(117)
Percentage	10.7	10.0	10.7	10.0
Not in labor force	0.630	0.540	1.162	0.802
N	(793)	(1052)	(193)	(1052)
Percentage	89.3	90.0	89.3	90.0
Standardized		0.518		0.745

females. Since females not in the labor force may often depend on the income of other family members, their family-income levels are not greatly disadvantaged compared to those of females in the labor force.

The low levels of between-group inequality indicate that there is a good deal of overlap in the income distributions of participants and nonparticipants—many nonparticipants will have higher income than many participants. More important in explaining inequality in the aged population is inequality among participants and among nonparticipants. In other words, differences in the amount of income going to high-income participants compared to that of low-income participants (or high-income participants compared to low-income participants) are larger than differences between income going to all participants compared to all nonparticipants. Over time, the levels of within-group inequality have declined. For family income of males, within-group inequality declined from 0.430 to 0.407.

Note that total within-group inequality is based on a weighted sum of inequality among participating and nonparticipating populations.[12] Thus with one exception (personal income of male nonparticipants), the decline in total within-group inequality is shown also in separate decreases in inequality among participants and nonparticipants.

In short, the decline in inequality among the aged occurs through two processual sources of change. First, there has been a decline in between-group inequality, showing that a greater proportion of income is going to the population of nonworkers. Second, a greater proportion of income primarily within the population of workers and secondarily within the population of nonworkers is going to the poorest persons.

Family Status and Declining Inequality

The analysis performed for work-status groups can also be performed for family-status groups (table 5-4). Ideally, causes of changes in inequality could be analyzed for groups cross-classified by work status and family status, but the sample size of the 1-in-10,000 *Public Use Sample* (PUS) does not provide sufficient numbers of aged persons for reliable cross-classification of the groups. A variation on the previous analysis, however, is to measure inequality in job income. By comparing inequality in job income with inequality in total personal income, the effect of transfer payments and nonwork income on reducing inequality can be determined (Danziger and Plotnick 1977). Such an analysis would be of little use in the previous section since nonworkers have little work income. The following discussion will focus first on personal and family income and will then turn to consideration of job income.

Total inequality for male and female personal and family income has declined from 1960 to 1970, as would be expected given the results in tables 5-1 and 5-2. An especially large drop in inequality has occurred for female personal incomes. Also, as shown in the previous tables, inequality is higher for unrelated individuals than for family members, with one exception. Personal-income inequality is higher for female family members than for female unrelated individuals. Although some female family members will have no income at all, it is unlikely that unrelated individuals could survive without some personal income. Since family members can often share the income of their families, their high levels of inequality for personal income may be misleading.

Given these differences between the family-status groups, the growth of unrelated individuals has generally had a modest inhibiting effect on the decline in overall inequality. Compositional changes have the greatest effect for family income, where the difference between inequality among family

Table 5-4
Decomposition by Family Status of Information-Based Measures of Inequality: PUS Males and Females Aged 65 and Over

	Job Income		Personal Income		Family Income	
	1960	1970	1960	1970	1960	1970
Males						
Total inequality	1.565	1.460	0.658	0.550	0.479	0.445
Between-group inequality	0.020	0.023	0.003	0.010	0.022	0.046
(Percentage of total)	1.3%	1.6%	0.5%	1.8%	4.6%	10.3%
Within-group inequality	1.545	1.437	0.655	0.540	0.457	0.399
Family members	1.500	1.408	0.643	0.518	0.426	0.365
N	(564)	(635)	(564)	(635)	(564)	(635)
Percentage	82.5	75.4	82.5	75.4	82.5	75.4
Unrelated individuals	1.933	1.594	0.725	0.636	0.729	0.639
N	(120)	(207)	(120)	(207)	(120)	(207)
Percentage	17.5	24.6	17.5	24.6	17.5	24.6
Standardized		1.441		0.540		0.357
Females						
Total inequality	2.545	1.748	1.054	0.748	0.601	0.519
Between-group inequality	0.005	0.056	0.049	0.046	0.130	0.117
(Percentage of total)	0.2%	3.2%	4.6%	6.1%	21.6%	22.5%
Within-group inequality	2.540	1.692	1.005	0.702	0.471	0.402
Family members	2.703	1.966	1.188	0.836	0.426	0.339
N	(594)	(672)	(594)	(672)	(594)	(672)
Percentage	66.9	57.5	66.9	57.5	66.9	57.5
Unrelated individuals	2.273	1.503	0.809	0.604	0.831	0.659
N	(294)	(497)	(294)	(497)	(294)	(497)
Percentage	33.1	42.5	33.1	42.5	33.1	42.5
Standardized		1.796		0.771		0.478

members and that among unrelated individuals is largest. Thus for males, changes in household composition prevented the level of inequality from falling to 0.357—0.088 points below the observed 1970 value.

As was the case for work status, compositional shifts and their effects on inequality are overshadowed by the decline in inequality owing to processual changes. However, the processual effects responsible for the decline occurred within family groups rather than between them. Note that as a proportion of total inequality, between-group inequality has increased for all comparisons. Within groups, however, inequality has declined. Since within-group inequality is a larger proportion of total inequality, especially for female personal income, the within-group decline outweighs the between-group increase. Substantively, then, there has been little redistribution of income from family members to unrelated individuals; but among unrelated individuals and families, income has been redistributed somewhat to those with the lowest incomes.

Finally, the effect of nonwork income on levels of inequality can be examined by comparing inequality for job income with inequality for total personal income. Naturally, inequality is much higher for job income than for personal income—all those who are not working have no job income, but do have personal income from nonjob sources. It is more important to compare the size of the reduction in inequality from job income to personal income in 1960 to the reduction in 1970. As transfer payments become a more important source of redistributing income, the differences between job-income inequality and personal-income inequality should become larger.

To test this argument, the percentage reduction in inequality from job income to personal income can be compared across years. For males, the percentage difference in 1960 is 58 [(1.565 − 0.658)/1.565]. For 1970, the percentage reduction is 62. The role of transfer payments and nonwork income in reducing income inequality has become only slightly larger between 1960 and 1970. Similar results hold for females; the 1960 percentage reduction is 59, and the 1970 percentage reduction is 64.

Summary and Discussion

Let me return to the original questions about changes in inequality raised in the first section of this chapter. First, what has been the trend in income inequality? The analysis showed that for the total aged population and nearly all subgroups in the population that were examined the trend has been downward. Substantial inequalities remain, but there is evidence that the increases in income demonstrated in chapter 2 have not further increased the gap between the haves and the have-nots in the aged population.

Second, how do levels of inequality of retired persons compare to those of workers, or those of families to those of unrelated individuals? Inequality is found to be higher among labor-force nonparticipants and among unrelated individuals, both growing segments of the aged population. Third, given the higher inequality among the expanding subgroups of the aged population, how have compositional shifts in their prevalence in the aged population affected inequality? Compositional changes have had a modest limiting effect on declining inequality; that is, without compositional changes in the proportion of retired and unrelated individuals, inequality would have declined slightly more than it actually did.

Fourth, how has the process of income redistribution affected income inequality? The comparisons of inequality between labor-force participants and nonparticipants show that processual effects have reduced both between-group and within-group inequality. Relative both to workers and to other nonworkers, low-income retirees have improved their income position. These processual effects are large enough to cause major declines in inequality despite the compositional effects in the opposite direction. For the comparison of family members and unrelated individuals, processual effects have been large enough also to reduce income inequality in the face of compositional effects. The processual changes involve changes within groups; between-group inequality, only a small proportion of the total, actually increased but had little effect relative to within-group declines.

The evidence supports the argument that modest redistribution of income has occurred within the aged population. It is not possible from the results of this chapter to identify what has caused the processual changes responsible for declining inequality. The data would suggest, however, that the major area of redistribution occurred among males in the labor force, females not in the labor force, and nonfamily members. Smaller redistribution has occurred among retired males and among females in the labor force. For men, this suggests that wages and salaries are being more progressively distributed, but that transfer programs to retirees have been less successful in directing income to the most needy retirees. For women, transfer of income to those not in the labor force probably reflects the increase in retirees and the decrease in housewives and widows. In contrast to that of males not in the labor force, inequality among females not in the labor force has declined and indicates progressive changes in distribution of income benefits.

As a final qualification, these results refer to income inequality rather than to inequality in economic welfare. Despite the decline in income inequality, those at the bottom of the distribution may have made little headway in reducing inequality of wealth. Conversely, nonmonetary transfer payments, if they were included, might further reduce income inequality. These are issues that need to be addressed by future research.

Notes

1. In a special report of the U.S. Bureau of the Census (1967), Gini indexes were calculated for a wide variety of social groups for the years 1947-1964. Among these calculations were Gini indexes for the population aged 65 and over. However, although these calculations were presented in tables, there was no attempt to analyze the changes. Moreover, the results are based on income distributions adjusted to maintain comparable categories over time. The adjustment of the data leads to some difficulties in interpretation and to much fluctuation in the measures of inequality; hence the need to analyze and discuss a consistent time series of inequality measures remains.

2. The data are published in series P-60, report numbers 5, 6, 7, 9, 11,

12, 14, 15, 16, 19, 20, 23, 24, 27, 30, 33, 35, 37, 39, 41, 43, 47, 51, 53, 60, 66, 75, 80, 85, 90, 97, and 101. Family-income data for 1949 and 1953 are not available.

3. As in chapter 2, it was necessary to recalculate the relative distribution for personal income because the published distributions present the proportion of persons in each category as a proportion of all persons receiving income; persons without income are therefore not included. I recalculated the distribution including all persons, whether they had received income or not, in order to avoid underestimating the level of inequality.

4. Inequality will be higher than for family income because of the inclusion of persons with no personal income in the calculations (see note 3). They may be excluded from the calculations on the assumption that those with no personal income must have income from some other source and that personal income of these persons is misleading. They may be included for other reasons. The number of persons with no personal income is an important aspect of the distribution of income. Even if such persons can share the income of others, they may face serious problems if disruption of family relations occurs. Excluding these persons would lead to underestimation of the level of inequality. In any case, calculations done with and without persons with no personal income show a similar pattern of change even if the absolute levels of inequality differ.

5. Although 1975 and 1976 data are available, the number of categories used to classify income was increased from 17 to 24. Because comparison with earlier years would be misleading, and because the 1975 and 1976 time points are insufficient for identifying trends, data are presented only for the years up to 1974.

6. An alternative method for dealing with the changing categories has been used in a publication by the Bureau of the Census (1967). The census bureau transformed the income data into a set of identical categories for the years 1947-1964. This was done by making assumptions about the distribution of cases within the categories so that identical categories could be calculated for each year. The results, however, are only as reliable as the assumptions made to transform the income distributions. In fact, the transformations appear to be unreliable, especially for income of unrelated individuals. The Gini ratios calculated from the transformed distribution show a great deal of fluctuation. For instance, the Gini indexes for the income of unrelated individuals show the following pattern for the years from 1951 to 1956: the 1951 value is approximately 0.49; 1952, 0.59; 1953, 0.49; 1954, 0.56; and 1955, 0.47. This shows a great deal more fluctuation than the untransformed calculations to be reported here.

7. Given a number of income categories, the cumulative proportions of the population in and below each category, and the cumulative propor-

tion of income owned by persons in and below each category, the formula for the Gini index is:

$$G = \Sigma \ X_i Y_{i+1} - \Sigma \ X_{i+1} Y_i$$

where X_i and Y_i are the cumulative proportions for population and income, respectively.

8. The formula for the Theil information-based measure, I, is:

$$I = \Sigma \ Y_i \ ln \ (y_i/x_i)$$

where x_i refers to the proportion of the population in category i, and y_i refers to the proportion of owned income of persons in category i. Unlike the Gini ratio, the upper limit for I varies depending on the number of categories.

9. The correlations between the Gini index and the Theil index were above 0.95 for all measures of income. Given the similarity of the trends, I present the more familiar Gini index here; results for the Theil index will be presented in the next section where decompositional analysis of inequality will be performed.

10. For females, it is not possible to distinguish between retirees and housewives. Thus inequality among older female nonparticipants only partially reflects distribution of retirement benefits.

11. The standardized index calculates income inequality for 1970 using the distribution of participants and nonparticipants for 1960 and the distribution of income for those groups in 1970. Processual differences are allowed to vary while compositional changes are held constant.

12. The weights used in calculating the total within-group inequality from the separate inequality for participants and nonparticipants are based on the proportion of income going to each group.

Appendix 5A:
Income Categories
Used in Calculations
of Gini Index and
Quintile Distribution
for CPR Data

Family Income Categories

1947-1950	*1951-1962*	*1963-1974*
$0-499	$0-499	$0-999
$500-999	$500-999	
$1,000-1,499	$1,000-1,499	$1,000-1,499
$1,500-1,999	$1,500-1,999	$1,500-1,999
$2,000-2,499	$2,000-2,499	$2,000-2,499
$2,500-2,999	$2,500-2,999	$2,500-2,999
$3,000-3,499	$3,000-3,499	$3,000-3,499
$3,500-3,999	$3,500-3,999	$3,500-3,999
$4,000-4,499	$4,000-4,499	$4,000-4,999
$4,500-4,999	$4,500-4,999	
$5,000-5,999	$5,000-5,999	$5,000-5,999
$6,000-9,999	$6,000-6,999	$6,000-9,999
$10,000+	$7,000-9,999	$7,000-7,999
	$10,000-14,999	$8,000-8,999
	$15,000-24,999	$9,000-9,999
	$25,000+	$10,000-11,999
		$12,000-14,999
		$15,000-24,999
		$25,000+

Personal Income Categories

1947-1951	*1952-1958*	*1959-1966*	*1967-1974*
$0-499	$0-499	$0-499	$0-499
$500-999	$500-999	$500-999	$500-999
$1,000-1,499	$1,000-1,499	$1,000-1,499	$1,000-1,499
$1,500-1,999	$1,500-1,999	$1,500-1,999	$1,500-1,999
$2,000-2,499	$2,000-2,499	$2,000-2,499	$2,000-2,499
$2,500-2,999	$2,500-2,999	$2,500-2,999	$2,500-2,999
$3,000-3,499	$3,000-3,499	$3,000-3,499	$3,000-3,999

$3,500-3,999	$3,500-3,999	$3,500-3,999	
$4,000-4,499	$4,000-4,499	$4,000-4,499	$4,000-4,999
$4,500-4,999	$4,500-4,999	$4,500-4,999	
$5,000-5,999	$5,000-5,999	$5,000-5,999	$5,000-5,999
$6,000-9,999	$6,000-6,999	$6,000-6,999	$6,000-6,999
$10,000 +	$7,000-9,999	$7,000-7,999	$7,000-7,999
	$10,000-14,999	$8,000-9,999	$8,000-9,999
	$15,000-24,999	$10,000-14,999	$10,000-14,999
	$25,000 +	$15,000-24,999	$15,000-24,999
		$25,000 +	$25,000 +

6 Compositional and Processual Changes in Determination of Income of Aged Males

Despite the arguments of early research that older persons face steadily growing financial problems and that the gap between the incomes of the aged and the non-aged was increasing (Burgess 1960; Palmore and Whittington 1971), the evidence in chapter 2 showed that all indicators of the income of the aged had risen. Decreasing labor-force participation seems not to have reduced the income of the aged, nor has it prevented the occurrence of a decline in income inequality within the aged population.

However, the inferences that can be made about aged individuals from aggregated data are limited. Moreover, the nature of time-series data limits the variables that can be controlled for: the effects on income of variables such as education, occupation, and family status, not treated previously, now need to be considered. By using individual-level data from the consecutive cross-sectional surveys, this chapter will be able to identify some of the individual-level determinants of income among the aged and will be able to test for compositional and processual explanations of the increases in the income of the aged population.

To review some of the arguments in chapter 1, explanations of the increase in income have focused on two types of change: (1) cohort replacement and compositional changes within the aged population and (2) increased levels of transfer income that have changed the process of income determination, especially in relation to the consequences of retirement.

Compositional Changes in the Aged Population

The importance of cohort change on the composition of the aged population is shown by the fact that 60 percent of the aged population was replaced during the decade of the 1960s (Uhlenberg 1977). Most writers have argued that these changes have improved the income of the aged; compared with earlier-born cohorts, newer cohorts have a higher proportion of members who are urban, highly educated, and current or former occupants of high-prestige jobs (Foner 1975; Neugarten 1975). These more recent cohorts were better able to participate in expansion of the educational system and upgrading of the occupational-prestige structure and to carry those advantages into old age, which has resulted, among other things, in higher income among the aged during the 1960s and 1970s.

With respect to income, however, this argument works in both directions. Although increases in urban residence, education, and occupational prestige may increase income of newer cohorts, other cohort characteristics may be responsible for lower income. First, since retirement income is seldom as high as preretirement earnings, increases in the proportion of retired persons in more recent cohorts is likely to lower the income of the aged population. Although average income levels have risen at the same time that retirement has gone up, income might have increased even more had not retirement become so common. Second, changes in marital and family living arrangements might have adversely affected family-income levels of the aged (Clemente and Summers 1973). Smaller household size may reduce family income, even if the share of family income for each person has remained constant.

Third, residual cohort effects need to be considered. Persons born in large cohorts, where competition for jobs and resources is intense, and persons born in cohorts that entered the labor force during periods of economic depression, are likely to have lower income than other cohorts (Spaeth 1976; Elder 1974). It is difficult to measure the level of competition that cohort members face or the state of the labor market they enter. It is possible, however, to measure the effects of these characteristics indirectly by examining the effect of birth-cohort membership on income attainment.

In summary, compositional changes may affect the income levels of the aged population in several directions. First, income improvements might have been greater than they were had it not been for increases in the proportion of persons retired, decreasing household size, and historical events affecting the financial situation of cohorts. Second, increases in urban residence, education, and occupational prestige may have changed the composition of the aged population sufficiently to explain the observed increase in income. Third, despite arguments to the contrary, compositional changes may have little effect on changes in the income of the aged.

Changes in the Process of Income Determination

At the extreme, income increases could be completely explained by compositional changes that increase the proportion of persons in the aged population with characteristics that favor higher income attainment. It is more likely, however, that processual changes have occurred independently of compositional change; that is, persons in the same structural position are likely to have higher income in later periods than in earlier periods. Thus time will change the process of income determination by affecting the way the compositional variables determine income. This kind of change is likely to result from increases in pension benefits, wages, and the standard of living.

There are three hypotheses concerning the direction these processual changes may take. First, the increase in income, net of compositional changes, may have occurred equally among subgroups of the aged population. In other words, the process of income attainment may have changed identically across the aged population. This pattern would be indicated by additive effects of time on income.

Second, the effect of time on income may have been different for different subgroups of the aged population. The process of income attainment may change in such a way that the independent variables become stronger over time and the income differences between groups become larger. If, for example, the net effects of education are stronger in more recent years, the income gap between the more and less educated persons in the aged population would increase. In short, this hypothesis predicts divergence in income levels between the highly educated and the less educated, the working and the retired, the young-old and the old-old, the urban and the rural, and the high-status workers and the low-status workers. Rather than affecting all groups equally, time would have the largest effects on income of the high-income group.

Third, if the effects of the independent variables are stronger in the earlier years, this would indicate convergence in income levels among groups in the aged population. The effect of time would thus be strongest for the low-income groups. Since the negative effects of being old, less educated, retired, rural, or a low-prestige worker would have declined, the income gaps between these groups would be smaller. Convergence of income levels over time would reduce the importance of background differences, yet would still lead to higher income as low-income groups approach the income of their high-income counterparts. Such changes might result from the growth of transfer payments, which are distributed more equally throughout the aged population than are salaries or wages (Danziger and Plotnick 1977; Moon 1977). This hypothesis is consistent with the results of the previous chapter.

Data and Methods

The compositional and processual hypotheses discussed previously suggest a model of family income that includes the time, age, education, former or current occupation, employment status, urban or rural residence, family living arrangements, and cohort.[1] The compositional hypotheses can be tested with the consecutive cross-sectional survey data by comparing the gross effects of time on family income with the net effects of time, controlling for these compositional variables. The difference between the gross and net effects will show the increase in income resulting from all compositonal changes. Furthermore, the effect of compositional changes in individual variables can be observed in the indirect effects of time on family income through the intervening compositional variables. The processual hypotheses can be tested by examining models of family income separately for each time period or, alternatively, by testing for significant interaction effects among time, family income, and the compositional variables. If significant interactions exist, then the direction of the effects can be examined to test the convergence and divergence hypotheses.

For the purposes of this chapter, only white males aged 60 and over from the SRC surveys will be examined.[2] The use of age 60 and over to define old age is somewhat arbitrary; yet it includes persons at ages at which retirement is common and does not exclude all but the very old. The analysis of income for nonwhites is postponed until chapter 8.

The SRC measure of income available for all the years is before-tax yearly family income. Although the measure does not distinguish the respondent's income from that of other family members, the two types of income are closely related, especially for heads of households ($r = 0.94$) (Henretta and Campbell 1976, p. 111). Theoretically, family income may be more appropriate since aged males benefit from income of other family members; the use of family income, however, will require controls for household size.

A more important problem with the measure of income, in this chapter as well as in all the others, is that it does not include in-kind benefits or assets. Nonmonetary income is likely to have risen in recent years, so that measures of famly income will underestimate actual economic resources (Moon 1977). Yet there is little evidence on whether the ratio of non-monetary income to dollar income has changed over time. If the ratio is stable, the results will not be greatly biased. In any case, since time-series data on in-kind benefits and assets are rare, I must rely on the best measure available—dollar income.

The SRC family-income measure was originally obtained in income in-tervals. Since the size and limits of these intervals changed over time, the value of the interval midpoints in hundreds of dollars was assigned to respondents.[3] To avoid spurious correlations between time and family in-come resulting from inflation, I also standardized income according to the Consumer Price Index (CPI) (1972 = 1). Since it is often argued that the aged suffer most from inflation, it is necessary to make sure the income gains they have made increase their real spending power.

Measures of the current occupation of workers and the former occupa-tion of retirees was obtained. However, the 1952 survey used a measure with only seven categories (see table 6-1); forty categories were used from 1956 to 1964 and several hundred were used from 1968 to 1978. In order to include the 1952 data, which is important since 1952 is the earliet year available, the more-detailed occupational categories for the following years have to be recoded into the original seven categories. Fortunately, the seven categories appear to represent fairly well the forty-category Duncan SEI scale. Using data for 1956 and after, two models of family income were estimated—one using the seven dummy categories and the other a continuous, forty-category Duncan SEI scale. The R-square adjusted for degrees of freedom for the model with the SEI measure is 0.370; with the dummy categories it is 0.367. Given the small difference in the variance explained, and the importance of preserving the earliest survey year, only the results for the seven-category scale will be presented.

Employment status was measured in two categories: employed and retired. A small number of unemployed persons (1.1 percent of the sample) were included in the retired category since unemployment is likely to lead to exit from the labor force at the older ages (Rosenblum 1975). Tests for interaction among occupation, employment, and family income were performed to determine whether the effects of employment and occupaton could be treated additively. The test was not significant ($F = 1.13$ at 6 and 1,262 degrees of freedom). Thus the effect of occupation on family income is the same for workers as for retirees, although the intercept for retirees is lower.[4]

Finally, there is the problem of measuring residual cohort effects. Since the lifetime labor-market experiences of cohorts are difficult to operationalize, it has been common to measure cohort by chronological birth date (Glenn 1976). Although the actual cause of cohort differences is not indicated by such measures, the existence of differences can be identified. However, when cohort is calculated from period minus age, there will be linear dependence between the three variables and models containing all three will be unidentified (Mason et al. 1973). In this chapter, cohort will be measured by a set of dummy variables based on four-year birth cohorts (the four-year groupings correspond to the four-year gap between many of the surveys; see table 6-1 for a listing). It may thus be necessary to constrain some of the cohort categories to be equal in the following analyses in order to avoid linear dependency.

Compositional Effects

Table 6-1 presents the multiple-classification-analysis (MCA) results for successive reduced-form models of family income of aged white males. Columns 1 and 2 present the sample size and gross deviations from the grand mean for the factor categories. The gross trend in constant income is up from $6,280 in 1952 to $9,180 in 1978—a linear increase of about $110 a year.[5] The trend for income in current dollars (not reported in table 6-1) is

Table 6-1
Multiple-Classification Analysis of Constant Family Income in Hundreds of (1972) Dollars for Successive Reduced-Form Models: SRC White Males Aged 61 and Over

Independent Variables	N (1)	Gross Deviations (2)	Model 1 Net Deviations (3)	Model 2 Net Deviations (4)	1 – 2 Indirect Effects Education (5)	Model 3 Net Deviations (6)	2 – 3 Indirect Effects Occupation (7)	Model 4 Net Deviations (8)	3 – 4 Indirect Effects Employment (9)	Model 5 Net Deviations (10)	4 – 5 Indirect Effects Family (11)
Year											
1952	105	−11	−13	−6	−7	−9	−3	−14	5	−16	2
1956	118	−16	−17	−12	−5	−11	1	−15	4	−15	0
1958	123	−15	−13	−6	−7	−7	1	−7	0	−8	−1
1960	126	−10	−10	−2	−8	−5	3	−7	2	−9	2
1964	117	−7	−5	−8	3	−10	2	−11	−1	−8	−3
1968	129	12	8	6	2	9	−3	10	−1	10	0
1970	131	5	7	7	0	6	−1	6	0	5	−1
1972	109	7	9	8	1	11	−3	14	−3	14	0
1974	130	10	9	4	5	4	0	5	−1	7	−2
1976	123	9	8	2	6	7	−5	9	−2	9	0
1978	99	18	17	5	12	6	−1	10	−4	11	−1
		0.16	0.15*	0.09	0.06	0.11*	−0.02	0.14*	−0.03	0.15*	−0.01
Covariate											
Age			−2.8*	−2.2*	−0.6	−2.4*	0.2	−1.6*	−0.8	−1.3*	−0.3
Education											
0-7	387	−29		−24		−17		−16		−18	
8	323	−20		−20		−17		−16		−15	
9-11	212	−1		−1		−3		−3		−2	
12	107	24		20		15		15		14	
12 + tech	87	31		24		16		16		16	
13-15	75	38		35		24		23		23	
16+	118	84		80		67		65		65	
		0.48		0.44*		0.35*	0.09	0.34*	0.01	0.34*	0.00

	N	(1)	(2)	(3)	(4)	(4a)	(5)	(5a)
Occupation								
Profess.	99	61		13	12	1	12	0
Managers	223	41		32	31	1	30	−1
Cler.-Sal.	123	15		1	−1	2	−2	−1
Skill BC	475	−14		−11	−9	−2	−8	−1
Prot. Ser.	22	−22		−22	−25	3	−23	−2
Unsk.-Ser.	145	−35		−24	−23	−1	−20	−3
Farm	223	−22		2	0	2	−1	−1
		0.41		0.24*	0.23*	0.01	0.22*	0.01
Covariate								
Rural				−14.2*	−14.7*	0.5	−15.0*	0.3
Employment								
Employed	516	24			15		14	
Retired	794	−15			−10		−9	
		0.26			0.16*	0.01	0.15	0.01
Covariates								
Married							8.2**	
Household							15.4*	
R^2		0.090	0.274	0.336	0.355		0.385	
Grand mean		73.8	73.8	73.8	73.8		73.8	
N		1359	1345	1310	1310		1310	
df		1347	1327	1285	1283		1281	

*$p < .01$

**$.01 < p < .05$

from $3,900 to $13,800; much of this increase is clearly the result of inflation. By comparing the trend in column 2 with the net trend in time controlling for all the compositional variables in column 10, we can see that standardization has little effect. The MCA beta coefficient for time drops by 1 percentage point, and the deviations change by at most only $600. Similar results hold when models are estimated for current dollar income or for the natural log of constant and current income.

Before using the reduced-form equation to apportion the compositional effects, it is worth examining the gross and net effects of the other independent variables (column 10). Education is by far the most important variable; the nonlinearity in its relationship to income is shown by the strong effect of college education. The effects of occupation on family income are smaller than those of education, but they are consistent with the prestige hierarchy. The exception is farmers, whose gross income is low but whose net income is higher when controls for education and rural residence are included. For employment, the results show that retired workers have $1,000 less family income than still-employed workers in their former occupation. Since the effects of retirement are additive, this drop preserves the occupational-status rankings that exist before retirement (Henretta and Campbell 1976). Finally, all the covariates are significantly related to family income; both household size and being married increase income.

The remainder of the table allows determination of the effects of individual independent variables on the time trend of family income. The successive reduced-form equations are based on a recursive model in which the following groups of variables are taken in order to causality. Time and age are exogenous, and education is the first intervening variable. Following the order of the life course, occupation and rural residence are the next intervening variables; since occupation and residence are closely related, especially for farmers, they are added to the model simultaneously. Next comes employment status, followed by living arrangements, which can be a function of changes in employment status. This completes the model.[6] By entering the variables into the model in this order, the indirect effects of time on family income through the compositional variables can be shown by comparing the effects of time with those in the previous reduced-form model.

First, column 3 presents the base model, showing the net effects of time and age on family income. Although controls for age have little effect on time, controls for education strongly affect time (column 4). The differences between the effect of time in column 3 and in column 4 are presented in column 5 and show the indirect effect of time on family income through changes in education. The net deviations for time converge as a result of controls for education; that is, the difference between the mean for the early years and that for the later years becomes smaller. The beta is also reduced and is no longer statistically significant.

The next model (column 6) includes the effects of occupation and residence. Occupation does not further reduce the effects of time; rather, the beta increases and returns to statistical significance. Similar but slightly stronger results occur in column 8, where the employment status variable is added. Thus occupation and employment both have a suppression effect on the relationship of family income and time. The suppression effect of employment is the result of the positive relationship between time and proportion retired, and of the negative relationship between proportion retired and family income. The suppression effect of occupation appears to be the result of a small decline during the 1970s in the proportion of aged males in lower-status white-collar occupations and an increase in those in higher-status blue-collar occupations. Finally, the effects of household size and marital status (column 11) have a weak suppression relationship with time and family income. In total, however, the beta is increased to its size in column 1. Thus the increases in income resulting from education are completely balanced by loss of income resulting from changes in occupational status, residence, employment status, marital status, and household size.

A variation on the preceding analysis can be performed by controlling for cohort as well as for time, age, and the other variables. One quick and easy way to look at the effects of cohort without facing the identification problem when including age, time, and cohort in the same equation, is to measure income in such a way that period effects are removed. In table 6-2 I have multiplied income of the respondents in each year by a factor based on the ratio of the grand mean to the category mean for each year. The effect of the adjustment is to make the means for each year equal to the grand mean of famiy income. This is simlar to standardizing by the CPI, except that the adjustment factor is based on the mean income levels for time in table 6-1, column 10.[7] Measuring income in this way allows time to be left out of the equation when age and cohort are included. The results show that the cohort effects are significant but that the direction of the net deviations fluctuates (early cohorts tend to be much younger and less educated than later cohorts, so the gross deviations for cohort are misleading). For the net effect, early cohorts are well above the grand mean, perhaps because many of the lower-status, low-income persons in these cohorts were selected out by mortality (Glenn 1976). The persons born just before 1900 have lower income than persons born just after, which supports the arguments of Cain (1967). The 1909-1912 cohort is well below the others, probably because the cohort entered the labor force at the beginning of the Depression. The next cohort, which entered the labor force later, has much higher net constant family income.

Although the model gives theoretically interpretable effects for cohort net of the other variables, it does not indicate how these cohort changes affect the trend over time in income. Since more recent cohorts do not show great advantages over earlier cohorts, net of other variables, it is unlikely

Table 6-2
Multiple-Classification Analysis of Cohort Effects on Adjusted and Constant Family Income in Hundreds of Dollars: SRC White Males Aged 61 and Over

	N	Gross	Net	Constant Family Income Net Deviations		
Year						
1952				−16	−16	−24
1956				−12	−11	−18
1958				−6	−5	−11
1960				−5	−5	−9
1964				−5	−5	−6
1968				11	10	11
1970				6	5	7
1972				14	13	17
1974				6	6	11
1976				5	4	10
1978				2	2	8
				0.12	0.12	0.18
Cohort						
Before 1880	88	−25	9	2[c]	2[b]	16
1881-1884	83	2	16	2[c]	2[b]	16
1885-1889	134	−14	0	2[c]	2[b]	2
1889-1892	143	−12	−5	−8[b]	−8	−6[b]
1892-1895	192	0	−4	−8[b]	−9	−6[b]
1896-1899	151	−5	−4	−8[b]	−6	−6[b]
1900-1903	153	0	3	4	5[b]	0[c]
1904-1907	167	16	2	5	5[b]	0[c]
1908-1911	124	14	−9	−2	−1	−9
1912+	75	28	4	24	25	14
		0.18	0.08	0.11*	0.11*	0.12*
Education						
0-7	387	−29	−19	−18	−18	−18
8	323	−20	−15	−15	−15	−15
9-11	212	0	−2	−2	−2	−2
12	107	21	13	13	13	13
12+ tech.	87	26	13	13	14	13
13-15	75	37	26	25	25	25
16	118	87	68	66	66	65
		0.46	0.34*	0.34*	0.34*	0.34*
Occupation						
Professional	99	64	15	11	11	11
Manager	223	44	33	31	31	31
Clerical-sales	123	17	−1	−1	−1	−1
Skilled blue-collar	475	−16	−8	−8	−8	−8
Protective service	22	−21	−23	−24	−25	−25
Unskilled-service	145	−37	−23	−21	−21	−21
Farm	223	−23	−5	−1	−1	−2
		0.42	0.23*	0.22*	0.22*	0.22*

Table 6-2 *(continued)*

	N	Adjusted Family Income[a] Gross	Net	Constant Family Income Net Deviations		
Employment						
At work	516	28	15	14	13	13
Retired	794	−18	−10	−10	−10	−10
		0.30	0.16*	0.15*	0.15*	0.15*
Covariates						
Age			−1.5*	−1.1*	−1.1*	−1.7*
Rural			−14.6*	−14.9*	−14.9*	−14.6*
Married			8.8**	9.8**	10.0**	9.6**
Household size			17.4*	14.9*	14.9*	14.9*
R^2			0.381	0.394	0.394	0.395
Grand mean			79	79	79	79
N			1,310	1,310	1,310	1,310
df			1,281	1,275	1,275	1,275

*$p < .01$

**$.01 < p < .05$

[a]Income adjusted by mean income of year of interview (see text).

[b]Constrained to be equal.

[c]Constrained to be equal.

that the effects of cohort will have large positive or negative compositional effects on income. However, it may be useful to estimate a model that includes age, period, and cohort. To do this, I use the Mason et al. (1973) technique of retricted least squares.[8] Rather than randomly constraining different sets of cohorts atheoretically (Knoke and Hout 1974), it is possible to use the results in table 6-2, column 3, to make the constraints. Since several of the category means for cohort are similar, and since combining some of the categories is consistent with theoretical predictions, the use of constraints has an empirical and theoretical basis. Three such models with three different sets of constraints are presented in table 6-2. Although the effect of time is no longer statistically significant when controlling for cohort, the size of the time effect remains large. The lack of statistical significance may be a result of collinearity among the age, period, and cohort variables. Given this problem, there is little evidence that residual cohort effects on the composition of the aged population explain the increase in income over time.

Processual Changes

In order to test for the interaction of time, family income, and the other independent variables, it was necessary to simplify the measurement of time.

Tests for curvilinearity using a quadratic for year (where 1952 = 1, 1956 = 5, and so on) showed that the time trend could be summarized by a single, linear term. Besides indicating that increases in income occurred uniformly throughout the time period, the single term allowed easy construction of multiplicative interaction terms to be used to test for interaction. First, I calculated the interaction terms by multiplying the dummy or interval variables in table 6-1 by the year variable. The interaction terms were then added to the basic model. While the R-square for the additive model is 0.381, the R-square model is 0.396. With degrees of freedom of 18 and 1,264, the F value of 1.8 is significant at the .05 level. However, given the sampling procedures of the SRC data, and the desire to reject unparsimonious models if possible, the interaction effects should be interpreted cautiously.

To examine the nature of these interactions, I estimated models of family income for three time periods: 1952-1960, 1964-1970, and 1972-1978. Since sample sizes are too small to estimate models for separate years, and since such models would be difficult to interpret with all the coefficients, this rough division of the surveys into three decades was used. In order to make the models comparable, the effects of time within groups must be removed. This was done by standardizing income for respondents in each year in such a way that the mean income for each year is equal to the within-group means for the three periods. The effect of time within the groups is therefore nil.[9]

The MCA results for the period-specific models are presented in table 6-3. Given the small number of cases for some of the categories, and the lack of statisical significance for many of the interaction terms discussed previously, the results must be interpreted cautiously. For occupation, there is a decline in the betas, which results primarily from the improved position of farmers. Similarly, the negative effects of retirement become smaller, although this may be the result of sampling error. The negative effects of age become stronger, and a major change in the effect of household size occurs from the 1960s to the 1970s. This change corresponds to the entrance into old age of cohorts with a high proportion of female workers. Since much of the increase in female labor-force participation occurred during and after World War II among middle-aged women (Oppenheimer 1970), cohorts entering old age during the 1960s and 1970s will reflect these labor-force experiences. Hence, multiperson households are more likely to have female workers or retirees in the 1970s than previously.

As a final summary of the previous results, and as a chance to compare the relative importance of compositional and processual effects, I have decomposed the change in mean family income across these three time groups using regression-standardization techniques. To review, regression standardization apportions the differences between the group income means into that resulting from changes in the intercepts, changes in the

Table 6-3
Multiple-Classification Analysis of Adjusted Family Income in Hundreds of Dollars for Separate Time Periods: SRC White Males Aged 61 and Over

	Adjusted Constant Family Income					
	1952-1960		1964-1970		1972-1978	
	N	Net	N	Net	N	Net
Education						
0-7	171	−8	112	−23	104	−25
8	141	−8	89	−15	93	−24
9-11	73	−3	63	1	76	−4
12	26	0	25	−4	56	26
12 + tech.	15	7	25	13	48	15
13-15	16	38	26	38	34	6
16	32	62	37	72	49	57
		0.32*		0.38*		0.34*
Occupation						
Professional	28	25	27	1	44	15
Manager	78	34	73	35	71	22
Clerical-sales	47	4	45	−7	32	−6
Skilled blue-collar	141	−5	136	−12	198	−8
Protective service	9	−1	3	−25	10	−43
Unskilled-service	64	−19	36	−22	44	−27
Farmer	105	−15	57	3	62	21
		0.32*		0.24*		0.22*
Employment						
At work	241	12	143	16	132	13
Retired	231	−12	234	−10	328	−5
		0.21*		0.17*		0.11**
Covariates						
Age		−0.2		−1.9*		−2.1*
Rural		−15.3*		−12.7		−19.4*
Married		6.4		5.9		1.8
Household size		13.5*		17.4**		26.9*
R^2		0.460		0.399		0.322
Grand mean		61		77		85
N		473		377		459
df		454		358		440

Note: Figures are adjusted to remove within-group period effects.
*$p < .01$
**$.01 < p < .05$

slopes, changes in the mean values of the independent variables, and changes caused by interaction between the changes in the means and slopes (Iams and Thornton 1973). The unstandardized-regression estimates corresponding to the MCA results in table 6-3 were used to calculate the decomposition.[10] The results are presented in table 6-4.

Table 6-4
Regression-Standardization Decomposition of Changes in Constant Family Income in Hundreds of Dollars: SRC Males Aged 61 and Over

	1952-1960 versus 1964-1970 Change in Income Owing to Different:			1964-1970 versus 1972-1978 Change in Income Owing to Different:		
	Coefficients	Means	Interaction	Coefficients	Means	Interaction
Education	-10.75	-6.48	1.98	2.79	-5.23	1.76
Occupation	-20.31	-1.09	-1.78	11.28	1.80	0.35
Employment	1.69	3.47	-0.36	-6.62	1.60	0.87
Age	117.17	0.25	-0.22	18.22	0.14	-0.02
Rural	-1.11	0.09	0.02	2.80	-0.54	0.19
Family	6.68	0.91	0.81	-28.74	1.18	-0.51
Total	93.38	-2.86	0.45	-0.28	-1.05	2.65
Differences in intercepts	-107.38			-9.53		
Differences in income	-16.43			-8.20		

The results for changes from period 1 to period 2 show that changes in coefficients and intercepts are the largest components of change in family income. The change in intercepts can be interpreted as the difference in mean income resulting from the additive effects of time, whereas the changes in the coefficients can be interpreted as differences in mean income caused by the interactive effects of time. These additive and interactive processual effects are in opposite directions, but even added together they overshadow the compositional effects. The negative difference between the intercepts results from the larger intercept in period 2 and indicates that the additive effects of time have increased income of all groups equally from the 1950s to the 1960s. The positive difference for regression coefficients indicates that if the coefficients were identical across time periods, income would be even higher than it is in period 2. Thus the interaction effects have served to limit increases in income. The major cause of this effect is the increased negative effect of age on income; the effects of changes in the coefficients of education and occupation work to increase the income of the aged but are much smaller than the effect of the changing age coefficients. Finally, compositional effects, although small, serve to increase the income of the aged; the small effect results from a positive effect of education slightly larger than the effect of employment and in the opposite direction.

The changes in income from period 2 to period 3 are smaller than those in the previous comparison. In largest part the change is the result of changing intercepts or the additive effects of time, which increase income of the aged. The overall effect of changes in the regression coefficients is near 0, but this results from counterbalancing effects of age-occupation with household size-employment status. The negative effects of age continue but are balanced by positive effects of larger household size. As mentioned, the increased effect of larger family size may result from the presence of additional workers or retirees in the family—something undoubtedly related to the rise of female labor-force participation in the last decades. The compositional effects are also small overall because of the counterbalancing effects of higher education, which increases income, and of a higher mean age of the population, which reduces income. Finally, the interaction of changes in the slopes and means for education has a small effect of reducing income of the aged.

Summary and Discussion

Overall, compositional effects have had little effect on the increase in family income among the aged population, but several individual changes have been more important (although in the opposite direction). Improvements in education of the aged population have helped their income status, but only enough to balance the loss of income caused by increased proportions of retired persons in the aged population. In terms of relative size, processual effects are more important in explaining the increase in income among the aged. The additive processual effects of time show that net of compositional changes, there were significant increases in income among all groups in the aged white male population. At the same time, there were also some interaction effects of time. Income grew more quickly among the young-old than among the old-old and among multiperson households than among single-person households. In general, then, although there is some evidence for the divergence hypothesis of processual effects, most support must go to the hypothesis predicting increase in income distributed equally among groups in the aged population.

Several issues are raised by these results. The first concerns the counterbalancing effects of compositional changes. Proponents of the view that cohort change has improved the status of the aged correctly predicted the positive effect of higher educational levels. Yet compositional characteristics more subject to change during old age have changed in ways that have limited the growth of income. Without higher education or improved income before old age, increased retirement or independent living arrangements might not have occurred. There may be some threshold of income that aged persons consider necessary to live comfortably during old age (Barfield and Morgan 1969). If it is possible to maintain that income level through higher education or through changes in the nature of income determination, then retirement levels are likely to increase.

Second, for the most part, the effects of time on family income are additive. In the long run, such changes can reduce aggregate income inequality within the aged population, as shown by declining Gini ratios (U.S. Bureau of the Census 1967); even if the dollar increases are the same across groups, the proportional increase will be larger for low-income groups than for high-income groups. For example, the mean incomes of workers and retirees in 1952 were $7,200 and $3,900, respectively. In 1972 the means were $9,900 and $6,600, which shows that the gap between workers and retirees declined and that the proportional increase in income was higher for retirees.

One exception to declining inequality concerns the increasing gap between the young-old and the old-old. There are several possible explanations for the growth of age inequality. First, for workers the difference between the old and young aged may be the result of changing proportions of full-time and part-time workers. In more-recent years, older persons who desire to remain in the labor force are more likely to work part time. This increase in the ratio of part-time workers to full-time workers at the older ages may cause a decline in income, even controlling for employment status. Second, for retired workers at the older ages, there may be an effect from the number of years retired. If age at retirement declines over time, workers at the older ages in the early years will have been retired for fewer years than retirees at the same age in later years. Since many pension programs are not adjusted for inflation, and since they reflect wage levels near the end of a person's employment, those retired for the most years—even when they are the same age—may have lower income. Finally, Burgess (1960) argued that with lower mortality rates, more unhealthy and disabled persons are able to survive into old age. If health is strongly related to family income, a decline in average health levels will reduce income. However, there is little direct evidence of declining health among the aged.

As discussed, the increased effects of household size correspond to entrance of cohorts into old age with a higher proportion of female labor-force participants. There has been some evidence that income of aged persons has been reduced because the aged prefer living alone even if their income suffers as a result. There is indirect evidence for this view here in the finding that multiperson households are improving their income position relative to unrelated individuals. In any case, the trend in female labor-force participation has implications beyond the status of the women themselves—it also affects the family income of aged males.

In summary, future changes in the income levels of the aged population will be likely to depend less on changes in the characteristics of the aged population than on period changes that affect all older persons regardless of their cohort backgrounds. Growth of social-security and private pension benefits (chapter 2), along with the rise in the standard of living for the total population, have been the major influences on income levels since the 1950s. Further changes in social-security benefits, which are adjusted by the rise in the CPI, and improvements in private pension plans and in other transfer programs in monetary and nonmonetary terms will be likely to outweigh compositional changes in retirement levels and education in determining income.

Notes

1. Health of the respondent may have some effect on income dependent of employment status, but an appropriate measure is not available from the SRC surveys. Cohort differences in health, to the extent that they affect family income, will appear in the effects of the dummy cohort variables.

2. Analyses were also performed for the Public-Use Sample (PUS) data, but these essentially replicate the SRC results for a shorter time span. To simplify the already detailed and numerous tables to be presented with the SRC data, I will not present or discuss the results from the census data.

3. For the open-ended category, the midpoint was calculated by multiplying the lower limit by 4/3. This multiple corresponds to the midpoint of the open-ended category in a Pareto distribution with a constant of 4 (Theil 1967; Treas and Walther 1978).

4. Evidence that the replacement rates of retirement income to previous wages is higher for low-status workers is inconsistent with these results (Kolodrubetz 1975). Although more precise occupational measures may lead to different results, the finding here is probably the result of the use of family income rather than personal income or retirement income.

5. When the net deviations are regressed on time and a time quadratic, significance tests show that there is no curvilinearity in the relationship. The trend appears to be steady throughout the time span.

6. Since former occupation is measured for retirees, occupation causally precedes employment status. Household size and marital status were included after retirement because changes in living arrangements often follow changes in work status. In some cases, however, marital status may affect age of retirement. If this is the case, some of the indirect effects attributed here to employment may actually be results of family status.

7. The strategy is similar to measurement of income as deviations from the mean of the appropriate year, except that the method used here maintains the grand mean of the sample rather than changing it to 0. For example, the grand mean of constant income is 74 (hundred dollars), whereas the net mean for 1952 respondents in constant dollars is 58 (hundred dollars). The family income in 1952 dollars is then multiplied by 74/58 (or 1.28). This adjusts the 1952 mean to 74 and, when done for all the years, removes the effect of time.

8. I am unable to describe in detail the problem involved in the simultaneous examination of age, period, and cohort; but I can provide a brief overview of the issues. Because cohort is equal to period minus age, independent effects of each variable cannot be determined. A person born in 1900 and interviewed in 1970 is by definition aged 70. In order to determine the effect of age on income while controlling for cohort and period, it is necessary to compare persons at different ages during the same year who were born in the same cohort. This is impossible unless certain assumptions are made.

The crux of the Mason et al. (1973) technique is to constrain a small number of age, period, or cohort categories to be equal. For example, assume that the effect on income of being born in 1900 or in 1901 is identical; thus persons born in these two years can be treated as members of the same cohort. Then it is possible to compare persons aged 70 and 69 in the year 1970; in other words, age is allowed to vary while period and cohort are constant. This example oversimplifies a more-complicated statistical procedure but indicates the nature and necessity of constraints. For a discussion of the weakness of the technique, see Glenn (1976).

9. The same procedure described in note 7 is used, except that the category means are standardized to the within-group means rather than to the grand mean for the total sample.

10. The latter of the two time groups is used as the standard in the calculation. Further, since differences between the components are shown by subtracting the latter period from the earlier period, a negative value indicates an increase over time and a positive value indicates a decrease over time.

7

Changes in the Labor-Force, Family, and Income Status of Aged Females

Perhaps the group of persons most subject to financial problems in old age is single women. Thirty-three percent of female unrelated individuals aged 65 and over in 1974 had incomes below the poverty level, compared with levels half as high for elderly male unrelated individuals or for family members of either sex (U.S. Bureau of the Census 1976). The problems of aged single women result from lifetime dependence on the income of their spouses. Many married women find themselves living alone during old age with little income of their own, no recent labor-force experience, and limited assets. It is argued that widows face especially severe problems compared to divorced and never-married women because widowhood provides less of a chance to prepare for living alone (Lopata 1973).

Yet chapter 2 showed that the median income of aged females has increased over time and that there has been a decline in inequality among female unrelated individuals. Despite the financial problems of many older women, some changes must have occurred to increase the average income levels of older women. It is likely that the hypotheses presented in the chapter concerning compositional and processual effects on income increases for aged males can be extended to explain increases in income of aged females. When family income is used as a dependent variable, the results for males and females will be similar in some ways since the family income of married females will be the same as that for married males.[1]

However, there have been two major trends in the position of women in society, which are likely to affect the family and personal income of women independent of men: (1) the increased proportion of female unrelated individuals in the aged population and (2) the increased proportion of aged women who have some labor-force experience. Since unrelated individuals typically have lower income than family members, and since labor-force participants have higher income than housewives, these changes become more important when a distinction is made between family income and personal income. Over time, average family income of females might decline because of the increased percentage of small, female-headed households and of primary individuals. Yet the personal income of women might have increased as a result of the loss of family ties, growth of government transfers, and increases in labor-force experience.

As was the case for male income, aggregate time-series data do not allow precise tests or the influence of household and work-status changes.

127

The objective of this chapter, then, is to use the Survey Research Center (SRC) and census consecutive cross-sectional surveys to examine individual variation in income and the effects of compositional and processual changes over time on the income of aged females.

More specifically, several questions are addressed in this chapter. First, how has the rise in income among aged females been affected by compositional changes in the population of aged females? On the one hand, increases in labor-force experience, educational levels, and urban status should increase income. On the other hand, the rise of unrelated individuals in the population and the aging of the aged population may limit increases in income.

Second, how have the trends of income within groups of heads and nonheads of households changed over time? The effects of time may be different for the two populations. To the extent that public-assistance programs, private insurance, and retirement benefits are increasingly directed toward the most needy widows, the income of heads of households may rise more quickly than the income of women who are wives or other family members. This is especially likely to be true for personal income, where improvements among heads of households will likely be greatest. For family income, the opposite pattern may emerge. Since family income will reflect income of wife and husband, and since husband's income has risen in the past, total family income will be likely to grow more quickly among family members than among unrelated individuals. Clearly, absolute levels will be higher for family members; but percentage growth should also be higher than for nonfamily members.

Third, in addition to seeing whether the process of income determination differs for heads and nonheads of households, we can ask whether the different processes have changed over time. For instance, if differences over time exist, have they increased, decreased, or remained constant over time? A decrease in differences or a greater similarity in the effects of the determinants on income for heads and nonheads of households would indicate greater equality between the groups. Alternatively, if differences between the groups grow over time, this would indicate greater inquality. Thus the results of chapter 5 on inequality can be expanded when considering the changing effects of background factors on income of aged females.

**Compositional and Processual Changes
in Family Income: SRC Results**

The first step in the analysis is to disentangle the effects of compositional and processual effects on changes in the income levels of aged females. The strategy for considering constant family income of females is similar to the strategy used for males: the combined SRC data are used to examine the effect of time on income net of compositional variables. The size of the net time effects indicates the importance of compositional and processual effects on income. Further, examination of successive reduced-form equations can be used to calculate the indirect effects of time on income separately for each compositional variable in the model. If the results are similar to those for males—as they should be for family income—compositional effects will be small and the processual effects of time will primarily be additive.

A variation on the anlaysis for females, however, will be the estimation of separate models for those who are heads of households and those who are not. It is necessary to estimate separate models for women who are the primary source of income of households from women who are not the primary source but who may depend on the income of a spouse or relative. Although it is not possible to determine which women are the chief sources of income of their households, it is possible to use the distinction between women who are heads of household, and thus likely to be the primary source of income, and women who are not household heads and who are likely to depend at least partially on the income of the household heads. The processes of income determination for the two groups will differ since the family income of female nonheads of households will depend on the status of the heads as well as on their own status. Based on this reasoning, persons classified as secondary individuals—persons living in a household headed by a nonrelative or in group quarters—will be grouped with heads of households. Although they are not classified as heads of households, secondary individuals do not typically share income with the heads as would wives, children, parents, or other relatives. Thus I will use nonheads of households to refer to women related to the heads, and heads of household to refer to women who head their own households or are unrelated to the heads of their households.

Nonheads of Households

Table 7-1 presents successive reduced-form models of the constant family income of women who are not heads of household but are related to the head. The variables in the model are similar to those examined in previous chapters, except that the labor-force and occupational status of the heads of the household as well as of the respondent are measured. For the head of household and the respondent, labor-force status and occupation are combined into one variable. This is necessary because occupational measures are not available for housewives, who must be treated as a separate occupational-labor-force category comparable to retired or working persons. A related

Table 7-1
Multiple-Classification Analysis of Constant Family Income in Hundreds of Dollars for Family Members Who Are Not Heads of Households: SRC White Females Aged 61 and Over

	N	Gross	Models of Constant Family Income				
			(1) Net	(2) Net	(3) Net	(4) Net	(5) Net
Time							
1952	54	− 29	− 24	− 13	− 21	− 22	− 22
1956	53	− 25	− 25	− 21	− 22	− 23	− 23
1958	52	− 8	− 7	− 12	− 7	− 4	− 6
1960	59	− 8	− 7	− 8	− 8	− 6	− 6
1964	77	− 6	− 6	− 5	− 10	− 12	− 12
1968	49	− 7	− 8	− 4	− 11	− 9	− 9
1970	59	10	12	6	4	5	5
1972	82	10	10	13	14	13	13
1974	53	22	15	10	22	23	23
1976	51	21	19	16	21	21	22
1978	51	17	18	12	16	12	13
		0.22	0.20*	0.16**	0.20*	0.20*	0.20*
Age							
60-64	203	14	14	12	6	8	9
65-69	194	1	1	− 3	− 4	− 4	− 3
70-74	115	− 9	− 5	− 5	1	0	− 1
75-79	72	− 16	− 19	− 14	− 7	− 7	− 9
80 +	55	− 16	− 13	− 4	− 2	− 6	− 9
		0.15	0.15*	0.12**	0.06	0.08	0.09
Education							
0-7	131	− 35		− 30	− 29	− 28	− 29
8	134	− 21		− 18	− 12	− 11	− 11
9-11	113	− 9		− 7	− 2	− 2	− 2
12	96	22		17	14	13	13
12 + tech.	46	29		25	18	17	17
13-15	65	27		26	19	19	20
16 +	55	58		54	42	38	39
		0.39		0.35*	0.28*	0.26*	0.27*
Household ocupation							
Housewife	7	− 43			− 31	− 30	− 38
Retired professional	27	20			− 2	− 2	1
Manager	73	26			10	9	11
Clerical-sales	31	− 2			− 14	− 17	− 16
Skilled	165	− 23			− 23	− 24	− 22
Service	33	− 40			− 28	− 22	− 20
Farmer	63	− 23			− 16	− 16	− 15
Working professional	21	61			44	42	42
Manager	44	94			91	88	86
Clerical-sales	37	9			10	8	5
Skilled	84	4			12	13	9
Service	21	− 34			− 17	− 16	− 18
Farmer	36	− 19			− 4	0	− 1
		0.46			0.40*	0.39*	0.38*

Table 7-1 *(continued)*

			Models of Constant Family Income				
	N	*Gross*	*(1)* *Net*	*(2)* *Net*	*(3)* *Net*	*(4)* *Net*	*(5)* *Net*
Retiree's occupation							
Housewife	477	−4				1	1
Retired—white-collar	56	16				13	11
blue-collar	39	−9				−1	−2
Work—white-collar	43	29				−5	−5
blue-collar	27	−34				−27	−27
		0.26				0.16*	0.17*
Covariates							
Rural						−8.4	−7.7
Household size							9.1
Not wife							11.5
R^2		0.064	0.183	0.333		0.363	0.370
Grand mean		78	78	78		78	78
N		695	692	653		639	639
df		680	671	620		593	591

*$p < .01$

**$.01 < p < .05$

result of this treatment is that the effects of occupation are allowed to differ for retired and working persons.[2] For the occupation-labor-force-status measure of respondents, occupation is coded into two categories: white-collar and blue-collar workers. Only a small number of women who are not heads of households are either working or retired; therefore, categories must be combined to provide enough cases. The only other variable measured differently than in previous tables is a dummy variable that distinguishes women who are married to the head of household from those that are other relatives of the head.

The equations in table 7-1 present the gross effects of all the variables on income along with the category sample sizes. The net effects are presented first for a model including time, age, and education—all completely exogenous variables determined before adulthood. The second column of net coefficients adds the other variables—those determined during adulthood—to complete the model. These two equations show the major compositional change without presentation of an equation for each individual variable.

The gross effects of time show a steady increase in income until 1978. When education and age are added to the equation, the effect of time is reduced—the beta declines from 0.22 to 0.16, although it remains significant. The main cause of the reduced time effect is education. Age has only a small effect on the trend in income over time. As was the case for men, then, increases in education brought into old age by newer cohorts have had modest effects on increasing income during old age.

The inclusion of other variables in the model after education, however, increases the effect of time on income. The effect of head's occupation on income, for instance, is strong (beta equals 0.38).[3] Its effect on increasing the relationship between time and income shows the existence of suppression: time increases income at the same time that it reduces income through higher retirement levels. Respondent's occupation has a small but significant effect on income but does not greatly affect the time-income relationship. For both head's work status and respondent's status, workers are generally better off than retirees.

These results for female income of related nonheads of households are similar to those for males, since the family income of a large number of these women is based partly on the income of male heads of households. Compositional effects have minor effects on income; education partly explains the rise but is balanced by negative effects of other variables. It is possible that higher income from education in some ways allowed increases in retirement with the consequent negative effect on income. Of more importance, however, are the processual effects shown by the additive effects of time. Separate models for different time periods, and the test for interactive time effects, are prevented by the small number of cases; such analysis will be postponed until the Public Use Sample (PUS) data are considered.

Heads of Households

We may now turn to the model for heads of households and secondary individuals (table 7-2). The model is the same for nonheads of households, except that only one measure of occupation-labor-force status is needed since the respondents are the heads of households. The pattern of results for the heads of households is again similar to those for males and nonheads of households. The effect of time on income is reduced by education but is raised by occupation. Overall, the size of the beta for time are nearly identical to those for nonheads. Yet the grand mean is much lower for the heads of households, and the spread around the mean is smaller. Despite lower family income, there has been an increase over time independent of compositional changes.

It is worth noting that for household heads, as well as for nonheads of households, the effects of age are no longer significant once occupational-labor-force status is thus controlled. The disadvantage of older women clearly results not so much from old age itself but more from the high levels of housewives and retired women.

There are some variables that have different effects on income for heads and nonheads of households. The effect of occupation-labor-force status is

Table 7-2
**Multiple-Classification Analysis of Constant Family Income in Hundreds
of Dollars for Heads of Households and Secondary Individuals: SRC White
Females Aged 61 and Over**

	N	Gross	Models of Constant Family Income			
			(1) Net	(2) Net	(3) Net	(4) Net
Time						
1952	64	−12	−11	−8	−11	−14
1956	70	−16	−17	−13	−14	−13
1958	62	−13	−11	−9	−12	−12
1960	84	−5	−4	−7	−6	−5
1964	85	0	1	1	0	−2
1968	102	1	1	1	0	1
1970	115	2	2	1	1	0
1972	96	6	6	7	7	7
1974	99	4	3	2	4	3
1976	101	4	4	2	4	6
1978	99	14	14	12	14	16
		0.20	0.20*	0.16*	0.19*	0.20*
Age						
60-64	182	10	11	9	6	6
65-69	178	3	3	0	1	1
70-74	184	−2	−1	0	0	−1
75-79	160	−6	−7	−6	−6	−5
80 +	273	−4	−4	−2	−1	−1
		0.13	0.15*	0.12*	0.09	0.08
Education						
0-7	208	−13		−12	−10	−10
8	234	−11		−11	−8	−8
9-11	179	−4		−4	−2	−2
12	117	5		6	5	6
12 + tech.	82	13		11	8	9
13-15	83	19		18	14	14
16 +	74	38		36	27	24
		0.36		0.34*	0.26*	0.25*
Retiree's occupation						
Housewives	485	−5			1	1
Retired-professional	56	31			10	11
Manager	31	6			2	2
Clerical-sales	103	1			−5	−5
Skilled	59	−10			−10	−10
Service	75	−16			−15	−14
Farmer	6	−11			−5	−10
Working-professional	27	42			18	18
Manager	19	27			21	23
Clerical-sales	42	22			12	12
Skilled	22	6			8	7
Service	43	−10			−9	−8
Farmer	11	−11			4	0
		0.32			0.19*	0.19*

Table 7-2 *(continued)*

	N	Gross	Models of Constant Family Income			
			(1) Net	(2) Net	(3) Net	(4) Net
Covariates						
Rural					− 12.7*	− 13.1*
Household size						18.6*
R^2			0.057	0.168	0.212	0.257
Grand mean			39	39	39	39
N			999	999	977	977
df			984	969	943	942

*$p < .01$
**$.01 < p < .05$

smaller for nonheads of household than are those for the heads of households in the previous tables. Similarly, the R-squared is smaller. These background characteristics are less able to predict income of heads of households. In other words, background differences are less distinguishing among the heads of households.

As a final test for heads of households, I examined the effect of marital status in the models for the years 1956 and after.[4] The variable did not significantly affect income—differences between never-married and divorced or widowed women are not large, controlling for household size and background characteristics.

To review, additive processual changes have increased the income of both female heads and female nonheads of households. The trends appear to be similar for both groups, indicating that little reduction of the gap between them has occurred. Given the gap, and given the increases in the proportion of females who head their own households, we need to consider the effect of compositional changes in household status on the income of aged females. These compositional effects can be examined through a simple exercise in standardization. Table 7-3 first presents the mean income (in hundreds of constant dollars) for the total population of females for the years from 1952 to 1978. These figures are calculated from a weighted average of the category net deviations and the grand means for heads and nonheads of households from tables 7-1 and 7-2. Thus the figures control for changes in other variables within the population of heads and nonheads of households, but do not equalize the population changes in household headship itself. The trend shows a steady increase.

To examine the compositional effects of household status, an average of the means for each year of heads and nonheads of households can be calculated holding the proportion of household heads and nonheads constant. Rather than using the distribution by household headship for each year, the distribution of household status in 1952 can be used to weight the means in each year. This shows what the mean income of the aged population would have been in each year had there not been an increase in household heads or in female-headed households. These results are presented in column 2. The results for 1952 are identical since that is the standard year. For the other years, the standardized income controlling for changes in household are not much higher than the acutal figures until the mid-1960s. After that time the gap between the standardized and actual becomes larger. At the highest, the average income would have been $700 higher if the heads of households had not increased. Thus compositional effects resulting from changes in household status have had a modest inhibiting effect on growth of income of aged females. In all, however, compositional effects appear smaller than processual effects. A more exact comparison of the two components is made in the next section.

Changes in Personal Income: Census Results

There are some major disadvantages in the census data that limit their use in explaining changes in female income. Figures are not available on the labor-force or occupational status of the heads of households, except when respondents are the household heads. Especially for family income, then, prediction will be weak and the results will be misleading. There is less

Table 7-3
Net Trend in Constant Family Income in Hundreds of Dollars and Net Trend in Income Standardizing for the Proportion of Heads of Households in the Aged Population: SRC Females Aged 61 and Over

Year	Net Trend	Standardized Trend[a]
1952	39	39
1956	38	39
1958	48	48
1960	50	51
1964	51	50
1968	49	53
1970	54	59
1972	67	68
1974	63	69
1976	63	70
1978	67	72

Note: Calculated from weighted average of net deviations of time for complete models in tables 7-1 and 7-2.

[a]The calculations assume the proportion of household heads for all the years has not changed from the 1952 value.

problem in examining personal income, which depends more indirectly on the household head's position, and more directly on the respondent's labor-force status and occupation. Thus the focus here will be on personal income only.

Nonetheless, several advantages are afforded by the PUS data. The sample size for each year is slightly larger, and separate models for household heads and nonheads in each time period can be estimated. The models in table 7-4, therefore, are estimated separately for 1960 and 1970 heads of households and nonheads of households. The variables include age, education, a simplified occupation-labor-force measure distinguishing blue-collar from white-collar workers, and covariates measuring rural residence and household size. The dependent variable is constant personal income.

These multiple-classification analysis (MCA) results can be briefly summarized without presenting more detailed tables. The results for heads and nonheads of households are similar: education and occupation-labor-force are consistently important predictors of personal income. The major difference is that the size of the effects of the independent variables and the total variance explained are smaller for the nonheads of households (as in the SRC data).

A simple but more useful way to present these differences is through regression standardization decomposition, which will show compositional and processual differences between groups and between time points without an excessive number of coefficients to interpret.[5] Table 7-4 presents the regression standardization for the four relevant comparisons: (1) 1960 nonheads of households compared with 1960 heads of households; (2) 1970 heads of households compared with 1970 nonheads of households; (3)

Table 7-4
Regression-Standardization Decomposition for Differences in Constant Personal Income in Hundreds of Dollars: PUS Females Aged 60 and Over

| | Differences in Mean Income | Differences in Income Owing to Different: | | | |
		Means	Coefficients	Interaction	Intercepts
1960 heads versus 1970 heads	−6.20	−0.32	−9.25	0.36	3.02
1960 nonheads versus 1970 nonheads	−5.70	−1.18	−9.44	−0.21	5.13
1960 nonheads versus 1960 heads	−15.29	−5.27	0.96	1.15	−12.14
1970 nonheads versus 1970 heads	−15.79	1.64	0.52	−3.71	−14.25

1960 heads of households compared with 1970 heads of households; and (4) 1960 nonheads of households compared with 1970 nonheads of households.

First, compare the differences across time between the mean income of female heads of households and that of secondary individuals. The mean in 1970 is about $600 higher than in 1960. Compositional changes over time in the makeup of the population of heads of households is not important in explaining the increase. Processual effects are much larger and are negative: if the process of income attainment had been the same in 1970 as it was in 1960, the income of heads of households would have been about $900 lower than it actually was. Thus processual changes have been beneficial to the income of this group.

Similar effects across time for related nonheads of households are found. Compositional changes are again small and negative: if the composition of the nonheads of households had been the same in 1970 as it was in 1960, income would have been $118 lower. Processual effects are much larger. If the process of income determination in 1970 had been the same as in 1960, income would be $944 lower.

Next, comparisons between heads and nonheads of households can be made controlling for time. The comparison of the two family groups in 1960 shows that compositional effects explain about one-third of the differences in means ($527/$1,529). The personal income of nonheads of households is higher partly because nonheads of households include a higher proportion of labor-force participants. Processual and interaction effects are small and positive. The largest component of the difference in mean income, however, is the difference between the intercepts of the regression equation. Much of the difference, in other words, is unexplained by the variables in the model. The comparison of heads and nonheads of households in 1970 shows a difference in mean income about the same size as that in 1960. In 1970, however, compositional effects are small and positive. The major component is again the difference between the intercepts.

Summary

This chapter has demonstrated increases in constant family and personal income among aged females. Further, the effect of several changes in the characteristics of aged women on the changes in income were considered. First, one of the major problems of the aged is the financial situation of widows and unrelated individuals. Since these women have had little labor-force experience and little or no income of their own, a high proportion are in poverty with even more just above the poverty level. Indeed, the data on family income presented in this chapter showed that in 1978 the mean income of women who headed their own households was $5,500; the mean for those who were not heads of households, controlling for household size and other variables, was $9,100. The gap is large.

Nonetheless, increases in income have occurred among all groups of aged females. Widows, housewives, workers, retirees, middle-aged women, and old women have experienced increases in constant income of about $2,600. Since this increase is in real dollars and does not reflect the trend in inflation, it indicates some improvement in the financial plight of older women. Furher, since the increase is constant across all groups studied, the lowest income groups experience the largest proportional increase.

The source of the change for elderly women, as for elderly men, is change in the process of income determination rather than change in the composition of the aged population. Environmental changes that affect all groups, such as the rise in the standard of living, wages, insurance benefits, and social-security benefits, appear responsible for the trend in income. Surprisingly, a number of compositional variables explain little of the trend. For instance, heads of households are clearly disadvantaged relative to nonheads of households in family income: the family income of nonheads benefits greatly from the income of the heads of households. Yet, the rise in female-headed households has not been large enough to limit the trend of rising income. Similarly, women with labor-force experience fare better than those without, but the rise in participation contributes only modestly to the rise in income. Thus, the income of aged women in the future is likely to depend less on the characteristics of the women themselves and more on the characteristics of the economy, employers, and transfer programs.

Notes

1. They would be identical for the total population of married persons, spouse present. Yet in this sample many of the married persons aged 60 and over will be married to persons under that age. Hence the results for married males and females will not be identical.

2. If labor-force status and occupation were treated as separate variables, a category of housewives would have to be included in both variables. The measures of the two variables would therefore be partially redundant.

3. There are only seven nonheads of households who report they live in households headed by housewives. This number is too small to provide reliable estimates, but the group is important enough theoretically to be treated as a separate category. A female respondent with little personal in-

come may be forced to share the household of another female relative, also a housewife with little presonal income. As shown by the result for the small number of cases, these households have low family income. Rather than treating these respondents as missing data, or combining them with one of the working or retired categories, I leave them as a separate category.

4. The 1952 data, as discussed earlier, distinguish only between married and unmarried persons. Since all these women are not married, the important distinctions are between widowed, divorced, separated, and never-married women.

5. See chapter 6 for a discussion of the details of regression standardization.

8

The Combination of Age, Race, and Sex in Determination of Income

Because the processes of income attainment differ, I have intentionally analyzed males and females separately. For the same reason, I have also excluded blacks and minorities from the previous analyses. Although it was possible to estimate income models for white females and males, it was not possible to do the same for nonwhites. The number of aged nonwhite males and females in the two data sets is too small to provide reliable estimates, given the large number of variables used in the previous models (often forty or more). For that reason, it is not my intention here to replicate the white models for nonwhites. Rather, I would like to make some simple comparisons between the effect of race on income and the effects of age and sex, to determine how these ascriptive variables combine to determine income, and to compare the effects across time.

The need to compare income of aged white and nonwhite males and females stems from debate over the hazards occupying multiple, negative, ascriptive statuses. The ascribed statuses of age, race, and sex clearly affect levels of income; but the ways in which the statuses combine to determine income is less clear. Some have argued that women and blacks are more vulnerable to the negative effects of old age—that blacks and women face double jeopardy because they grow old while already occupying a minority status. In fact, elderly black women may face triple jeopardy. On the other hand, old age may serve as a leveler of the status differences that persons bring into old age. Since there is less income to go around in old age, the differences between men and women or between blacks and whites may become smaller. Or, finally, the differences in status or income between men and women and between blacks and whites may be maintained during old age, with old age reducing the status of all but maintaining the relative positions of the groups.

Most studies of multiple jeopardy have focused on sex and race during the younger years (Almquist 1975) or on sex and ethnicity (Lieberson 1970). Studies of multiple jeopardy during old age have typically examined measures of psychological variables such as morale and adaptation. This chapter focuses specifically on one indicator of status—income—over several decades using a national sample. By using consecutive cross-sectional surveys, changes in the way in which multiple jeopardy affects income can be considered.

Models of Multiple Jeopardy

To determine how sex, race, and age may combine to affect the income of aged persons, consider the effects of age on income for four groups: white males, white females, nonwhite males, and nonwhite females. With age taken as a continuous variable predicting income, figure 8-1 describes the several ways in which the effects of age may differ for each combination of statuses. The graphs in figure 8-1 start with the heuristic assumption that at age 55 the income of white males is highest, followed by that of black males, white females, and black females. The situations illustrated by the graphs in figures 8-1(a)-8-1(c) indicate whether these already existing gaps get larger, get smaller, or stay the same during old age.

Figure 8-1(a) presents the situation in which the gaps between the groups remain the same during old age. Income of all groups declines with old age, but the already existing inequalities are maintained. This is referred to as the additive model: income of persons can be predicted by subtracting the effect of each negative status they occupy. White males lose income for each additional year of age, the amount of which is determined by the slope of the line relating age to income. The income of black males at the same age is determined by subtracting the effects of age plus a negative constant resulting from being black; the income of white females is calculated from the effects of age plus a negative constant resulting from being female; and the income of black females is calculated from the effects of age plus the negative constants resulting from being both black and female.

Figure 8-1(b) presents a model in which the effects of age, race, and sex interact—where the effects of the negative statuses cannot be added. In other words, the race and sex background of persons specifies how old age reduces income. In figure 8-1(b), the effects of race and sex become smaller in old age—that is, growing old has the largest negative effect on the group that begins with the highest income (Kent 1971). This model is referred to as the leveling model (Dowd and Bengston 1978). The reasoning behind the model is that greater equality exists among inferior groups (Palmore and Manton 1973). Since there is less income to be unequally distributed among old people than among young people, age and sex inequalities will be reduced during old age. Although equality between the groups may not be reached, those groups with less to lose when they enter old age will do well relative to higher-status groups with more to lose.

The third model, figure 8-1(c), is also interactive, but the sex and race differences are predicted to grow during old age. In this model, the negative effects of old age are greatest for the most disadvantaged groups and smallest for the most advantaged group of white males. Old age thus makes the negative effects of race and sex more serious. This is the basis of the double- and triple-jeopardy hypotheses, which suggest that high-status

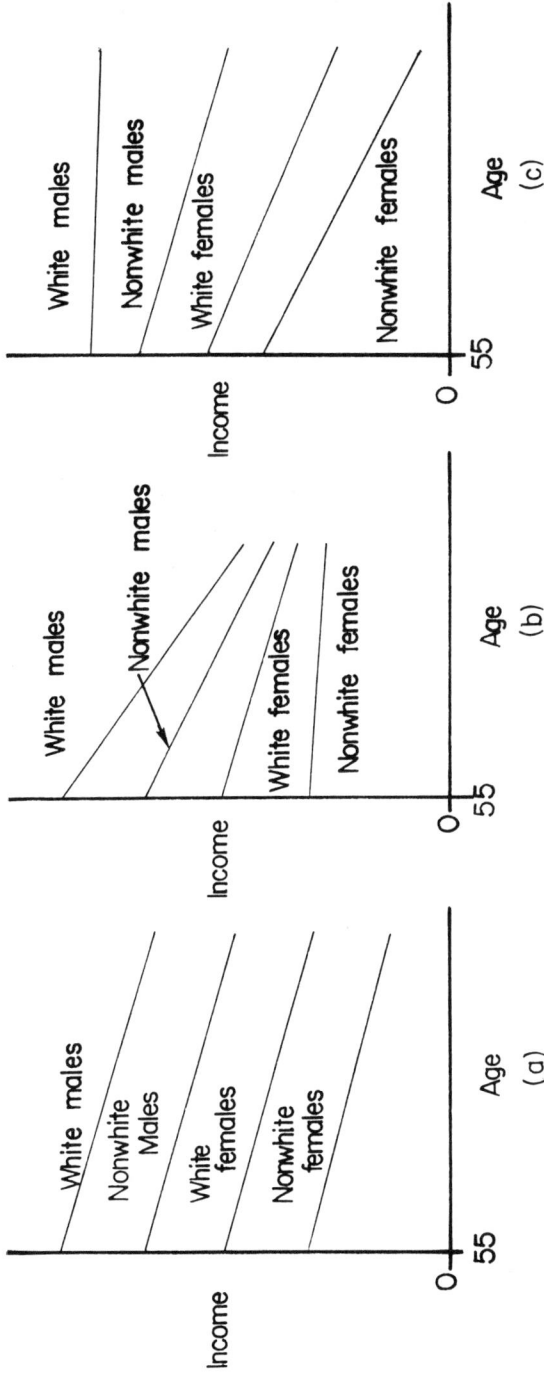

Figure 8-1. Hypothetical Models of Income Determination during Old Age for Race-Sex Groups

groups have more resources to limit the negative influence of old age (National Council on Aging, 1972). Those groups already disadvantaged, without as many resources, are more vulnerable to old age. The combination of age, race, and sex thus leads to greater loss of status than would be predicted from the individual, additive effects of each.[1]

Before we consider in more detail the predicted regression effects from each of the models, several other issues must be considered. First, the models ignore the effects of time. Income has increased over time; but has the increase been equally distributed across the age, race, and sex groups? If the effects of time on income are additive, then the pattern of additivity, leveling, or multiple jeopardy found for the early years will be the same in later years, except that mean income for all the groups will be higher. Alternatively, the effects of time may change the way in which age, sex, and race combine. Without describing the large number of possible combinations, the time interaction effects can be divided into two groups. Time may *reduce* group differences, in which case multiple jeopardy would be reduced or the pattern of leveling further strengthened. In the other direction, the effects of time may *increase* differences. Multiple jeopardy, if it exists, will be strengthened; leveling, if it exists, will be reduced.[2]

The second theoretical issue to consider here concerns the cause of the observed patterns. I have merely described the possible ways in which the ascriptive patterns may relate to income without suggesting explanations of the observed patterns. The question is whether the observed age, sex, and race patterns remain once controls are added. In the last chapter, the effect of age on the income of females was found not to be significant once controls were included. In the same way, the age, sex, and race combinations may disappear once controls for other variables are considered. As mentioned, it is difficult to construct models of the complexity of those in previous chapters when examining the small number of cases for nonwhites. Yet it will be possible to examine the effect of some simple controls for labor-force status, household size, education, and residence.[3] It is possible that race differences may be explained by educational differences, or that sex differences may be explained by differences in labor-force status.

In summary, the objective of this chapter is to address three questions: (1) What are the additive and interactive effects of age, race, and sex on income of the aged? (2) What effects do differences in education, labor-force status, household size, and residence have on the observed differences between the age, sex, and race groups? (3) How have the observed patterns, with and without controls, changed over time?

Testing for Multiple Jeopardy

Palmore and Manton (1973) have attempted to measure multiple jeopardy by using indexes of similarity to compare the income (or education or occupational status) distribution of old versus young, male versus female, and white versus nonwhite. The smaller the index of similarity, the greater the disadvantage of the negative status. To check for double jeopardy, similarity indexes can be calculated for distributions of older females compared with younger males, or for white males compared with nonwhite females. However, the use of the similarity index has been criticized because it does not identify the location of the differences in the distributions (Johnson 1973). Moreover, the similarity index fails to use the ordinal or interval properties of the indicators of status (Lieberson 1975). Finally, it is difficult to control for additional variables (other than age, race, and sex) when using similarity indexes.

For these reasons, I take an approach that utilizes fully the ratio property of income measures—regression analysis. Age is taken as a continuous predictor of income, whereas race and sex are dummy variables that provide the context in which age affects income. The loss of income because of negative statuses will thus be shown by the size of the regression coefficients. Under the assumptions of the additive model, the slope of income on age will be raised or lowered by membership in female or nonwhite groups. The usual tests for interaction may then be performed to determine whether the slope of income on age differs for the race-sex groups—as is predicted by the leveling and multiple-jeopardy models. Multiplicative interaction terms will show whether the combination of two or three negative statuses is different (either larger or smaller) than expected based on addition of the effects of the negative statuses. If the interaction effects are significant, the additive model can be rejected. Then the direction of the interaction effects can be examined to test the leveling and multiple-jeopardy hypotheses.

To complete the analysis, the additive and interactive effects can be examined with controls for education, household size, residence, labor-force status, and time. Given the number of interactions and the limited number of nonwhite aged persons in the sample, the number of controls must be limited to the most important variables. Finally, the additive and interactive effects of age, race, and sex, plus additive controls for the background variables, must be considered in the context of social change. Time can first be used as an additive control to adjust for general increases in income levels over time. Tests can then be performed to determine whether time interacts with the other variables. By multiplying time by all the other variables, and by adding these interaction terms to the equation, tests for changes in the process of income determination can be made.

The age range chosen for study is 55 and over. Many studies compare the young with the old, but the processes of income determination of persons in their twenties or thirties and of those in their sixties or seventies are too different to consider in one model. My approach will be to examine the negative effects of age after middle age. Age 55 includes persons who are at the peak of their earning power but are close to old age. Moreover, the limited time span controls in some ways the effects of cohort on age and reduces the effects of extraneous factors.

In the following analysis, the ascriptive status variables will be measured to show the effects of the negative status. Thus age is measured in single years beginning with 55,[4] sex as a dummy variable with females coded 1, and race as a dummy variable with nonwhites coded 1.[5] Otherwise, time takes the form of a dummy variable for the PUS data, where 1970 is coded 1; for the SRC data, time measures number of years from 1952, the year of the first survey. Education is measured in number of years of completed schooling. Labor-force status distinguishes those at work from those not currently employed and not currently in the labor force.[6] Residence is a dummy variable, with rural coded 1. And household size is the number of persons in the respondent's household.

SRC Results

Table 8-1 uses the SRC data to present a variety of models predicting income that can be used to test the double- and triple-jeopardy hypotheses. The first model in column 1 is based only on year of survey, age, sex, and race. The control for time is necessary to account for the growth in income over time (whether the increase over time is the same across the negative-status groups will be examined shortly). All the status variables are related negatively and significantly to income. For each increase in age of one year, persons lose, on the average, $266 in family income. Nonwhite respondents, on the average, have family incomes $3,764 lower than those of whites. The effects are smaller for sex, since the family variable allows men and women to share income; but the average female family income is still $1,800 lower than that for males. This is no doubt the result of income differences of unrelated males and females.

The second step of the analysis is to include measures of double jeopardy—the two-way multiplicative interaction effects. The additional variance explained by inclusion of these interaction terms is significant, as shown by an F-test value of 6.057. Two of the individual interaction terms, both involving age, are significant. In each case, the loss of income with age is greater for the high-status groups of men and whites than for the low-status groups of women and nonwhites. This supports the leveling hypothesis.

The three-way interaction term, which is added to the equation in the next column, is not significant; nor does it explain significantly more variance than the previous model. The effects of triple jeopardy, in contrast with the effects of double jeopardy, do not significantly affect the process of income attainment in either direction.

To determine whether the age, sex, and race patterns found so far can be explained by compositional differences in employment status, residence, education, and household size, these variables are included in the model in column 4. These controls are all related to income: being not employed or a

Table 8-1
Unstandardized Regression Coefficients for Models of Constant Family Income in Hundreds of Dollars: SRC Males and Females, Whites and Nonwhites, Aged 55 and Over

Independent Variables	Unstandardized Regression Coefficients					
	(1)	(2)	(3)	(4)	(5)	(6)
Constant	234.31	265.69	266.27	72.05	−29.86	46.29
Time	1.64*	1.62*	1.63*	1.31*	8.08*	2.90**
Additive						
Age	−2.66*	−3.13*	−3.14*	−1.63*	−0.14	−0.72**
Sex	−18.54*	−62.13*	−63.15*	−37.38*	58.78**	42.04
Race	−37.64*	−118.27*	−125.51*	−97.80*	−76.98	−76.51
Interaction						
Age*sex		0.65*	0.67*	0.38**	−0.98**	−0.79
Age*race		1.19*	1.30*	1.18**	1.11	0.95
Sex*race		5.07	17.54	−4.62	−10.09	−3.84
Age*sex*race			−0.19	0.11	0.05	−0.01
Controls						
Not employed				−13.29*	−13.71*	−5.09
Rural				−12.32*	−12.13*	−14.74*
Education				6.61*	6.59*	4.21*
Household size				24.22*	24.01*	14.86*
Time interaction						
Age					−0.10*	−0.06*
Sex					−6.40*	−5.44*
Race					−1.86	−1.79
Age*sex					0.09*	0.08*
Age*race					0.01	0.02
Sex*race					0.66	0.52
Age*sex*race					—	
Not employed						−0.55*
Rural						0.19
Education						0.16**
Household size						0.62*
R^2	0.15984	0.16282	0.16283	0.33397	0.33833	0.34479
df	5,107	5,104	5,103	5,099	5,093	5,089
F-increment test		6.057	0.061	327.642	5.59	12.549

*$p < .01$
**$.01 < p < .05$

rural resident decreases income, whereas higher education and larger household size increase income. These controls reduce the size of the age, race, and sex effects but do not remove the statistical significance of the effects. Thus beyond these simple controls, other factors are responsible for the negative effects of the ascriptive statuses and their interaction.

Have these effects changed over time? Column 5 adds interaction terms to the equation that are based on multiplication of each of the age, sex, and race main and interaction terms by time. The *F*-test for the additional variables is significant, indicating that some changes have occurred in the process over time. The results show that the main effects of age and sex (also of race, although it is not significant) are getting stronger over time: the loss of status is stronger in more recent years than in the past. Also, the leveling effects of age combined with sex are getting stronger over time. These results may result partly from growth of income levels and variance in income—since there is more to lose, those in the negative statuses lose more. At the same time, some of the main effects are reduced to insignificance, perhaps because of the presence of multicollinearity.[7]

Finally, the last model includes time interaction terms for the control variables. The negative effects of not being employed become stronger over time, while the positive effects of education and household size become stronger. The time interaction effects for age, sex, and race are maintained despite the inclusion of the time-control variable interaction.

In summary, the results support the leveling argument. As persons grow old, differences between whites and nonwhites and between males and females grow smaller. There is loss of income for all groups, but the losses are smaller for the low-status groups. Over time, the negative effects of age, race, and sex become larger; consequently, the leveling effects become larger also. The pattern remains much the same in the later periods, but the income levels start higher with larger differences.

PUS Results

Similar analyses can be performed for the census PUS data, except that the time span covers ten years and two data points. Also in contrast to the SRC data, the census sample includes institutionalized persons. The initial estimates of the effects of age, sex, and race on family income, shown in table 8-2, are significant controlling for time. Persons in 1970 have, on the average, $1,573 more than those in 1960. Given this difference, each year of age leads to about $200 less income. Females have about $1,000 less than males and nonwhites about $1,200 less than whites.[8]

Inclusion of the two-way interaction effects significantly increases the variance explained, but only one interaction term is significant—age by sex. Again, the direction of the interaction effects is positive, supporting the leveling hypothesis. The three-way interaction term is not significant.[9]

Controlling for the background variables explains many of the main and interaction effects found in the previous equations. All terms except for age and time are reduced to insignificance, although the direction of the effects found in the previous equations is not changed. These results therefore differ from those for the SRC data, where the control variables do not explain the age, sex, and race relationships to income.

Table 8-2
Unstandardized Regression Coefficients for Models of Constant Family Income in Hundreds of Dollars: PUS Males and Females, Whites and Nonwhites, Aged 55 and Over

Independent Variables	Unstandardized Regression Coefficients					
	(1)	*(2)*	*(3)*	*(4)*	*(5)*	*(6)*
Constant	220.77	243.48	252.73	37.45	14.21	47.43
Time	15.73*	15.71*	15.69*	12.97*	55.28*	−9.69
Additive						
Age	−2.08*	−2.43*	−2.57*	−0.63*	−0.29	−0.62**
Sex	−10.07*	−47.87*	−63.96*	−2.56	3.24	−11.39
Race	−12.63*	−18.23	−55.07**	−38.86	−34.29	−38.64
Interaction						
Age*sex		0.57**	0.81*	0.01	−0.06	0.11
Age*race		0.08	0.64	0.38	0.30	0.37
Sex*race		0.78	67.23	37.85	35.80	41.46
Age*sex*race			−1.00	−0.61	−0.48	−0.56
Controls						
Not employed				−24.06*	−24.16*	−17.89*
Rural				−28.65*	−28.84*	−31.20*
Education				6.25*	6.24*	5.66*
Household size				21.88*	21.87*	18.43*
Time interaction						
Age					−0.62	0.02
Sex					−11.79	13.15
Race					−7.60	−3.86
Age*sex					0.17	−0.13
Age*race					0.13	0.08
Sex*race					−3.09	−11.29
Age*sex*race					−0.13	−0.02
Not employed						−11.89*
Rural						4.48
Education						1.13**
Household size						6.93*
R^2	0.05366	0.05440	0.05482	0.26200	0.26304	0.26711
df	6,955	6,952	6,951	6,947	6,940	6,936
F-increment test		3.760	3.089	487.56	1.399	9.630

*$p < .01$
**$.05 < p < .01$

The interaction effects of time by the other variables in the model are shown in column 5. None of the individual interaction terms are significant, and the additional variance explained is not significant. Except for the additive effects of time, the processes are similar across time. Again, this result differs from the SRC results, where the negative effects of age, race, and sex became larger. The shorter time span prevents the interaction effects from emerging as they did for the SRC data. The 1960-1970 time span also does not include the later years in which the negative effects of status are strongest. Hence the effects of age, race, and sex independent of the control variables are smaller than for the SRC data.

In summary, the PUS family-income results show a pattern similar to that of the SRC data. Yet the short time span prevents emergence of results as strong as those found for the SRC data. Although the initial models show loss of income from the negative statuses, and leveling from the interaction terms, these patterns are largely explained by the control variables. Further, there has been little change in the pattern of age, sex, and race effects on income over the 1960-1970 time span.

We may now turn to the same analysis for personal income of the PUS respondents (table 8-3). In the initial equation, which includes measures of time, age, sex, and race, all variables are significant. The negative effects of age and race are smaller for personal income than they were for family income. However, the effects of sex are much larger for personal income than family income. Women, who may share the family income of their spouses, are more disadvantaged with respect to personal income.

The two-way interaction terms contribute significantly to the variance explained, and the two terms involving sex are individually significant. The direction of the effects is again positive, indicating support for the leveling hypothesis. The low levels of personal income of females get closer to the income of males in old age. Similarly, the disadvantage of black females is less than expected based on the additive effects of sex and race. The three-way interaction term is again not significantly different from zero.[10]

Controls for the background variables do not explain the effects of age, race, and sex on income—both the direction and the significance of most of the variables remain the same as in previous models. In fact, as found earlier, household size has no significant effect on personal income.

Tests to determine whether the processes of income attainment have changed over time indicate some differences across the periods. In particular, the loss of income of females relative to males becomes larger in 1970 than in 1960. Although female income has increased over time, as demonstrated in the last chapter, the position of females relative to males has declined.

Thus for personal income, the negative effects of sex are stronger than for family income; and these effects seem to be getting stronger over time. Otherwise, the pattern of status loss and the leveling effects of the interaction terms are similar to the previous results.

Summary

Previous chapters have shown the loss of income that generally occurs with old age. This chapter directly compares the losses of nonwhites and females with those of whites and males. The results show strong negative effects of

Table 8-3
Unstandardized Regression Coefficients for Models of Constant Personal Income in Hundreds of Dollars: PUS Males and Females, Whites and Nonwhites, Aged 55 and Over

Independent Variables	Unstandardized Regression Coefficients					
	(1)	*(2)*	*(3)*	*(4)*	*(5)*	*(6)*
Constant	140.36	221.58	226.19	111.65	96.35	113.11
Time	10.99*	10.90*	10.89*	6.33*	35.08*	3.49
Additive						
Age	−1.25*	−2.47*	−2.54*	−0.95*	−0.75*	−0.93*
Sex	−40.98*	−178.04*	−186.06*	−131.91*	−105.99*	−112.60*
Race	−5.47*	−23.70**	−42.06**	−36.95**	−33.23	−36.59
Interaction						
Age*sex		2.04*	2.17*	1.48**	1.16**	1.25*
Age*race		0.22	0.50**	0.46	0.45	0.49
Sex*race		7.14*	40.25	37.12	10.44	12.97
Age*sex*race			−0.50	−0.49	−0.14	−0.17
Controls						
Not employed				−36.67*	−36.98*	−33.99*
Rural				−12.36*	−12.48*	−14.50*
Education				3.74*	3.72*	3.15*
Household size				−0.05	−0.05	−0.58
Time interaction						
Age					−0.35	−0.04
Sex					−47.96**	−37.47
Race					−8.99	−6.38
Age*sex					0.58	0.45
Age*race					0.04	0.02
Sex*race					46.20	43.80
Age*sex*race					−0.59	−0.57
Not employed						−5.51
Rural						3.97
Education						1.09
Household size						1.11
R^2	0.15674	0.17802	0.17824	0.32225	0.32393	0.32567
df	6,955	6,952	6,951	6,947	6,940	6,936
F-increment test		59.99	1.861	369.03	2.46	4.526

*$p < .01$
**$.05 < p < .01$

age, race, and sex on income, even when controlling for a small number of background variables. However, tests for interaction showed that the loss of income during old age is greater for high-status groups than for low-status groups. In other words, status differences are leveled during old age. There is little evidence for the multiple-jeopardy hypotheses for either personal income or family income using persons aged 55 and over. Thus there is less inequality across groups among the very old than among the younger old.

The SRC analysis showed that the negative effects of the ascriptive statuses were becoming larger over time. In more recent years the differences between groups at age 55 are larger, and the loss of income of the groups as they grow older is greater. At the same time, the interaction effects increase over time: the leveling of group differences during old age gets stronger over time—a change that partially counteracts the larger negative effects of old age, being female, and being black. With higher mean income and greater dispersion of income, gaps between many of the groups are larger in the more recent periods. Referring back to Palmore and Manton's (1973) argument, group differences will be greater when there is more income to go around.

The age, race, and sex effects are, for the most part, maintained with controls. Controls greatly reduce the size of the effects for the PUS data, but with the larger number of time points in the SRC data the control variables do not remove the statistical significane of the ascriptive status variables. Employment status explains some of the differences between younger and older elderly persons or between males and females; education explains some of the differences between blacks and whites; and household size explains some of the differences between males and females. Yet since age, race, and sex are proxies for underlying processes, other factors must be involved in explaining the net effect of these variables. Perhaps net differences can be explained by discrimination, perhaps by unmeasured variables. What is needed is a larger sample size of nonwhites that will allow more reliable comparisons and the use of more detailed controls.

The results of this chapter are consistent with the results of previous chapters showing declining inequality in the aged population. Differences between sex and race groups are major components of inequality. As the process of leveling ascriptive group differences gets stronger over time, inequality will decline. The gap between the advantaged and disadvantaged groups has by no means disappeared. Yet, patterns of aging do appear to be converging over time, at least with respect to income.

Notes

1. The three models presented are, of course, oversimplified. The ordering of the group at age 55 will differ depending on whether personal or family income is measured, and the gaps between the groups will not be equally spaced. More importantly, there may be partial support for one pattern and partial support for another. Thus the effects of sex may be additive but the effects of race interactive, or there may be double jeopardy but not triple jeopardy. These graphs are suggestive of abstract patterns.

2. Again, this simplifies the possible results. Time may affect sex differently than race, or race differently than age.

3. Tests of interaction for the control variables with time will be performed, but there will be no interaction tests performed for the control variables with one another or with the age, sex, or race groups. Education or labor-force status may interact with household size; but, given the limited number of cases in some of the categories, it is necessary to limit the number of interactions to be included. Separate analysis of these kinds of interaction are, in many cases, explored in previous chapters.

4. Tests for curvilinearity show that age can be treated as a linear, continuous variable.

5. Over 90 percent of the nonwhites are blacks, but the category also includes Asian-Americans, Native Americans, and persons with Spanish surnames.

6. Unemployed persons are included with those out of the labor force.

7. It was not possible to include the interaction term based on time multiplied by age, race, and sex. The variable was so highly correlated to the other variables in the equation that it could not be included.

8. The coefficients for the SRC data are larger than those for the PUS data, especially for the effects of race. This is the result of the differences in time span of the two data sets. The SRC includes the high-income years after 1970.

9. The additional variance explained is significant, but the ratio of the standard error to the coefficient is not. With interaction terms, it is best to use significance tests carefully. Therefore, I use the test for the coefficient, which shows no significant relationship, as the final arbitrator.

10. Note 9 also applies here.

9

The Effect of Increases in Personal Income on the Living Arrangements of Unmarried Aged Persons

There is little support for arguments that the aged suffer in contemporary society because of loss of extended family ties, isolation of parents from their adult children, and complete dependence of aged persons on government services and housing.[1] Shanas (1979) has attacked the myth that aged persons are alienated from their children and other relatives. Although they seldom share the same household, parents and their adult children maintain strong ties. In fact, there is no evidence that older persons living in multigenerational households are better off than those who do not. Family relationships tend rather to be based on modified kin relationships where emotional, social, and financial exchanges across generations are common despite maintenance of separate households (Sussman 1965). In cases where older persons face severe financial or health problems, children are willing to provide needed help (Bane 1976) and unwilling—except when there is no other choice—to place their relatives in institutions (Brody 1977).

Although the extent of separation between older persons and their families has been exaggerated, some important changes in the nature of the living arrangements of the aged have occurred, particularly in the proportion of older persons who maintain their own households. Michael, Fuchs, and Scott (1980) find that the mean percentage of widows living alone for the fifty states increased from 24.5 in 1950 to 64.5 in 1976. Similarly, Kobrin (1976) finds a large increase in primary individuals (that is, household heads who live alone or with unrelated persons), especially among older females.

Given the arguments cited previously that adult children have not rejected the responsibility of caring for needy parents, what accounts for the observed increase in independent living arrangements among the aged? Many suggest that increases in income among older persons have increased their ability to afford independent living arrangements (Michael, Fuchs, and Scott 1980; Beresford and Rivlin 1966). A large number of surveys have shown that both older and younger persons prefer to maintain separate households and that only when financial or health problems necessitate it do aged parents desire to share the household of their children (Troll 1973). Given the improvements in income demonstrated in the last several chapters, fewer older persons should face the financial difficulties that force them to live with relatives; rather, older persons should be able to afford to live as they choose, namely, in their own households.

Cross-sectional studies have supported these arguments by showing that independent living arrangements depend on the personal-income levels of aged persons, but studies of the relationship between changes in income and changes in living arrangements are rare. A study by Michael, Fuchs, and Scott (1980) examines changes in the percentage of widows living alone as a result of increases in social-security benefits for dependents. However, this study uses aggregated cross-sectional data for states to estimate the effects of the income measure on living arrangements, and then uses those estimates to calculate implied changes in living arrangements over time from changes in income levels. This assumes, of course, that the effects of income on living arrangements have been constant over time and that compositional changes account completely for changes in living arrangements. It is possible that the effects of income on living arrangements have changed over time—in other words, that the process of determining living arrangements has changed. These types of effects have not been tested for in the literature; thus results such as those found by Michael, Fuchs, and Scott (1980) may be misleading.

The objectives of this chapter, then, are first to present more detailed time series on the family living arrangements of the aged than have heretofore been presented and, second, to use consecutive census cross-sectional surveys to explain some of the causes of the changes.[2] An especially important determinant is the income of older persons, since theoretical arguments suggest that higher income is responsible for independent living arrangements. The compositional and processual explanations of changes in family living arrangements briefly mentioned in the preceding paragraphs will be expanded and tested in the following sections. Again, this chaper contributes to literature on changes in the living arrangements of the aged by actually analyzing changes rather than by inferring changes from estimation of cross-sectional relationships.

The focus of the following analysis is on unmarried persons. Married persons are by definition family members, and their proportion in the aged population responds to changes in mortality and divorce rates rather than to their ability to afford independent housing. In fact, the proportion of husband-wife households in the older population has increased since 1960 because of lowered mortality rates (Soldo 1977). Thus there is the need to focus on changes in nonfamilial living arrangements independent of changes in marital status, to examine the probability that unmarried persons will live without other family members. In this chapter, then, it will be necessary to take marital status as an exogenous determinant of living arrangements of the aged.

The chapter will also focus on personal income of individuals rather than on family income. Family income is determined by living arrangements of persons and by household size rather than being a determinant of living arrangements. In contrast, personal income was found not to be determined by household size or living arrangements and can best be taken as a determinant of living arrangements. This issue will be discussed in more detail later, but the compositional and processual arguments discussed in the next section will refer to personal income.

Compositional and Processual Arguments

Soldo's (1977) study of the 1960 and 1970 *Public Use Samples* (PUS) of the census explained changes in living arrangements of the aged using the compositional variables of age, sex, and race. The increase in females and very old persons in the aged population has had a substantial influence on changes in family living arrangements. However, Kobrin (1976) has shown that increases in unrelated individuals have occurred independent of compositional changes in age, sex, race, and marital status. Others have therefore argued that the compositional effects of another variable—income—must be considered. Carliner (1975), for instance, found that increases in headship probably result from increases in income. Beresford and Rivlin (1966) also found a postive relationship between income and the likelihood of living alone among unmarried women, and they suggest that increases in income explain increases in independent living among both young and old. Perhaps the most detailed study of the influence of income on living arrangements was that of Michael, Fuchs, and Scott (1980) for elderly widows. They estimated the effects of several measures of income on living alone, using aggregate, state-level data for 1970, and used the findings to apportion the change in living alone resulting from changes in income. Although the measurement of income as average social-security benefits for dependents is less than ideal, they found positive effects from income that explained 75 percent of the increase in the percentage of aged widows living alone.

Theoretically, arguments predicting the importance of income on living arrangements take a consumer-demand approach (Michael, Fuchs, and Scott 1980). Privacy and autonomy, which come from living alone, are seen as goods desired by older persons (as well as by younger persons). Given that these desires exist, increases in income will provide the means for more older persons to live alone or with nonfamily members. It may be that a specific threshold level of income must be reached before persons feel they have sufficient income to afford living alone; persons below that threshold may feel they cannot adequately support themselves in their own households and thus may move in with relatives. The greater the number of older persons above that threshold, the greater the number who will live alone. In summary, this is a compositional argument in which the composition of the aged population is said to change through increases in the proportion of the population that can afford their own households.

The processual argument suggests that the effect of income on living arrangements will change over time. If the desire to live alone, the norms supporting living alone, or the demand for autonomy and privacy have increased in recent years, then people will be more willing to live alone given the same income. They will be more willing to subsist on less income, or will be willing to sacrifice income that would come from moving in with family members, in order to enjoy living alone. Even if income levels were identical across time, living alone would increase because preferences have changed.

As with other changes in the status of the aged, the processual effects may show up in additive or interactive form. If the change in the process of deciding to live alone is additive, all income groups in the aged population will experience similar increases in the probability of living alone. The differential in living alone for different income groups may remain the same over time, yet the additive effects of time will raise the levels for all these groups. If there is interaction among time, income, and living arrangements, then the trend in living arrangements for different income groups will differ. For instance, high-income groups may have always had a high proportion of persons living independently, which would allow little room for change; but low-income groups, where the level of independent living is lower, may experience much larger increases in independent living arrangements. This would indicate convergence in patterns of living arrangements.

In summary, the arguments reviewed take several different predictions. According to the compositional argument, controls for income should explain increases in nonfamilial living arrangements among the aged. According to the processual argument, increases in nonfamilial living arrangements will increase independent of income because of changes in preferences for living alone. These processual changes may occur additively, with increases in nonfamilial living arrangements increasing similarly for all income groups. Or the changes may occur interactively, with increases in nonfamilial living arrangements being stronger for low-income groups than for high-income groups.

Modeling Changes in Living Arrangements

Before testing the compositional and processual explanations, I would like to consider three issues concerning the model of living arrangements to be tested in this chapter. First, how are living arrangements of the aged to be conceptualized? Second, what role will marital status play in predicting living arrangements? And third, what types of causal relationships exist between income and living arrangements?

First, it is necessary to discuss conceptualization of living arrangements. I have referred generally to nonfamilial living arrangements, but the concept is more complicated than that. Census definitions distinguish persons who are members of a family from unrelated individuals who head their own households (primary individuals), unrelated individuals who do not head their own households (secondary individuals), and unrelated individuals who live in group quarters or institutions. One aspect of living arrangements, then, concerns whether persons live with other family members or with unrelated individuals. Unrelated individuals will not benefit from the social contact and income provided by relatives to older persons who are family members. Yet some of the older persons who are unrelated individuals may share their household with nonrelatives. These roommates may not be as close as relatives, but they do provide companionship and share expenses. Thus there is a need to make a second distinction, between persons who live alone and persons who do not.

Third, persons who live in households differ from those who live in group quarters. Group-quarters residents, who live primarily in boarding houses and institutions, do not live alone. Yet they do not actually share an independent household with the other residents of their group quarters. They can therefore be differentiated from persons who live in households with only one person or with several persons. It is important to make this distinction because increases in income may allow persons to avoid group-quarters living by setting up their own households. In some ways, the trend away from family living may be reflected in a trend away from institutional living. In summary, there are three aspects of living arrangements to consider: whether persons are unrelated individuals or members of families; whether persons live alone or in multiperson households and group quarters; and whether persons live in group quarters or in households. The first category of unrelated individuals is the broadest—persons living alone and persons living in group quarters are exclusive but not exhaustive subsets of unrelated individuals.[3]

A second issue to consider is who should be included in the analysis of living arrangements. If the spouse is present, married persons are by definition family members. Changes in the proportion of persons who are married respond to rates of divorce and mortality, topics that cannot be studied here in detail. Of greater interest is the change in living arrangements of persons who are unmarried or separated. The major change in living arrangements has not been in the proportion of older persons who are married, but in the proportion of widowed and other unmarried and separated persons who live alone or without family contacts. Thus marital status will be taken as exogenous, and living arrangements of unmarried and separated persons only will be examined. With the time-series data, where it is impossible to remove married persons from the aggregate figures, statistical controls for percentage married will be used in predicting living arrangements. In the cross-sectional data, married persons, spouse present, will be excluded from the analysis altogether, thereby allowing calculation of the probability of living alone independent of changes in the proportion of married persons in the aged population.

Finally, the direction of the causal relationship between income and living arrangements needs to be discussed in more detail. In considering family income, I argued that the direction of causality is from family relationships and household size to family income. When considering the personal income of individuals rather than of families, I argue that causality is in the opposite direction—from personal income to living arrangements and household size. This implies that there is no simultaneous, nonrecursive feedback relationship between income and living arrangements. Although household size predicts family income, family income does not determine household size; although personal income determines household size, household size does not determine personal income.

In defense of this specification, it is clear first of all that household size increases family income since additional members bring in additional income (tables 6-1 and 7-2). If, on the other hand, higher family income leads to larger household size, then older persons would be attracted to living with their families based on their families' income levels. Although there is probably some family income level below which families cannot afford to take in other relatives, the evidence on living arrangements of the aged suggests that such pull factors are less important than push factors, or the income of the older persons themselves. Despite the family income of relatives, older persons will live in their own households if they can afford to; when older persons find it difficult for financial or other reasons to support their own households, they are likely to move in with relatives regardless of those relatives' family income. Thus personal income of the respondents determines whether or not they live alone, and family income will not be treated as an independent variable.

When personal income is used as a predictor of living arrangements, there is no simultaneous feedback relationship: previous results showed that household size and other measures of family living arrangements are not significant determinants of personal income (tables 6-5 and 7-5). The advantage of such a specification is that ordinary least squares rather than two-stage least squares can be used to estimate the model. If the model was nonrecursive, estimates of the relationships could be obtained only if strong instrumental variables were available. In this case, it would require variables strongly related to income but unrelated to living arrangements and other variables strongly related to living arrangements but unrelated to income. Such variables are not available in the data for this study. Even if they were, two-stage least squares are most inefficient with cross-sectional survey data, such as those to be used here. Given these problems, I will depend on the simpler, recursive specification, which allows use of ordinary-least-squares estimation techniques.

Time-Series Trends

Before testing the compositional and processual arguments, a preliminary examination of the yearly trends in one aggregate measure of living arrangements—the percentage of aged persons living as unrelated individuals—is useful. Unrelated individuals are persons living alone or with nonfamily members (in either households or institutions). All persons who are not unrelated individuals are therefore family members.[4] Although the measure of percentage of unrelated individuals in the aged population does not provide the detail of the conceptualization discussed in the last section, it is available from the *Current Population Reports* for the years from 1954 to 1978 and provides more long-term baseline information than can the analysis of the individual-level measures that will be analyzed shortly.

To begin the analysis of the trends, table 9-1 presents some equations predicting the percentage of males aged 65 and over not living with family

Table 9-1
Unstandardized Regression Coefficients and *T*-Ratios for Models of the Percentage of Males Aged 65 and Over Living as Unrelated Individuals

Independent Variables	Unstandardized Regression Coefficients and T-Ratios		
	(1)	*(2)*	*(3)*
Time	−0.288	0.058	
	(1.87)	(0.48)	
Time^2	0.010	0.007	
	(1.77)	(1.72)	
Percentage of married males$_t$		−0.654	−0.770
		(5.44)	(5.13)
Median male income$_t$ (constant $)			0.383
			(4.15)
Constant	22.51	63.38	64.41
R^2	0.0595	0.5913	0.5220
Durbin-Watson	1.232	1.327	1.086
df	22	21	22

members. To describe the trend, equation 1.1 regresses the percentage of unrelated individuals on measures of time and time squared. The effect of time is designed to show the increase or decrease in the dependent variable on the average for each year from 1954 to 1978. The squared term is included to measure any curvilinearity in the trend. The effect of time is negative and significant in equation 1.1, whereas the effect of time squared is positive and significant. This indicates that there has been a downward trend in the percentage of male unrelated individuals but that this trend has become smaller in more recent time periods. The r-squared is low, however, and indicates little clear-cut trend over the time period.

The downward trend in the percentage of unrelated individuals is not in the predicted direction. The cause of the negative time term is likely to be related to the treatment of married persons. As argued earlier, the appropriate population for study of changes in living arrangements is unmarried persons because married persons are by definition family members and have no choice of living alone. It is necessary, therefore, to control for changes in marital status in examining the trends in the percentage of unrelated individuals. The next equation in table 9-1 includes a measure of the percentage of males who are married as an independent variable predicting the percentage of unrelated individuals. Using the percentage married as a predictor of the percentage of unrelated individuals is not tautological. If widows or divorcees immediately (within a year-long time period) move in with other relatives, changes in marital status will have no effect on the percentage of unrelated individuals. Otherwise, the effect of the percentage married will indicate the proportion of older persons who do not live with family members after marital disruption.

With the percentage of married males controlled, the direction of time effects in equation 1.2 shows increases in the percentage of unrelated individuals. The upward trend is getting larger in more recent years according to the positive time-squared term. The higher the percentage married, the lower the percentage of unrelated individuals. The negative effects of time on the percentage of unrelated individuals found in the previous equation thus results from increases in the percentage married. In this equation, as in the last one, the Durbin-Watson statistic is in the indeterminant range, which does not allow rejection or acceptance of the null hypothesis of no autocorrelation. If autocorrelation exists, the estimates are not biased; but the variance of the estimates are underestimated and consequently the size of the t-ratios is overestimated.

To explain the net trend of time, equation 1.3 uses constant median personal income of males aged 65 and over as a predictor of unrelated individuals, and deletes the time and time-squared terms.[5] Use of median income as a predictor is based on the compositional arguments discussed earlier: the effect of income on the percenage of unrelated individuals is assumed to be constant over the period, but increases in income will lead to increases in unrelated individuals given a constant positive effect. In the equation, the effect of the percentage married is again negative, whereas the effect of median income is in the predicted positive direction. Since median income is measured in hundreds of dollars, an increase of one unit of income increases the percentage of unrelated individuals by a little over 0.33 percent. The constant median income of males increased by about $1,200, which explains an increase in the percentage of unrelated individuals of about 5 percent (12 times 0.38). This is not a large change, but the total net change in the percentage of unrelated individuals as predicted by the time terms in equation 1.2 is only 5.8 percent.[6] It is important to keep in mind, however, that these results assume that all changes have resulted from compositional effects. The baseline results based on this assumpton will be refined in later analysis. At least the trend and the relationship in income has been demonstrated.

The results reported in table 9-2 present similar models of percent unrelated individuals for elderly females. In equation 2.1, the percentage of unrelated individuals is regressed on time. Tests for curvilinearity showed that the time-squared term was not significant; time is therefore linearly related to the dependent variable. The coefficent for time shows a much steeper increase in the percentage of unrelated individuals for females than for males. For females, each year shows an increase of 0.6 percent—an increase of 15 percent over the twenty-five-year time span. Controlling for the percentage married in equation 2.2 does not reduce the size of the effect of time. The percentage of married, aged females has increased almost 3 points;

Table 9-2
Unstandardized Regression Coefficients and T-Ratios for Models of the Percentage of Females Aged 65 and Over Living as Unrelated Individuals

Independent Variables	Unstandardized Regression and T-Ratios		
	(1)	*(2)*	*(3)*
Time	0.615	0.663	
	(22.67)	(40.05)	
Percentage of married females$_t$		−1.062	−0.982
		(7.19)	(2.58)
Median female income$_t$ (constant $)			1.762
			(14.93)
Constant	31.14	63.63	51.77
R^2	0.9553	0.9861	0.9074
Durbin-Watson	0.963	1.451	0.494
df	23	21	22

when controlling for this increase, the coefficient for time becomes slightly larger than it was in equation 2.1. Further, the r-squared in equations 2.1 and 2.2 is large, indicating a strong trend in the percentage of female unrelated individuals.

Equation 2.3 finds a strong effect of income on the percentage of unrelated individuals. An increase of $100 in constant, median personal income of aged females increases the percentage of unrelated individuals by more than 1 percent. Although the existence of autocorrelation may exaggerate the size of the t-ratio, the effect of income is more strongly related to the percentage of unrelated individuals for females than for males. It may be that increases in income have been especially important in increasing the percentage of unrelated females who have had little income. The effect of income on the percentage of unrelated males may be smaller since income levels have been higher and males have traditionally desired independent living. This argument can be tested in more detail in the next section.

Changes in Living Arrangements:
Individual-Level Results

The time-series results presented in the last section, as well as other time-series studies (Michael, Fuchs, and Scott 1980), assume that changes in living arrangements are the result of compositional changes in income levels. In this section, the 1960 and 1970 PUS census surveys can be used to test this assumption by comparing the size of compositional and processual effects on living arrangements. Just as it was necessary in the time-series results to examine changes net of exogenous change in marital status, it will be necessary to control for marital status changes in the cross-sectional data by excluding married persons from the analysis. Hence the probability that unmarried or separated persons will live with nonfamily members, live alone, or live in group quarters rather than move in with relatives can be determined. Married persons who are separated, or whose spouse does not share the same household, will also be included in the analysis.[7]

The model of living arrangements is as follows. There are three measures of the dependent variable. First, a dummy variable is used to indicate whether a person is an unrelated individual or a family member, with unrelated individuals coded 1. Unrelated individuals do not necessarily live alone, but they do not live with relatives. A second dummy variable indicates whether persons live alone or in multiperson households or group quarters. Third, a dummy variable indicating whether persons live in group quarters or institutions rather than in households is used.

The independent variable of most interest is income. It will be measured as personal income in constant dollars divided into six categories. The categorization of the variable, and treatment as a factor in the MCA analysis, allows for nonlinear relationships between income and living arrangements. In addition to income, several control variables need to be included in the model. Age, education, rural residence, and race (nonwhites equal 1) are measured as they were in previous chapters. A dummy variable for employment status (at work and not at work) is included. Current marital status includes categories for widowed, divorced, never-married, separated, and married with spouse absent. Finally, a dummy variable for time, where being a 1970 respondent is coded 1, is included: the effect of this time variable on living arrangements independent of the effects of income and the other independent variables will show processual changes or changes in preferences.

Before we present the results, tests for interaction of the variables over time need to be discussed. Regression equations that add multiplicative time interaction terms to the equations including the additive variables were estimated. Such tests were performed for males and females for all three dependent variables. Of the six tests for time interactions, only one was significant at the .01 level—the probability of living in group quarters for aged females. Since most of the models do not show the interaction over time, the following results include only the additive effects of time. The one exception, female group-quarters living, will be considered in more detail after presentation of the additive results.

Table 9-3 presents the additive models for males. The results show only two significant predictors of the probability of being an unrelated individual. The first is marital status: currently widowed males are the least likely to be unrelated individuals, whereas divorced and separated males are most likely to be unrelated individuals. The second is time: in 1970, 15 percent more of the males are unrelated individuals than in 1960. This increase occurs despite changes in income, marital status, or any of the other variables. The r-squared in the model is low; many causes other than those included in the model may relate to not living with family. Yet the factor often argued to be most important—income—has little effect, and the trend over time is fairly large.

Many unrelated individuals who live with friends or other nonrelatives may share income in ways similar to sharing expenses with family members. Thus being an unrelated individual may not purchase autonomy or privacy, and income will not have the expected effect. A more valid test of the effect of income, however, can be made with the probability of living alone as the dependent variable. Since more autonomy or privacy can be purchased by living alone than by living as an unrelated individual, the effect of income should be larger.

The results for living alone are presented in the next column of table 9-3. Here, in addition to the significant effects of marital status and time,

Table 9-3
Multiple-Classification Analysis of Measures of Nonfamilial Living Arrangements: PUS Males Aged 60 and Over

Independent Variables	N	Unrelated Individual		Live Alone		Group Quarters	
		Gross	Net	Gross	Net	Gross	Net
Age							
60-64	153	4	2	1	0	0	3
65-69	138	3	4	5	6	-1	0
70-74	141	-1	0	6	6	-6	-6
75-79	99	-4	-6	-9	-8	3	1
80+	128	-4	-2	-6	-6	5	2
		0.07	0.07	0.12	0.12	0.10	0.09
Education							
0-7	290	-5	-2	-6	-4	0	0
8	151	3	3	8	7	-2	-2
9-11	88	3	0	2	2	3	0
12	66	4	0	-5	-8	6	5
13-15	35	0	-3	7	3	-11	-7
16	29	17	11	10	8	3	5
		0.11	0.06	0.13	0.10	0.10	0.08
Employment							
At work	187	-1	-5	6	1	-12	-12
Not at work	472	0	2	-2	-1	5	4
		0.01	0.06	0.07	0.02	0.22	0.18*

Constant personal income						
None	54	−5	−5	−25	−20	28	24
$1–499	52	−2	2	−9	6	5	7
$500–999	67	−11	−8	−8	−6	1	0
$1,000–2,499	237	0	−1	1	2	−1	−2
$2,500–4,999	118	7	7	9	8	−4	−3
$5,000–9,999	92	−2	−3	4	2	−7	−4
$10,000+	39	14	9	15	7	−14	−10
		0.12	0.11	0.20	0.16**	0.27	0.23*
Marital status						
Widowed	326	−6	−5	4	5	−7	−7
Divorced	62	15	10	17	11	−8	−6
Separated	100	6	6	−13	−13	7	9
Never married	171	2	2	−6	−5	8	7
		0.15	0.13**	0.18	0.17*	0.27	0.25*
Covariates						
Rural			−5.2		−4.2		−1.8
Black			−5.9		−2.8		−9.9**
Time			15.3*		12.9*		4.1
R^2			0.077		0.111		0.190
Grand mean			66		41		14
N			659		659		659
df			634		634		634

Note: Coefficients are multiplied by 100.

*$p < .01$

**$.05 < p < .01$

the effects of income are also significant. The higher the personal income of aged males, the more likely they are to live alone. Marital status is related to living alone, but the direction is different than it was for being an unrelated individual: widowers are more likely to live alone but are less likely than others to be unrelated individuals. Most widowed unrelated males live alone, whereas unrelated males of other marital status are more likely than widowers to live with nonfamily members. The third significant variable is time. Despite increases in income levels, which have raised the ability of older males to live alone, the demand for living alone has also grown. Thus persons with the same income are more likely to live alone in 1970 than in 1960. The net increase is fairly large—12.9 percent over ten years.

The third dependent variable, living in group quarters, includes persons living in institutions, hospitals, and rooming or boarding houses. The grand mean is 14 percent. Since national figures show that less than 5 percent of aged males are in nursing homes, many of the respondents in table 9-2 must live in noninstitutional settings. Income is related to living in group quarters, but in the direction opposite to that found for living alone. Those with high incomes are more likely to be able to afford to live outside of group quarters. Naturally, employment is related to living in group quarters; few persons in such quarters hold jobs. Especially for those in institutions, health problems are probably responsible for both work status and living arrangements. As for marital status, never-married and separated men are most likely to live in group quarters. Finally, time has no significant independent effect on living in group quarters. The mean level is 4.1 percent higher for 1970 than for 1960, but the increase is not significantly different from 0. Thus the increase in living alone has not necessarily been accompanied by an increase in the percentage of males living in group quarters.

Table 9-4 presents simlar models for females. Females are less likely than males to be unrelated individuals but are slightly more likely to live alone. Thus it is less common for females to share households with nonrelatives, and women are less likely to live in group quarters. National statistics show that females are more likely than males to live in nursing homes, so the differences in group-quarters living are the result of differences in the percentages living in rooming and boarding houses.

The model predicting unrelated living arrangements shows income, marital status, and time to be related significantly to the dependent variable. In contrast to that of men, the personal income of women allows them to live with nonfamily members. Separated persons are most likely to be unrelated individuals, and divorced persons are least likely to be unrelated individuals, although the differences are not large. Finally, time is again significant, indicating an increase in unrelated living independent of income and marital-status changes.

Table 9-4
Multiple-Classification Analysis of Measures of Nonfamilial Living Arrangements: PUS Females Aged 60 and Over

Independent Variables	N	Unrelated Individual		Live Alone		Group Quarters	
		Gross	Net	Gross	Net	Gross	Net
Age							
60-64	336	1	−5	3	4	−4	−6
65-69	369	0	−1	1	0	−4	−4
70-74	362	0	0	4	4	−2	−2
75-79	291	2	5	1	3	0	0
80+	333	−1	2	−11	−11	11	12
		0.03	0.07	0.11	0.11	0.22	0.23*
Education							
0-7	551	−6	−3	−5	−2	1	0
8	394	0	1	−1	1	0	−1
9-11	249	1	0	1	−1	0	0
12+	284	3	0	6	2	−1	−1
13-15	112	6	3	3	0	−1	−1
16+	101	14	10	7	3	3	3
		0.10	0.06	0.08	0.03	0.03	0.04
Employment							
At work	316	8	5	7	−1	−5	0
Not at work	1,375	−2	−1	−2	0	1	0
		0.08	0.05	0.07	0.01	0.09	0.00
Constant personal income							
None	217	−6	−13	−25	−21	12	11
$1-499	121	−11	−9	−11	−6	3	0
$500-999	289	−8	−7	−5	−5	0	−2
$1,000-2,499	575	4	4	4	3	−2	−1
$2,500-4,999	274	10	8	10	9	−4	−2
$5,000-9,999	157	10	6	13	12	−4	−4
$10,000+	58	13	9	11	11	−2	−3
		0.19	0.16*	0.24	0.20*	0.19	0.16*
Marital status							
Widowed	1,260	0	0	2	3	−2	−2
Divorced	110	−2	−3	5	0	−3	0
Separated	78	1	3	−18	−14	16	16
Never married	243	2	−1	−7	−10	5	6
		0.06	0.08**	0.10	0.11*	0.20	0.21*
Covariates							
Rural			−1.4		3.4		−1.2
Black			−4.0		−4.5		−4.5**
Time			8.1*		9.8*		1.2
R^2			0.056		0.085		0.128
N			1,691		1,691		1,691
df			1,666		1,666		1,666

Note: Coefficients are multiplied by 100.

*$p < .01$

**$.05 < p < .01$

The results for living alone are similar to those for living as unrelated individuals. Income and marital status are related to living alone, and there has been an increase of 9.8 percent independent of compositional changes. The r-squared for living alone, as for being an unrelated individual, is low; clearly other factors help explain the living arrangements of women.

Finally, the results for living in group quarters are much the same for women as for men. Poorer women, separated women, and white women are most likely to live in group quarters and institutions. But, there has been no significant increase over time. As mentioned, however, evidence indicates a change in the process of living in group quarters for women across time. Without going into detail, the interaction effects can be summarized as follows. The ability of high personal income to prevent institutionalization has increased over time; income differences are much larger in 1970 than in 1960. Since the levels of group-quarters living for women are low, this change has not had a major effect on reducing group-quarters living.

Summary

The results indicate not only increases owing to compositional changes in the proportion of older persons with sufficient income to avoid living alone, but also increased demand for the privacy and autonomy of such living arrangements as shown by the additive, processual effects of time. The probability of living alone for all income groups in the aged population, and for all other groups, has increased for both males and females. At the same time, there has been little increase in the percentage of older persons living in group quarters.

There are other possible explanations for the net increase over time in living alone, in addition to increased demand for privacy and autonomy. No measure of health or disability is available for the 1960 PUS data. Reductions in disability may allow older persons to live outside their families. Yet according to the data on disability limitations that will be presented in chapter 11, there are only 3 percent more disabled persons in 1970 than in 1960. This is not sufficient to explain the effects of time. It is likely that changes have allowed more persons with the same activity limitations to maintain separate households in 1970 than in 1960. Further, other unmeasured characteristics related to birth cohort are likely to explain the increase since the effects of age are not significant.

It may be that increases in mobility of children have separated them from their parents, preventing parents from moving in with their children. Yet evidence on cross-county migration shows that the percentage of persons age 35 to 44 who moved across county lines in the last three years remained around 10 percent; from 1960 to 1970 there has been a change of less than 1 percent. Further, the decline in rural residents, controlled for in the analysis, cannot explain the increase over time. Even the decline in the number of children is probably not large enough to have major effects on living arrangements over a ten-year time span.

Thus this chapter provides more evidence that the nature of aging, in contrast to the characteristics of the aged, have changed considerably. Increases in income are not sufficient to explain the trend in living alone or with unrelated individuals. Along with changes in economic variables, changes in sociocultural tastes must also be considered. Using the data analyzed here, it is difficult to identify the nature of the tastes involved. It may be that norms and values sanction against living with relatives, that preferences for maintaining one's own life style have increased, or that government services for the elderly have made it safer and easier to live alone. Whatever the nature of this change, it is clear that persons are more likely to live alone on less income in recent years than in the past, and that regardless of changes in income in the future, independent living will continue to increase.

Notes

1. Burgess (1960), for instance, argued that the nuclear family isolated old persons from their families when compared to the extended families of the past, with old and young sharing the same household. Yet a great deal of literature (for example, Laslett and Wall 1972) has shown that the extended family has never been very common in the United States. The loss of family ties from preindustrial to industrial societies is often exaggerated, just as the lack of family ties of older persons in postindustrial societies is sometimes exaggerated.

2. Only the census survey data will be analyzed in this chapter. The Survey Research Center (SRC) cross-sectional data are missing the variable most crucial for explaining changes in living arrangement of the aged—personal income.

3. The category of unrelated individuals is made up of persons living alone, persons living in group quarters, and persons living in households with nonrelatives. Analysis will be made of changes in persons living alone and living in group quarters, but not of persons living with nonrelatives. These persons are of little theoretical interest in themselves, but they are important as persons not living in families or as persons not living alone. Thus in the conceptualization of living arrangements, persons living with nonrelatives are included either with persons not living with family members or with persons not living alone.

4. Institutional inmates are included with unrelated individuals in this

variable. Until 1971 the number of institutional inmates was included in the *Current Population Reports* (CPR), but after 1971 it was not. To deal with this problem, inmates are included as a residual category to be combined with unrelated individuals. The number of persons in families is divided by the total number of persons aged 65 and over obtained from independent population estimates. This proportion is then subtracted from 1 and multiplied by 100 to give the percentage of persons living as unrelated individuals and institutional inmates. Since institutional inmates seldom live with family members, I will use the term *unrelated individuals* to refer to all persons not living with family members, whether they live in households or in institutions. In the CPR figures, persons living in group quarters, such as boarders or roomers, are already included with unrelated individuals.

5. Results for income measured in current dollars differ little for males. For females, in the equations to follow, measurement of income in constant dollars performs better than measurement of income in current dollars. To be consistent, the results of males and females are presented with the constant-income measure.

6. This is calculated from the time and time-squared coefficients multiplied by the twenty-five-year time span: $0.058 \times 25 + 0.007 \times 25^2$.

7. Married persons whose spouse is absent from the household are not necessarily classified as family members—this depends on whether they live with children or other relatives. Thus it is necessary to include these married persons in the analysis. They will be included with formally separated persons in the analysis to follow.

10 The Effect of Income Levels on the Financial Satisfaction of the Aged

All the indicators of the status of the aged studied so far have been measures of objective conditions. In particular, the growth of income and its effect on changes in living arrangements and labor-force participation have been demonstrated. The objective consequences of higher income, however, can be supplemented by information on the subjective evaluation by the aged of their higher income. In other words, changes in subjective financial satisfaction can be compared with changes in actual income levels. Without some information on the subjective meaning of income to the aged, it is hard to tell how well their financial needs are being met.

Cross-sectional studies of the aged have shown, for the most part, a positive relationship between income and financial satisfaction (Campbell, Converse, and Rogers 1976; Peterson 1973).[1] Given a positive cross-sectional relationship between income and financial satisfaction, and given the increase in income over time, a simple compositional argument would predict that financial satisfaction should also increase. If a certain income level is needed to bring about financial satisfaction, an increase in the proportion of the aged population above that level should increase financial satisfaction. This assumes, of course, that the standards for evaluating income—or the effects of income on financial satisfaction—remain the same over time.

An alternative explanation would argue that the process of evaluating the adequacy of income has changed over time in ways that will prevent an increase in financial satisfaction from occurring. For example, aged persons may have developed higher expectations for their standard of living in recent years; thus higher income may be no more satisfying than the lower levels of the past (Easterlin 1973). Duncan (1975) finds no change in the satisfaction with standard of living of Detroit adults from 1958 to 1972, because the income of the total population rose and few persons experienced improvement in their position in the income distribution relative to others. It remains to be seen whether similar results hold for the aged.

The objective of this chapter is to examine changes in financial satisfaction among the aged when controlling for income and other background variables. If the compositional argument previously discussed is correct, then financial satisfaction among the aged will have increased. If the processual explanation is correct, then there will be either no change in financial satisfaction (if expectations rise at the same rate as income) or a decline (if expectations rise faster than income). These arguments thus correspond to the compositional and processual arguments considered throughout this book: changes in the income compostion should increase financial satisfaction unless changes in the process of determining financial satisfaction have occurred that limit the effect of higher income.

Data and Sample

There are two sources of data on financial satisfaction. The first is the Survey Research Center (SRC) data, which include measures of financial satisfaction for only four years: 1956, 1958, 1960, and 1964. It is necessary to supplement the analysis of these data with more recent figures. The second data set is the National Opinion Research Corporation (NORC) General Social Surveys for all the years from 1972 to 1978. The NORC data for each of the seven years includes measures of financial satisfaction as well as the demographic-background variables. In fact, the NORC data provides the advantages of yearly surveys for the time span and some more detailed measures of financial situation. The only other problem of comparability of the SRC and NORC data is that the early NORC surveys were based on block quota sampling rather than on probability samples. Yet modified probability sampling was used on the later surveys, making the surveys similar to the SRC surveys (House 1979).

The measure of financial satisfaction is identical for the SRC and NORC data. The question is stated: "We are interested in how people are getting along financially these days. So far as you and your family are concerned, would you say that you are pretty well satisfied with your present financial situation, more-or-less satisfied, or not satisfied at all." There are thus three alternatives with "pretty well satisfied" scored 3 and "not satisfied at all" scored 1.

It will be useful in considering changes in financial satisfaction to make reference to a measure—available only for the NORC data—of perceived relative financial standing. Respondents were asked whether, compared with American families in general, their family income was far above average, above average, average, below average, or far below average. "Far above average" is coded 5 and "far below" is coded 1. This variable may help explain changes in financial satisfaction (Liang and Fairchild 1979) as well as allowing examination of changes in relative standing on its own.

The first step in the analysis will be to take financial satisfaction as a function of time, income, and the other control variables. The control variables are the same as those used in previous chapters: education, age, labor-force status, sex, rural residence, household size, race, and marital status. The variables are measured as they were in previous chapters for both the SRC and NORC data. Then, for the NORC data, the measure of perceived relative standing can be included in the model to determine whether changes in perceptions of financial position help explain financial satisfaction. When financial satisfaction is treated as an interval variable, ordinary-least-squares techniques can be used to estimate the relationships. Time will be treated as a set of dummy variables with the trend in financial satisfaction shown by the gross coefficients and the trend controlling for compositional changes shown by the net coefficients. The SRC and NORC data will be analyzed separately so that comparisons of the trend in financial satisfaction can be made within the eight-year time span of the SRC data (1956-1964) and the seven-year time span (1972-1978) of the NORC data. Comparison of levels of financial satisfaction can also be made between the two data sets. Separate models for the two groups will also allow tests for interaction of the coefficients across time and regression-standardization decomposition of the size of compositional and processual effects.

Before examining the changes over time, however, it is necessary to determine which measure of income best predicts financial satisfaction. Income can be measured in current and constant dollars to determine whether old persons adjust for inflation when judging their financial satisfaction. Income can be measured linearly or measured as a natural log to determine whether increases in income of persons at the higher levels have a smaller impact on financial satisfaction than increases at the lower levels of income distribution (Duncan 1975; Vaughan and Lancaster 1979). Income can also be measured relative to that of other respondents in the year of interview to determine the effect of changes in economic standing: it may be that increases in income have no effect if relative standing has changed little. For all these measures, the variance explained in financial satisfaction can be compared to determine which is most useful in explaining financial satisfaction (Duncan 1975).

Form of the Relationship between Income and Financial Satisfaction

First, the ability of several different measures of income to explain variance in financial satisfaction can be compared to determine the "best" predictor. Whichever measure of income is found to be most useful will suggest how persons judge the adequacy of their income. Do they evaluate income in current or constant dollars? Does the ability of additional income to increase satisfaction decline at the higher income levels? Do persons make judgments based on their absolute income or on income relative to that of others? Specifically, I will examine the effect of six measures of income on the measures of financial satisfaction: (1) income in current (1972) dollars,

(2) income in constant dollars, (3) the natural log of current dollars, (4) the natural log of constant dollars, (5) income in current dollars standardized by the mean and standard deviation of the aged population in the respondent's year of interview, and (6) income in current dollars standardized by the mean and standard deviation of the total population in the respondent's year of interview.

The standardized measures subtract the appropriate mean and divide by the appropriate standard deviation. By using the mean and the standard deviation of income for the respondent's year of interview, this standardization differs from typical standard scores, which would use the grand mean and standard deviation for all the years combined. The method used here provides a measure of the person's position at one time point rather than the position of persons at all different time points combined. The scores are standardized by the income of both the aged population and the total population to determine whether older persons compare their income to that of other older persons or to that of the total population.

To assess the effect of these income measures on financial satisfaction, the control variables of year of interview, marital status, sex, labor-force status, age, education, race, and household size will be used. Table 10-1 presents the net effect of each income measure in the form of a standardized regression coefficient and r-squared for the dependent variable of financial satisfaction. Included as a comparison is the variance explained by a model that includes no measure of income, only the control variables. The first part of the table includes the results for the SRC data and the second part the NORC results.

For the NORC results, the variable that has the largest standardized coefficient and r-squared is income measured in current dollars. The log measures are clearly inferior to the untransformed measures. This indicates that the relationship of income and financial satisfaction is not curvilinear; there is no threshold above which returns in financial satisfaction relative to income become smaller. The other measures, income in constant dollars and both standardized measures, differ little from the current-income measure in the size of their effects. There is some evidence that current income is more important than constant income, and that income relative to the total population is more important than income relative to the aged population. However, the differences are too small to attribute major significance to them. The results do suggest, however, that current income is satisfactory for use in the following analyses.

The results for the SRC data cover four years—1956, 1958, 1960, and 1964—and provide a contrast with the NORC data. In contrast to the NORC data, the standardized coefficients and r-squared are largest for the logged measures in the SRC data. This indicates a change in the process of evaluating increases in income at the upper levels of the distribution. In the

Table 10-1

Net Regression Effect of Alternative Income Measures on Financial Satisfaction: SRC and NORC Males and Females, Aged 60 and Over

Alternative Income Measures	SRC: 1956-1964		NORC: 1972-1978	
	Standard Coefficient	R^2	Standard Coefficient	R^2
Income, current dollars	0.240	0.08869	0.254	0.10218
Ln (income, current $)	0.333	0.11376	0.192	0.08620
Income, constant $	0.240	0.08892	0.250	0.10111
Ln (income, constant $)	0.332	0.11376	0.192	0.08620
Standardized by aged income[a]	0.240	0.08882	0.245	0.10104
Standardized by total income[b]	0.240	0.08854	0.253	0.10205
No income measure		0.04849		0.06052

Note: Control variables: year, education, age, marital status, race, sex-labor-force status, household size, rural (see table 10-2).

[a]Standardized income is calculated from the respondent's family income minus mean income of persons aged 60 and over in the respondent's year of survey divided by the standard deviation of persons aged 60 and over in the respondent's year of survey.

[b]Based on the same formula as in the previous note except that the means and standard deviations for the total population aged 18 and over are used.

late 1950s and early 1960s, increases in income at the higher income categories add little to financial satisfaction. During the 1970s, the reduced effect of income on financial satisfaction disappears. Apparently, expectations or desires have risen enough so that few persons have income so high that further increases do not add to financial satisfaction.

Changes in Financial Satisfaction

The last section showed that income measured in current dollars better predicts financial satisfaction than income in constant dollars. Judgments of the adequacy of income are thus made on the basis of actual income without clear adjustments for the value of the income relative to inflation. Whether income should be treated linearly or not depends on the time period being examined. However, to make the analyses comparable over time, the unlogged measure of income will be used. The differences in the income relationship for the SRC data should be reflected in a smaller effect of income in current dollars, and should thereby shown differences across time.

A model predicting financial satisfaction using income in current dollars is presented in table 10-2. The variables in the model are measured as

Table 10-2
Multiple-Classification Analysis of Financial Satisfaction: SRC and NORC Males and Females Aged 60 and Over

		SRC			NORC		
	N	Gross	Net	N	Gross	Net	Net
Time							
1956	300	−0.04	−0.02				
1958	271	0.08	0.08				
1960	270	−0.13	−0.15				
1964	361	0.07	0.06				
1972				325	−0.05	0.00	−0.01
1973				274	−0.04	0.02	−0.02
1974				289	0.01	0.01	0.01
1975				312	0.07	0.07	0.07
1976				342	0.00	−0.03	−0.02
1977				270	−0.05	−0.09	−0.04
1978				302	0.07	0.01	0.03
		0.07	0.12*		0.06	0.06	0.05
Marital status							
Married	669	0.06	0.06	1,234	0.03	0.04	0.03
Widowed	409	−0.05	−0.03	619	0.01	−0.03	−0.02
Divorced	27	−0.26	−0.27	97	−0.23	−0.21	−0.15
Separated	15	−0.29	−0.32	53	−0.46	−0.26	−0.21
Never married	82	−0.14	−0.16	111	0.03	0.01	0.03
		0.11	0.11*		0.12	0.10*	0.07*
Sex-labor-force status							
Male working	280	0.03	−0.04	314	0.07	−0.01	0.01
Male retired	276	−0.02	0.00	658	−0.06	−0.06	−0.06
Female working	112	0.04	0.08	202	−0.05	0.00	−0.01
Female retired	115	−0.02	0.07	265	−0.01	0.01	0.01
Female homemaker	419	−0.01	−0.01	675	0.04	0.06	0.06
		0.03	0.05		0.07	0.07**	0.07*
Covariates							
Nonwhite		−0.251	−0.200*		−0.314	−0.146*	−0.054
Age		−0.004	0.003		0.007	0.013*	0.010*
Education		0.024	0.080		0.032	0.009*	0.005
Household size		0.031	−0.061		−0.006	−0.081	−0.072
Income		0.004	0.004*		0.002	0.002*	0.001*
Relative financial situation							
Far below average				117	−0.72		−0.63
Below average				622	−0.32		−0.27
Average				1,098	0.18		0.17
Above average				240	0.37		0.24
Far above average				19	−0.16		−0.26
					0.42		0.35*
R^2			0.089			0.102	0.208
GM			2.29			2.27	2.27
df			1185			2,094	2,090
N			1202			2,114	2,114

*$p < .01$
**$.05 < p < .01$

follows. Time of survey and marital status are presented as factors or sets of dummy variables. Sex and labor-force status are combined into one variable, which allows them to interact with one another in determining relative financial situation. The effect of not being in the labor force may be perceived differently by a woman than by a man. The covariates include a dummy variable for race (where nonwhites are coded 1), measures of age and education in single years, and household size counting the number of adults in the household. Tests for curvilinearity show the covariates to be linearly related to relative financial situation.

First, examine the gross trend in financial satisfaction over time. In the years of the SRC data, financial satisfaction fluctuates: beginning below the mean, it goes above, below, and then above. For the NORC data, the gross effects of time also fluctuate, beginning below the grand mean, rising above, going below, and rising above again. The grand means for the SRC and NORC data are nearly identical. Although the changes between years are small, they correlate partially with trends in economic conditions. The unemployment rate and mean financial satisfaction for the four years of the SRC data are correlated at 0.413; for the seven years of the NORC data they correlate at 0.422. In particular, the improvement in economic conditions experienced by the country in 1975 is accompanied by an increase in financial satisfaction.

The next question to consider is the role that changes in income and other variables play in the trend over time. To determine this, it is first necessary to examine the cross-sectional relationships of the variables in the model to financial satisfaction. First, income is positively related to financial satisfaction (as shown also in table 10-1). In addition, marital-status groups vary in their levels of financial satisfaction. Married persons are generally much more satisfied with their financial situation than are unmarried persons, even when household size and income are controlled. Divorced and separated persons are especially dissatisfied, perhaps because these persons evaluate their income relative to the greater levels of income they had when they were married. Blacks are less satisfied with their income even when it is at the same level as that of whites; this may reflect dissatisfaction of blacks with their position in the stratification system above and beyond their actual income. In any case, the hypothesis that blacks have lower expectations for income than whites, and that they will be satisfied with less income, does not hold for either data set. Finally, age and household size are related to financial satisfaction only for the NORC data, where persons with a large household at the younger ages are less satisfied with their financial situation. Given the greater needs of persons in this situation, it is not surprising that given the same income they will be less satisfied than older persons in smaller households.

Despite the existence of these relationships, controls for them do not change the gross relationship between time and financial satisfaction. The eta and beta for time are nearly identical for both the SRC and NORC data. Thus the increase in income has had little effect on financial satisfaction; levels of financial satisfaction are essentially independent. This would suggest that decisions about financial satisfaction are made independent of improvements in income or compositional changes in income; in other words, some kind of processual changes might have occurred.

To better summarize the effect of compositional changes with other causes of the change or lack of change in financial satisfaction, regression-standardization techniques can be used to decompose the change between the SRC and NORC data. Although there are no major increases in levels across periods, the regression standardization can help determine whether there are counterbalancing compositional and processual forces that have prevented an increase. Thus increases in income, which should have increased financial satisfaction, may have been reduced by processual changes. The results of the decomposition are presented in table 10-3.

The only compositional change of importance is the increase in mean income. If income had not increased, financial satisfaction would have been nearly 0.1 point lower. This is not a large effect, but it is in the predicted direction. Further, the processual and interaction changes contribute to the same direction: both are responsible for an increase in financial satisfaction (the negative sign indicates that if there had been no change from period 1 to period 2, the financial satisfaction would have been lower; thus the change is responsible for the increase). Of special importance to the processual change is age: the positive effect of growing older on financial satisfaction has a major effect on increasing financial satisfaction over time. The processual change for income shows that it has a smaller effect on

Table 10-3
Regression-Standardization Decomposition of Changes in Mean Financial Satisfaction

Independent Variables	Changes in Mean Satisfaction Owing to Different:		
	Means	Coefficients	Interaction
Marital status	−0.018	0.006	−0.002
Sex-labor-force status	0.046	0.006	−0.014
Income	0.176	−0.098	−0.093
Race	−0.004	0.001	0.000
Age	−0.748	−0.005	0.004
Education	−0.089	−0.009	0.008
Household size	0.026	0.001	0.000
Total	−0.611	−0.097	−0.097
Differences in intercepts		0.829	
Differences in means		0.025	

financial satisfaction in earlier periods. This income effect is much smaller than the other processual changes increasing financial satisfaction.

Given that the processual, compositional, and interaction effects are responsible for increases in financial satisfaction, why has no increase been observed over time? The results show that the component measuring differences between the intercepts is positive, which effectively balances the other changes. What does the effect of the intercepts mean? It actually refers to changes that are unmeasured in the model. Thus there have been changes in the means of evaluating financial satisfaction independent of changes in income and the other variables. These processual changes mitigate the positive effect that higher income should have on financial satisfaction.

It may be, as suggested by Duncan (1975) and Easterlin (1973), that financial satisfaction has not risen with income because the perceived relative position of persons in the income distribution has not changed. A measure of perceived position in the NORC data allows a test of this hypothesis. Table 10-4 presents the gross and net effects of time on perceived relative financial standing. Over time, the gross effects do not show major improvement in the relative standing of aged persons. The net effects show that controlling for income, perceived financial standing declines: if there had been no increase in income over time, financial standing would be

Table 10-4
Multiple-Classification Analysis of the Effect of Time on Perceived Relative Financial Standing: NORC Males and Females Aged 60 and Over

		Relative Financial Standing[a]	
	N	Gross	Net[b]
Time			
1972	324	−0.06	0.04
1973	280	0.06	0.11
1974	288	0.07	0.07
1975	310	0.02	0.03
1976	340	−0.04	−0.07
1977	272	−0.04	−0.12
1978	301	0.01	−0.07
		0.06	0.10 *
R^2			0.270
Grand mean			2.72
df			2,095
N			2,115

[a]Far above average = 5, above average = 4, average = 3, below average = 2, far below average = 1.

[b]Control variables: Income in current dollars, marital status, sex-labor-force status, race, age, education, household size (as in table 11-2).

lower. Since income did increase, financial satisfaction did not decline. Thus, given that there has been little change in perceived relative standing, it is not surprising that there has been little change in financial satisfaction.

Summary

Changes in the income levels of the aged should increase levels of financial satisfaction according to a compositional argument. Yet, financial satisfaction has changed little among the aged over the last twenty-five years—there is only a small fluctuation corresponding to fluctuations in economic growth. The reason for the lack of change in financial satisfaction seems to be that older persons have not perceived improvement in their relative financial position. Over time, the standards for evaluating the adequacy of income or the expectations for income have increased in ways that have prevented increases in financial satisfaction from occurring. This is again further evidence for processual changes in the determination of financial satisfaction; it replicates the results of Duncan (1975) for a local sample of adults of all ages.

The results have shown that at least financial satisfaction did not decline over time. But at the same time it did not increase along with improvements in income. This may reflect, first, misperceptions of the aged about changes in their relative financial standing. Increases in the income of the aged relative to that of the non-aged may not have been large enough to influence the financial satisfication of older persons. O'Gorman (1980) documented from the results of the Harris (1972) survey that older persons tend to overestimate the levels of financial and social problems in the aged population. Second, the use of subjective indicators of the status of the aged may be of limited use because subjective expectations rise as quickly as objective circumstances. Any long-run change in subjective measures such as financial satisfaction may be rare. This is not to say that objective improvements are unimportant because they do not translate into subjective improvements. On the contrary, policy-related programs to help the aged must focus on objective circumstances because they have little control over subjective expectations. Thus researchers may need to focus primarily on objective rather than subjective indicators in the study of social change and the aged in the future.

Note

1. Liang and Fairchild (1979) and Liang, Kahana, and Doherty (1980) also use a measure of change in financial situation in the last year to predict current financial situation. This measure, along with perceived relative

financial standing, is argued to mediate the effect of income on financial satisfaction. Although the measure of change in financial situation is available for both the SRC and the NORC data, I have chosen not to include it in the models to follow. When analysis is being made of consecutive cross-sectional surveys, the effects of time are intended to capture changes in financial satisfaction. Inclusion of a variable measuring change in situation may remove the effects of most interest. Further, it is not clear that change in financial satisfaction causally precedes current financial satisfaction; both may be determined simultaneously and one cannot be considered a determinant of the other.

11

A Note on Changes in Health Levels in the Aged Population

The previous chapters have shown that increases in retirement, income, and independent living arrangements have occurred independently of changes in the compositional characteristics of the aged population. However, I have been unable to measure a number of characteristics of the aged population, one of the most important of which is health. According to the Harris (1972) survey, 20 percent of aged persons said they faced serious health problems (only one other problem—fear of crime—was said to be serious by more aged persons). Further, health problems are closely related to the variables studied in this book. Persons with poor health are likely to be out of the labor force, to have low income, and to share the households of relatives. If there have been changes in health levels, these may explain some of the changes in retirement levels, income, and living arrangements demonstrated in the previous chapters. In other words, health may be a neglected compositional variable, the influence of which must be identified before the compositional explanation can be rejected and the processual explanation accepted.

The effect of health levels on the position of the aged depends on the direction of changes in health. On the one hand, if health levels have declined, they may help explain increases in retirement since persons with health problems may find it difficult to work. On the other hand, if health levels have improved, they may help explain increases in income and independent living arrangements.[1]

The literature on health of the aged is of little help in identifying the direction of the changes or the effect on other trends. Most studies of health of the aged have been cross-sectional, and those that have studied changes over time have provided contradictory evidence. Burgess (1960) argued that prolongation of life has changed the composition of the aged population so that less healthy, less robust persons have been more likely to survive into old age in recent years than they were in the past. The survival of more people past age 65 may have changed the nature of the aged population to include older, less healthy persons and to reduce the mean health levels of the aged population.[2] Others have similarly argued that the health of older persons may have declined, but for different reasons. Bowen and Finegan (1969) suggest that the entrance of World War I veterans into old age increased the disability levels in old age, and Parsons (1978) suggests that increased disability benefits have led more persons to interpret their health as disabling.

In contrast, Palmore (1976) has argued that cohort improvements in nutrition, health care, and standard of living have increased the health levels of persons entering old age in more recent years. Further, improvements in medical care offered to older persons in more recent years may have improved the health of the aged.

Thus there is contradictory evidence on changes in health levels and their effects on retirement levels, income, and living arrangements. It would be ideal to have individual-level data on health or disability that cover several time periods so that compositional effects of health on the indicators could be examined. Since such measures are not available, the alternative is to examine macrolevel trends in measures of health.[3] Depending on the extent of changes in the macrolevel data, inferences can be made about the influence of health on processual changes found for retirement levels, income, and living arrangements. If there is little or no change in health levels, the support for the processual explanation will remain. If health levels decline, they can be assumed to have partly affected the upward trend in retirement. If health levels improve, they can be assumed to explain partially increases in income and independent living arrangements. Thus this brief chapter will examine the trend in several macrolevel indicators of health and will discuss the implications of the results for findings in the previous chapters.

Data

Time-series data since 1961 on health levels of the population have been published from the results of the National Health Survey done by the National Center for Health Statistics. The survey from which the indicators are calculated is based on a probability sample of the civilian noninstitutional population. The results of the survey are then tabulated and published for sex and age groups of the population. Before considering the exact measurements of health that are used by the survey, a major problem in the sampling procedures must be mentioned: institutionalized persons, a category usually including those with the most severe health problems, are not included. Although survey results will therefore underestimate the health problems of the aged, the bias will not be large and is unlikely to change much over time. The proportion of persons in institutions is small—less than 5 percent—and has increased little since 1961. Thus improvements in health may be only slightly exaggerated in the data by the exclusion of persons with poor health who enter institutions and nursing homes.

The specific measures used by the surveys are the average number of restricted-activity days per person per year and the average number of disability days per person per year. A restricted-activity day involves reduction of usual activity due to illness or injury. A bed-disability day, which is also counted as a restricted-activity day, involves confinement to bed for the greater part of a day because of illness or emergency. Both measures focus on identifiable behavior rather than on general statements of self-rated health. These indicators are disaggregated by sex and age and can be measured for males and females aged 65 and over. These data are available only for 1961 and later. This time span is not as long as those in the earlier chapters, but the figures provide eighteen time points, which are enough to identify trends.

Trends for the average number of restricted-activity days per male and female aged 65 and over are presented in figure 11-1. For males, the figures show a decline in restricted-activity days until a low point is reached in 1970, followed by an increase to a point above the previous high point. Although there is a good deal of fluctuation in the trends, the figures reflect more than random error. Regression analysis shows that time has a significant curvilinear effect on male restricted activity and that the variance explained by a time quadratic is significantly greater than 0.[4] For females a similar pattern is apparent: levels decline during the 1960s only to increase back to original levels during the 1970s.

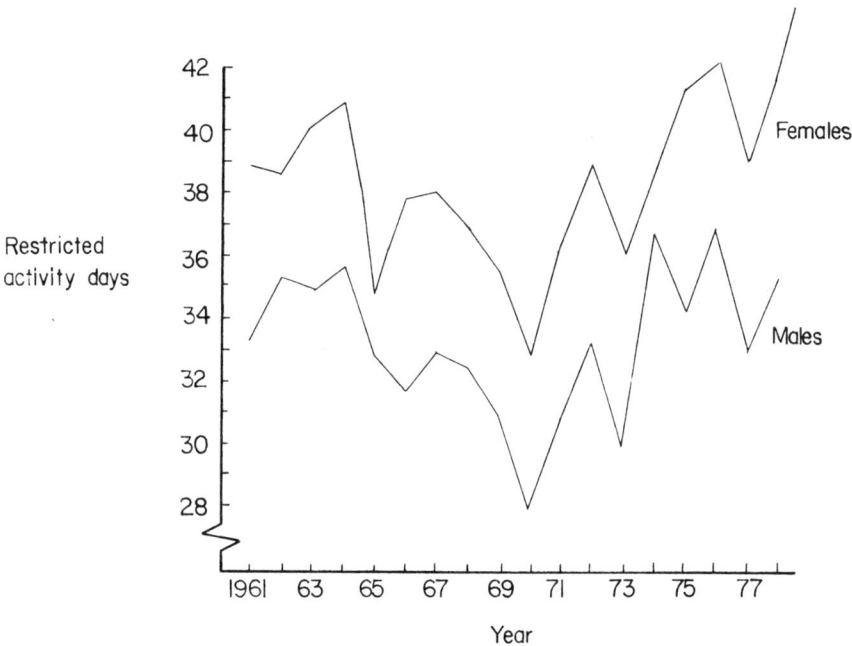

Figure 11-1. Trend in Restricted-Activity Days per Person per Year for Males and Females Aged 65 and Over

Despite the existence of the trends, there is not much variation in the measures of health. Table 11-1 presents the means and standard deviations for both measures of restricted-activity days. The means and standard deviations are larger for females than for males, perhaps because there are more females at the oldest ages. Yet neither group shows much variation over time in restricted-activity days. The coefficients of variation, or the standard deviation divided by the mean (Blalock 1979), are not large. Thus relative to the mean, there has been only a 7- to 8-percent change on the average.

For bed-disability days, the pattern of change is similar to those for restricted-activity days (figure 11-2). There is an initial decline, followed by an increase. The mean levels of disability, however, are much lower than the mean levels of restricted activity; and the standard deviations are also smaller. Regression analysis shows that the trend results from more than random fluctuation but that the levels of change are again relatively small compared to the mean.

Summary

Given the pattern of change in these indicators of health, it is unlikely that they can explain much of the change that has occurred in retirement levels, income, and living arrangements. Whereas health levels showed a curvilinear pattern of change, the other indicators have increased steadily since 1961. Further, the amount of change that occurs in the indicators of health is not large enough to account for the major trends in the other indicators. For instance, in 1978 the average number of bed-disability days per person for the male and female aged population was 14.5. That translates into 331 billion disability days for the 22 million aged persons. An increase of 1 disability day per person (about the size of the standard deviation for the years from 1961-1978) would add 22 million disability days to the aged

Table 11-1
Means and Standard Deviations for Indicators of Health for the Years 1961-1978

	$\overline{X}$	S	$S/\overline{X}$
Restricted-activity days			
Males	33.19	2.38	0.072
Females	38.14	2.81	0.073
Bed-disability days			
Males	12.73	1.18	0.093
Females	14.64	1.13	0.077

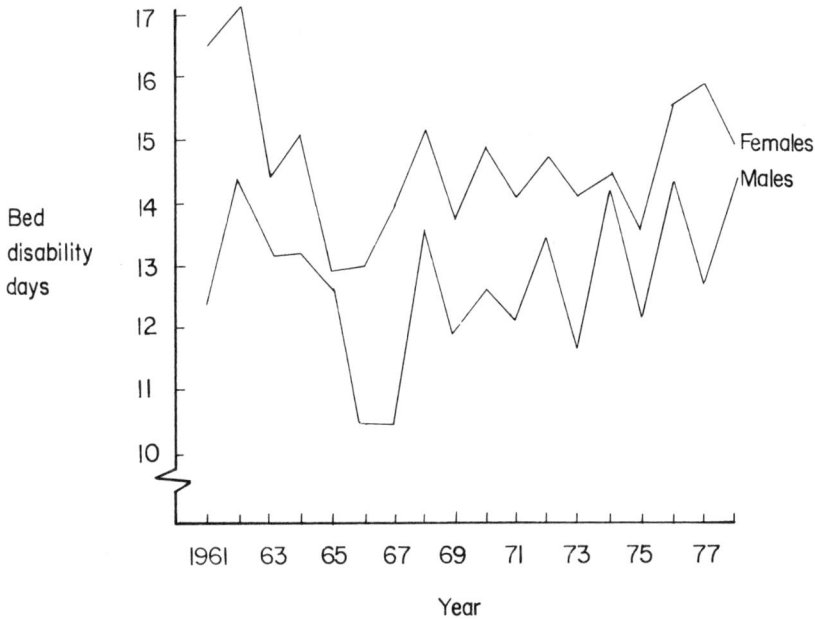

Figure 11-2. Trend in Bed-Disability Days per Person per Year for Females and Males Aged 65 and Over

population. One disability day per person is not likely to affect labor-force participation, income, or living arrangements. It is unlikely that the disability days will be distributed equally among all persons in the aged population, however. Another way to look at the increase of 1 disability day per person is that 3.3 percent of the aged population experiences a change in disability days of 60 days. In either case, the percentage of the population involved is small and unlikely to explain the larger trends in other indicators of the position of the aged.

Whatever is responsible for the curvilinear trend in restricted activity and bed-disability days among the aged has also affected non-aged persons. When the measures of disability for older persons are divided by the corresponding measures for persons aged 18 to 64, the ratios show a small, steady decline without a significant curvilinear trend (Palmore 1976). The increases in disability among the aged shown in figures 10-1 and 10-2 are smaller than the increases for the younger population. The cause of the changes in health levels is not unique to aged persons and would be unable to explain unique changes in the position of the aged in society.

At best, the recent increase in disability levels may be related to early retirement and the existence of disability benefits for those who are unable to work. Parsons (1978) compares self-rated health with an objective measure—mortality within five years—and finds that self-rated health is declining and participation increasing when higher levels of disability benefits are made available. The disability program was instituted in the late 1950s, however, and cannot explain the initial decline in disability days. Only during the 1970s can increases in transfer programs explain higher disability and higher nonparticipation. For the most part, then, support for the processual explanation of changes in the social position of the aged is maintained.

Notes

1. The effect of poor health on labor-force participation and living arrangements is direct, since persons who face physical limitations may find it difficult to work or live alone. The effect of health on income, however, must be more indirect. Income can be affected when persons are forced out of the labor force without desired pension benefits.

2. Most of the reduction of mortality in the aged population has involved immunity from infectious diseases. Since these diseases strike at all ages, the chances of survival to and past age 65 have increased. During old age, however, degenerative diseases are becoming more common; and medical advancements against these diseases have been less successful. An increase in the number of people who reach old age may have the ironic effect of subjecting more people to the incidence of chronic degenerative diseases. In short, the expansion of the aged population with the increase in incidence of chronic diseases at the expense of infectious diseases may decrease the health status of the aged.

3. The census has gathered data on disability in the 15-percent survey of the population. However, I have data available for individual-level analysis only from the 5-percent survey, which does not contain the disability measures.

4. The analysis involved regression of the indicators of disability on a time variable where 1961 is coded 1, 1962 is coded 2, and so on, until 1978 is coded 18. Time is treated as a quadratic; that is, terms for time and time squared are included in the equation to allow for curvilinearity. The significance of the time-squared term in the equations shows the existence of the curvilinear relationships. Further, significant F-tests for the variance explained provided further evidence for the existence of a significant trend.

12 Summary and Discussion

This study has been concerned with changes in the social position of the aged-in the postindustrial United States, specifically from 1948 to 1978. For a long time, the evidence suggested that the status of the aged declined with the industrialization and urbanization of Western countries. It was argued that occupational changes separated older workers from the work roles; that geographic mobility and urbanization isolated older persons from family contacts; and that health problems, retirement, and family isolation all combined to reduce the income of the aged. More recently, literature has suggested that the loss of status that occurred with industrialization has been reversed in postindustrial societies. Changes in both the characteristics of aged persons and the nature of aging have occurred to mitigate the effects of the trends that are said to harm the status of the aged in industrial societies. Yet studies of the more recent changes have been rare, and documentation of the improvement in the position of the aged has been inadequate. One objective of this study, then, has been to provide a more detailed description of changes in several indicators of the position of the aged—labor-force status, income, living arrangements, and health—in the United States from 1948 to 1978.

A second objective is to test some of the theoretical arguments that have been offered as explanations of improvements in the status of the aged in postindustrial countries. One explanation focuses on the effect of the process of cohort replacement on the composition of the aged population. A number of authors have argued that cohorts entering old age in the last fifteen or twenty years are better prepared for the problems of old age by virtue of having higher levels of education, higher-status occupations, more urban residents, better health, and higher income. Replacement of older cohorts by the "new old" has improved the position of the aged in society. Cohort analysis is recommended as a means of identifying the influence of these changes—indeed, analysis of the aged without reference to cohort differences is argued to be misleading (Riley, Johnson, and Foner 1972). An alternative, but not mutually exclusive, explanation focuses not on the changing characteristics of older persons but on the changing environment that they face. For instance, period changes in government support for service and transfer-income programs for the aged, the influence of interest groups acting on behalf of the aged, and the normative support for retirement have all improved the standing of aged persons in every age and cohort group. These two analytically separable explanations have been implicit in the literature on aging but have not been explicitly tested before.

This study has attempted to describe changes in the indicators of the position of the aged through analysis of two types of data. The first type, which is most often studied by researchers, consists of macrolevel, time-series data based on summary measures of characteristics of the total aged population for specified time periods, usually years. The second type of data consists of consecutive cross-sectional surveys that measure identical variables for different samples of older persons over a number of time points. These data allow examination of changes in the characteristics of individual aged persons rather than in summary measures for all aged persons. For both types of data, three major indicators of the status of the aged in contemporary society are examined: labor-force participation, income, and living arrangements. Consideration of changes in financial satisfaction, using the cross-sectional data, and in health levels, using the time-series data, are also made. Further, in all cases the indicators are studied separately for males and females and, in some cases, separately for whites and nonwhites.

The results of the analysis cover a great deal of material; in fact, each chapter provides a problem and analysis that can stand alone. But there have been several themes running through each of the chapters. In the following sections, I provide an overview of the results along with a discussion of their major implications.

Review of Results

The analysis begins with an examination of changes in labor-force participation. For males, the downward trend in participation is shown to result partly from increases in retirement income and occupational changes increasing the proportion of workers in nonagricultural, wage and salary occupations. Nonetheless, increases in the probability of retirement are found to occur above and beyond these compositional changes. In other words, persons in the same occupational and financial situation are more likely to retire in later years than in earlier years. Thus processual effects on changes in retirement levels and labor-force participation outweigh the effect of compositional changes and indicate that period events have occurred that increase the likelihood of retirement for all groups in the aged population.

For females, the increase in labor-force participation of the more recently born cohorts entering old age was demonstrated. Once controlling for the decline in housewives during middle age, however, changes in retirement levels among women have been similar to such changes among men: there have been both compositional and processual changes in levels of retirement, with the latter changes dominating. The results, then, demonstrate the existence of counterbalancing forces—increases in participation among cohorts entering old age and decreases resulting from retirement during old age.

Despite increases in retirement levels among males and females, income for both groups in constant dollars has increased since the 1940s, and income relative to that of the non-aged has increased since the 1960s. Although increases in educational levels across cohorts have had a small positive effect on income, they have been balanced by other compositional changes that have a negative effect on income. Overall, however, these compositional effects are small compared with processual effects that have increased the income of all educational, occupational, labor-force status, and cohort groups. The major cause of the increases involves improvements in transfer benefits and the standard of living. For females, these increases in income have occurred among low-income widows and unrelated individuals as well as among married, working women.

The results show that income differences between males and females and between whites and nonwhites decline during old age. Although the growth of income has increased the differences in income that the groups bring into old age, the process of leveling has at the same time increased so that the differences are reduced more in recent time periods. Overall, this has led to a decline in income inequality within the aged population, which is all the more surprising given the increase in low-income, high-inequality groups such as retirees and unrelated individuals. These findings thus indicate changes in the distribution of income in the aged population that primarily benefit the low-income aged.

One result of the change in income has been the growth of nonfamilial or independent living arrangements. The data show major increases in female and male unrelated individuals and persons living along (the proportion of persons in group quarters and institutions shows no real increase). The results show that levels of nonfamilial living arrangements have increased faster than would be expected on the basis of growth in income alone; they suggest that older persons perceive living alone as more desirable now than they did in the past. Persons with the same income are more likely to live alone in more recent periods than in the past, which means that persons are more willing to sacrifice the income they might gain from moving in with others in order to live alone. These trends are examined only for nonmarried persons, and therefore control for small increases in the proportion of older persons who are married.

Analysis of time-series results shows that small changes in levels of disability have occurred but that they are too small and fluctuate too much to explain changes in the other indicators. Since health levels can be seen as a neglected compositional variable, the results of the analysis indicate that compositional changes have not had a large effect on the indicators studied and that the processual effects found in the previous chapters cannot be explained by changes in health levels.

Finally, I have supplemented the analysis of the objective indicators with analysis of one subjective measure—finanacial satisfaction. Compositional changes in income should increase levels of financial satisfaction, but processual changes counteract the increases in income so that financial satisfaction changes little over the last twenty years. The process of evaluating the adequacy of income has changed to prevent higher income from increasing financial satisfaction. In general, then, subjective measures do not appear to change much over time despite objective changes; and I argued that objective changes may be the more useful focus of study for those interested in social change.

Compositional Changes and Cohort Analysis

A major implication of this study is that compositional changes in general and cohort analysis in particular explain little of the change in the indicators of the social characteristics of the aged in the United States since World War II. Historical changes in the educational system, occupational structure, and urbanization have affected the characteristics that cohorts have brought into old age during the last several decades, but such changes have not had large effects on any of the indicators studied. Other compositional changes in retirement levels and income likewise have had no more than modest effects on most indicators.

Consider some of the findings that show lack of support for the compositional and cohort arguments. First, income has increased among nearly all groups in the aged population—that is, increases have occurred independent of compositional characteristics. In fact, an analysis considering age, period, and cohort effects simultaneously shows little increase in income resulting from the entrance of new cohorts into the population. Second, it has been suggested that compositional changes in the labor-force experience and living arrangements of older women affect the income experiences of older women. Yet income among females in all labor-force-status and household-status groups has increased over time. The increase in older women living alone has modestly reduced mean family income, and the increase in labor-force experience has modestly increased mean family income; but neither effect is large compared to processual increases in income. Third, compositional changes in income should increase retirement levels, nonfamilial living arrangements, and financial satisfaction. For each of the indicators, income is able to explain only part of the changes over time. Retirement and independent living arrangements have increased to levels beyond those that would be predicted to occur through the effect of increasing income, and financial satisfaction has not changed at all despite increases in income.

The one exception to the lack of large compositional effects concerns the labor-force participation of females. More recently born cohorts have experienced greater opportunities for labor-force participation during middle age (Farkas 1977). Once in the labor force, persons in more recent cohorts bring their participation into old age, where they either continue to work or retire. The cohort changes almost completely explain the changes in the levels of housewives in the aged population in the last several decades. Once controlling for these changes, trends in retirement for women—as well as for men—reflect the influence of period events rather than of cohort differences in the predispositions to retire.

In short, period events or processual changes better explain changes in the social characteristics of the aged than do compositional or cohort changes. This supports Atchley and Seltzer's (1976) criticism of the work of Riley, Johnson, and Foner (1972) that the influence of cohort characteristics tends to become less important as cohorts grow older and reach old age. Atchley and Seltzer suggest that the similarities and cohesion of persons in the same cohort will decline over time. Differences across cohorts are not likely to exert great influence for persons in their sixties or seventies.

These findings also have implications for economic theories of retirement and living arrangements. Economic theories focus on the ability of persons to afford or purchase the leisure of retirement and the autonomy of living alone. Increases in income are argued to have allowed more persons to purchase this leisure and autonomy. In fact, these conceptualizations present income as a compositional variable explaining the rise in retirement levels and independent living arrangements; for the most part, they do not consider normative changes in preferences or tastes for these goods. The results here show that even if income had not increased, retirement and independent living arrangements would nonetheless have grown significantly. Shifts have occurred in the way income affects decisions to retire or live alone; these shifts are seldom captured by economic models of the change. Changes in tastes or preferences need to be considered along with changes in income in order to explain changes in the characteristics of the aged population.

Macro- and Microlevel Analysis

One advantage of this analysis in identifying the influence of compositional effects compared to processual effects, or the effects of income compared with the effects of tastes, is the use of individual-level cross-sectional data to supplement the more commonly measured macrolevel time-series data. The analysis of cohort differences has typically involved comparison of aggregate characteristics (Cain 1967; Uhlenberg 1977). The effect of aggregate differences across cohorts on indicators of the position of the aged may be misleading, however. In time-series analyses, the effect of aggregated, compositional variables on other aggregate indicators were overestimated because they spuriously captured processual changes in attitudes or tastes. For example, the effect of occupation change on labor-force participation levels was shown to be exaggerated in the aggregate time-series data. Similarly, the effect of increased income on independent living arrangements was found to be much larger with the aggregate data than with the cross-sectional data. Analysis of consecutive cross-sectional surveys thus provides the opportunity to estimate more precisely the effect of compositional and cohort changes and should be used to supplement time-series analysis of aggregate data in the study of social change.

Processual Effects

I have defined processual effects as changes in the indicators of the position of the aged that occur independently of compositional changes; they involve a change in the way compositional factors affect the indicators being studied. The extent of processual effects is shown by the net effects of time on the dependent variables. The effects of time show increases in the probability of being retired or living alone, or increases in mean income, that affect all groups in the aged population. When treated this way, processual effects are primarily descriptive rather than explanatory: time is a proxy variable summarizing a large number of forces that affect the aged population.

Rejection of the compositional arguments and demonstration of the existence of processual effects, then, set the stage for more detailed consideration of the meaning of the processual changes. I have discussed briefly some of the changes responsible for the processual effects of time. Increases in the standard of living for the total population, along with higher public and private pension benefits, have increased the income of the aged population; normative changes in the support of leisure and independence have affected labor-force participation and living arrangements; and efforts of interest-groups and intellectuals in the support of the aged have diminished the stereotyping and discrimination faced by the aged (Calhoun 1978). These changes, although they cannot be measured well with the data analyzed in this book, are consistent with the findings of the previous chapters. With the detailed description of the processual changes provided by this research, future research using new and different types of data can further identify the sources of the processual changes.

Convergence in Patterns of Aging

I stated that processual effects affect all groups in the aged population. But the results provide evidence that some groups are affected more than others and that there is convergence in the patterns of retirement, income determination, and living arrangements among different groups in the aged population. Henretta and Campbell (1976) have argued that status differences between persons during middle age are maintained during old age. The evidence in this book supports the existence of status differences within the aged population, but shows also that some of the differences have been declining over time. The prime evidence for this contention is that income inequality within the aged population has occurred. Despite increases in retirees and unrelated individuals—both groups with low income and high income inequality—overall inequality within the aged population has been lower in more recent years. (This conclusion, however, refers only to income inequality and might differ had measures of in-kind benefits or assets been available.) Further, chapter 8 showed that income differentials between whites and nonwhites or between males and females decline during old age. In other words, old age levels income differences between ascribed status groups. Over time, income gaps between the groups entering old age have increased while the process of leveling has also increased so that the income gaps are further reduced during old age. Finally, there is modest evidence that educational and residential differentials in retirement levels, income, and living arrangements have declined over time. Thus convergence in the effects of the background variables on the indicators studied, and convergence in the indicators themselves, has occurred.

Postindustrialization and the Aged

What implications do the results have for theories of the changing status of the aged? I have avoided a simple interpretation of the indicators studied here as "quality of life" measures, since such interpretations involve value judgments. Yet the analysis in earlier chapters provides some information on the meaning to the aged of changes in their social position and whether or not the changes can be interpreted as improvements. First, theories of modernization and aging typically consider retirement a loss of status. Cowgill and Holmes (1972) and Burgess (1960) argue that the aged are valued in societies where they continue to perform valued and useful functions. Since retirement is seen as loss of productive function, the higher retirement rates experienced recently may be interpreted as an indication of declining status. Yet this interpretation depends on the cause of retirement. Are older persons forced to retire against their will because they are no longer valued, or are older persons attracted to retirement by the promise of leisure time and pension benefits? Based on the analysis of the cross-sectional data, and on the findings of Schulz (1976), I have argued that increases in retirement are primarily the result of increased normative support and demand for retirement and leisure. Increases in transfer benefits have also been important in attracting persons to retirement, but alone are not able to explain the trend in the last several decades. There is little evidence that changes in the occupational structure, generational competition for jobs, obsolescence of jobs, or cohort differences have strongly affected the trend in retirement. Thus in postindustrial societies increases in retirement need to be reinterpreted as involving partial improvement in the status of the aged.

The improvement in the income status of the aged, in relative and absolute terms, provides the clearest indication of the improved status of the aged. This is especially true when the trend is accompanied by increases in retirement and leisure time. The cause of the increase is not that persons bring the financial benefits of middle age into old age, but that persons are treated more favorably in old age in recent years than they were in the past. Further, the decline in income inequality shows that increases in income have gone to the neediest groups in the aged population as well as to the most advantaged.

Changes in family living arrangements have often been viewed as the result of older persons being forced to live alone and to depend on state support because of lack of family support. More recent studies suggest that independent living arrangements are desired by both parents and their adult children. Accordingly, increases over time in nonfamilial living arrangements were found to result from increases in income that allow older persons to live alone and increases in demand for autonomous living arrangements, which lead some persons to live alone despite low income. Thus there is little evidence that this trend indicates forced segregation or loss of status of the aged.

In summary, the results of this book support the contention that, after a decline during industrialization, the status of the aged improves in postindustrial society (Palmore and Manton 1974; Cowgill 1974). The objective resources measured here—increases in income, the ability to retire, and the opportunity to live alone—have improved. These indicators do not measure components of the status of the aged such as prestige or respect, nor do they show that all the disadvantages of the aged relative to the non-aged have disappeared. Yet the resources studied here are important aspects of the status of the aged, greatly affect the relationships between the aged and non-aged (Dowd 1975; Gubrium, 1973), and show improvements over the last several decades in the United States.

Bibliography

Achenbaum, W. Andrew. 1978. *Old Age in the New Land: The American Experience since 1790*. Baltimore, Md.: Johns Hopkins Press.

Almquist, E. 1975. "Untangling the Effects of Race and Sex: The Disadvantaged Status of Black Women." *Social Science Quarterly* 56:129-135.

Althauser, R.P., and Wigler, M. 1972. "Standardization and Component Analysis." *Sociological Methods and Research* 1:97-135.

Andrews, Frank M.; Morgan, James N.; Sonquist, John A.; and Klem, Laura. 1974. *Multiple Classification Analysis*. Ann Arbor: Institute for Social Research, University of Michigan.

Atchley, Robert C. 1976. *The Sociology of Retirement*. Cambridge, Mass.: Schenkman.

_____ . 1977. *The Social Forces in Later Life*. Belmont, Calif.: Wadsworth.

Atchley, Robert C., and Seltzer, M.M. 1976. "Age Grading and the Life Course." In *The Sociology of Aging*, edited by Robert C. Atchley and Mildred M. Seltzer, pp. 1-4. Selected Readings. Belmont, Calif.: Wadsworth.

Bane, Mary Jo. 1976. *Here to Stay: American Families in the Twentieth Century*. New York: Basic Books.

Barfield, Richard E., and Morgan, James. 1969. *Early Retirement: The Decision and the Experience*. Ann Arbor: Institute for Social Research, University of Michigan.

Barfield, Richard E., and Morgan, J.N. 1978. "Trends in Planned Early Retirement." *The Gerontologist* 18:13-18.

Bell, Daniel. 1973. *The Coming of Post-Industrial Society*. New York: Basic Books.

Beresford, J.C., and Rivlin, A.M. 1966. "Privacy, Poverty, and Old Age." *Demography* 3:247-258.

Berk, R.A. 1977. "Proof? No. Evidence? No. A Skeptic's Comment on Inverarity's Use of Statistical Inference." *American Sociological Review* 42:652-656.

Blalock, Hubert M., Jr. 1979. *Social Statistics*. Rev. 2nd ed. New York: McGraw-Hill.

Boskin, M. 1977. "Social Security and Retirement Decisions." *Economic Inquiry* 15:1-25.

Bowen, William G., and Finegan, T. Aldrich. 1969. *The Economics of Labor Force Participation*. Princeton, N.J.: Princeton University Press.

Brennan, Michael J.; Taft, Philip; and Schupack, Mark B. 1967. *The Economics of Age*. New York: Norton.

Brody, Elaine M. 1977. *Long-Term Care for Older People*. New York: Human Sciences Press.

Burgess, E.W. 1960. "Aging in Western Culture." In *Aging in Western Societies*, edited by Ernest W. Burgess, pp. 3-28. Chicago: University of Chicago Press.

Butler, Robert N. 1975. *Why Survive: Being Old in America*. New York: Harper and Row.

Cain, Glen. 1966. *Married Women in the Labor Force*. Chicago: University of Chicago Press.

Cain, L.D., Jr. 1967. "Age Status and Generational Phenomena: The New Old People in Contemporary America." *The Gerontologist* 7:83-92.

_____ . 1974. "The Growing Importance of Legal Age in Determining the Status of the Aged." *The Gerontologist* 14:167-174.

Calhoun, Richard B. 1978. *In Search of the New Old: Redefining Old Age in America, 1945-1970*. New York: Elsevier North Holland.

Campbell, Angus; Converse, Philip E.; and Rogers, Willard L. 1976. *The Quality of American Life: Perceptions, Evaluations, and Satisfactions*. New York: Russell Sage.

Carliner, G. 1975. "Determinants of Household Headship." *Journal of Marriage and the Family* 37:28-38.

Clark, R.C.; Kreps, J.; and Spengler, J. 1978. "Economics of Aging: A Survey." *Journal of Economic Literature* 16:919-962.

Clemente, F., and Summers, G.F. 1973. "A Comment on Palmore and Whittington's Relative Status of the Aged." *Social Forces* 51:494-495.

Cowgill, D.O. 1974. "Aging and Modernization: A Revision of the Theory." In *Late Life, Communities and Environmental Policy*, edited by Jaber F. Gubrium, pp. 123-146. Springfield, Ill.: Charles C. Thomas.

Cowgill, D.O., and Holmes, Lowell D. 1972. *Aging and Modernization*. New York: Appleton-Century-Crofts.

Danziger, S., and Plotnick, R. 1977. "Demographic Change, Government Transfers, and Income Distribution." *Monthly Labor Review* (April):7-11.

Dowd, J.J. 1975. "Aging as Exchange: A Preface to Theory." *Journal of Gerontology* 30:584-594.

Dowd, J.J., and Bengston, V.L. 1978. "Aging in Minority Populations: An Examination of the Double Jeopardy Hypothesis." *Journal of Gerontology* 33:427-436.

Dualabs. 1973. *Technical Documentation for the 1960 Public Use Sample*. Rosslyn, Virg.: Dualabs.

Duncan, O.D. 1975. "Does Money Buy Satisfaction." *Social Indicators Research* 2:267-274.

Durkheim, Emile. 1947. *The Division of Labor in Society*. Glencoe, Ill.: Free Press.

Easterlin, R.A. 1973. "Does Money Buy Happiness?" *The Public Interest* 30:3-10.

———. 1978. "What Will 1984 Be Like? Socioeconomic Implications of Recent Twists in the Age Structure." *Demography* 15:397-432.

Elder, Glen H., Jr. 1974. *Children of the Great Depression: Social Change in Life Experience*. Chicago: University of Chicago Press.

Farkas, G. 1977. "Cohort, Age, and Period Effects Upon the Employment of White Females: Evidence for 1957-1968." *Demography* 14:33-42.

Firebaugh, G. 1978. "Cross-National Versus Historical Regression Models: Conditions of Equivalence in Comparative Analysis." Paper presented at the annual meeting of the American Sociological Association, San Francisco.

Fischer, David Hackett. 1978. *Growing Old in America*. Expanded ed. Oxford: Oxford University Press.

Foner, A. 1975. "Age in Society: Structure and Change." *American Behavioral Scientist* 19:144-165.

Friedman, E.A., and Orbach, H.L. 1974. "Adjustment to Retirement." In *American Handbook of Psychiatry*, edited by Silvano Arieti, pp. 605-645. New York: Basic Books.

Fuguitt, G.V., and Lieberson, S. 1974. "Correlation of Ratios or Difference Scores having Common Terms." *Sociological Methodology 1973-1974*, edited by Herbert L. Costner, pp. 128-144. San Francisco: Jossey-Bass.

Fuguitt, G.V., and Tordella, S.J. 1980. "Elderly Net Migration: The New Trend of Nonmetropolitan Population Change." *Research on Aging* 2:191-204.

Glenn, N.D. 1976. "Cohort Analysts' Futile Quest: Statistical Attempts to Separate Age, Period, and Cohort Effects." *American Sociological Review* 41:900-903.

Gubrium, Jaber F. 1973. *The Myth of the Golden Years: A Socio-Environmental Theory of Aging*. Springfield, Ill.: Charles Thomas.

Harris, Louis and Associates, 1972. *The Myth and Reality of Aging in America*. New York: National Council on Aging.

Henretta, J.C., and Campbell, R.T. 1976. "Status Attainment and Status Maintenance: A Study of Stratifiation in Old Age." *American Sociological Review* 41:981-992.

Hochschild, Arlie R. 1973. *The Unexpected Community*. Englewood Cliffs, N.J.: Prentice-Hall.

———. 1975. "Disengagement Theory: A Critique and Proposal." *American Sociological Review* 40:553-569.

House, J.S. 1979. "The University of Michigan Election Surveys as a Data Resource for Sociologists." *Contemporary Sociology* 8:46-53.

Iams, H.H., and Thornton, A. 1973. "Decomposition of Differences: A Cautionary Note." *Sociological Methods and Research* 3:341-352.

Irelan, L.M. 1972. "Retirement History Study: Introduction." *Social Security Bulletin* 35(11):3-8.

Jaffe, J.J. 1971. "Has the Retreat from the Labor Force Halted?" A Note on Retirement of Men 1930-1970." *Industrial Gerontology* 9:1-12.

Johnson, M. 1973. "A Comment on Palmore and Whittington's Index of Similarity." *Social Forces* 51:490-492.

Kalish, R.A. 1979. "The New Ageism and the Failure Models: A Polemic." *The Gerontologist* 19:388-402.

Kasshau, P.L. 1976. "Retirement and the Social System." *Industrial Gerontology* 3:3-8.

Kent, D.P. 1971. "The Elderly in Minority Groups: Variant Patterns of Aging." *The Gerontologist* 11(1, pt. 2):26-29.

Kitagawa, E.M. 1964. "Standardized Comparisons in Population Research." *Demography* 1:296-315.

Kmenta, Jan. 1971. *Elements of Econometrics*. New York: Macmillan.

Knoke, D. 1976. "A Comparison of Log-Linear and Regression Models for Systems of Dichotomous Variables." *Sociological Methods and Research* 3:416-434.

Knoke, D., and Hout, M. 1974. "Social and Demographic Factors in American Political Party Affiliation." *American Sociological Review* 39:700-713.

Kobrin, F.E. 1976. "The Fall of Household Size and the Rise of the Primary Individual in the United States." *Demography* 13:127-138.

Kolodrubetz, W.W. 1975. "Earnings Replacement from Private Pensions and Social Security." In *Reaching Retirement Age: Findings from a Survey of Newly Entitled Workers, 1968-1970*. Social Security Administration Report no. 47. Washington, D.C.: Social Security Administration.

Kreps, Juanita M. 1971. *Lifetime Allocation of Work and Income: Essays in the Economics of Aging*. Durham, N.C.: Duke University.

Kreps, Juanita M., and Clark, Robert. 1975. *Sex, Age, and Work: The Changing Composition of the Labor Force*. Baltimore, Md.: Johns Hopkins University.

Kuznets, S. 1974. "Demographic Aspects of the Distribution of Income Among Families: Recent Trends in the United States." In *Essays in Honor of Jan Tinbergen*, edited by Willy Sellekaerts, pp. 223-246. London: Macmillan.

Land, K.C. 1975. "Social Indicator Models: An Overview." In *Social Indicator Models*, edited by Kenneth C. Land and Seymour Spillerman, pp. 5-36. New York: Russell Sage.

Land, K.C., and Spillerman, Seymour, eds. 1975. *Social Indicator Models.* New York: Russell Sage.

Langbein, Laura Irwin, and Lichtman, Allan J. 1978. *Ecological Inference.* Beverly Hills, Calif.: Sage.

Laslett, P. 1976. "Societal Development and Aging." In *Handbook of Aging and the Social Sciences*, edited by Robert H. Binstock and Ethel Shanas, pp. 87-116. New York: Von Nostrand Reinhold.

Laslett, P. and Wall, Richard. 1972. *Household and Family in Past Time.* Cambridge, England: Cambridge University.

Liang, J. and Fairchild, T.J. 1979. "Relative Deprivation and Perception of Financial Adequacy Among the Aged." *Journal of Gerontology* 34:746-759.

Liang, J.; Kahana, E.; Doherty, E. 1980. "Financial Well-Being Among the Aged: A Further Elaboration." *Journal of Gerontology* 35:409-420.

Lieberson, S. 1970. "Stratification and Ethnic Groups." In *Social Stratification: Research and Theory in the 1970s*, edited by Edward Laumann, pp. 179-181. Indianapolis, Ind.: Bobbs-Merrill.

————. 1975. "Rank-Sum Comparisons Between Groups." In *Sociological Methodology 1976*, edited by David R. Heise, pp. 276-292. San Francisco: Jossey-Bass.

Lopata, Helena Z. 1973. *Widowhood in an American City.* Cambridge, Mass.: Schenkman.

Maddox, G.L. and Wiley, J. 1976. "Scope, Concepts and Methods in the Study of Aging." In *Handbook of Aging and the Social Sciences*, edited by Robert H. Binstock and Ethel Shanas, pp. 13-34. New York: Van Nostrand Reinhold.

Mason, K.O.; Winsborough, H.H.; Mason, W.M.; and Poole, W.K. 1973. "Some Methodological Issues in Cohort Analysis of Archival Data." *American Sociological Review* 38:242-258.

McEaddy, B.J. 1975. "Women in the Labor Force: The Later Years." *Monthly Labor Review* 98 (November):17-35.

Michael, R.T.; Fuchs, V.R.; and Scott, S.R. 1980. "Changes in the Propensity to Live Alone: 1950-1976." *Demography* 17:39-56.

Moon, Marilyn. 1977. *The Measurement of Economic Welfare: Its Application to the Aged Poor.* New York: Academic Press.

Moore, W.E. 1966. "Changes in Occupational Structures." In *Social Structure and Mobility in Economic Development*, edited by N.J. Smelser and S.M. Lipset, pp. 194-212. Chicago: Aldine.

National Council on Aging. 1972. *Triple Jeopardy: Myth or Reality.* Washington, D.C.: National Council on the Aging.

Neugarten, B.L. 1975. "The Future and the Young-Old." *The Gerontologist* 15:4-15.

Neugarten, B.L., and Datan, N. 1973. "Sociological Perspectives on the Life Cycle." In *Life-Span Developmental Psychology: Personality and Socialization*, edited by Paul B. Baltes and K. Warner Schaie, pp. 53-69. New York: Academic Press.

O'Gorman, H.J. 1980. "False Consciousness of Kind: Pluralistic Ignorance Among the Aged." *Research on Aging* 2:105-128.

Oppenheimer, Valerie K. 1970. *The Female Labor Force in the United States*. Berkeley, Calif.: Institute of International Studies.

Orbach, H. 1979. "Retirement: The Changing Pattern." Paper presented at the Leonard Z. Breen Symposium, West Lafayette, Ind.

Ostrom, Charles W., Jr. 1978. *Time Series Analysis: Regression Techniques*. Beverly Hills, Calif.: Sage Publications.

Palmore, E. 1965. "Differences in Retirement Patterns of Men and Women." *The Gerontologist* 5:4-8.

_____ . 1971. "Why Do People Retire." *Aging and Human Development* 2:269-283.

_____ . 1976. "The Future Status of the Aged." *The Gerontologist* 16: 297-302.

Palmore, E., and Manton, K. 1973. "Agism Compared to Racism and Sexism." *Journal of Gerontology* 28:363-369.

_____ . 1974. "Modernization and Status of the Aged: International Correlations." *Journal of Gerontology* 29:205-210.

Palmore, E., and Whittington, F. 1971. "Trends in the Relative Status of the Aged." *Social Forces* 50:84-91.

Parcel, T.L. 1979. "Race, Religion Labor Markets and Earnings." *American Sociological Review* 44:262-279.

Parnes, Herbert S.; Nestel, Gilbert; and Andrisani, Paul. 1973. *The Pre-Retirement Years*, vol. 3. U.S. Department of Labor, Manpower Administration, Manpower Research Monograph no. 15. Washington, D.C.: U.S. Government Printing Office.

Parsons, D.O. 1978. "The Decline of Labor Force Participation among Prime Age Males." Paper presented at the meeting of the Western Economics Association.

Parsons, T. 1954. "Age and Sex in the Social Structure of the United States." In *Essays in Sociological Theory*, pp. 89-103. Glencoe, Ill.: Free Press.

Peterson, D.A. 1973. "Financial Adequacy in Retirement: Perceptions of Older Americans." *The Gerontologist* 12:379-383.

Rainwater, Lee. 1974. *What Money Buys: Inequality and the Social Meaning of Income*. New York: Basic Books.

Reno, V.P. 1972. "Compulsory Retirement among Newly Entitled Workers." *Social Security Bulletin* 35(3):3-15.

Riley, Matilda White, and Foner, Anne. 1968. *Aging and Society*, vol. 1: *An Inventory of Research Findings*. New York: Russell Sage.

Riley, Matilda White; Johson, Marilyn; and Foner, Anne. 1972. *Aging and Society*, vol. 3: *A Sociology of Age Stratification*. New York: Russell Sage.

Rose, A.M. 1965. "Group Consciousness among the Aging." In *Older People and Their Social World*, edited by Arnold M. Rose and Warren A. Peterson, pp. 19-36. Philadelphia: Davis.

Rosenblum, M. 1975. "The Last Push: From Discouraged Worker to Involuntary Retirement." *Industrial Gerontology* 2:14-22.

Rosow, I. 1965. "And Then We Were Old." *Transaction* 2:23-31.

Ryder, N.B. 1965. "The Cohort as a Concept in the Study of Social Change." *American Sociological Review* 30:843-861.

Schulz, James H. 1976. *The Economics of Aging*. Belmont, Calif.: Wadsworth.

Shanas, E. 1979. "Social Myth as Hypothesis: The Case of the Family Relations of Old People." *The Gerontologist* 19:3-9.

Sheppard, H.L. 1976. "Work and Retirement." In *Handbook of Aging and the Social Sciences*, edited by Robert H. Binstock and Ethel Shanas, pp. 286-309. New York: Van Nostrand Reinhold.

Sherman, S.R. 1974. "Labor Force Status of Nonmarried Women on the Threshold of Retirement." *Social Security Bulletin* 9 (September): 3-15.

Shryock, Henry S., and Siegel, Jacob S. 1975. *The Methods and Materials of Demography*. Washington, D.C.: U.S. Government Printing Office.

Slavick, Fred. 1966. *Compulsory and Flexible Retirement in the American Economy*. Ithaca, N.Y.: Cornell University Press.

Soldo, B.J. 1977. "The Role of Demographic Composition in Accounting for Changes in the Distribution of Living Arrangements Among the Elderly: 1960-70." Paper presented at the annual meeting of the Population Association of America, St. Louis, Mo.

Spaeth, J.L. 1976. "Cognitive Complexity: A Dimension Underlying the Socioeconomic Achievement Process." In *Schooling and Achievement in American Society*, edited by William H. Sewell, Robert M. Hauser, and David L. Featherman, pp. 103-131. New York: Academic Press.

Stearns, Peter N. 1976. *Old Age In European Society: The Case of France*. New York: Holmes and Meier.

Streib, Gordon F., and Schneider, Clement J. 1972. *Retirement in American Society*. Ithaca, N.Y.: Cornell University.

Sussman, M.B. 1965. "Relationships of Adult Children with Their Parents in the United States." In *Social Structure and Family: Generational Relations*, edited by Ethel Shanas and Gordon Streib, pp. 62-92. Englewood Cliffs, N.J.: Prentice-Hall.

Sweet, James A. 1973. *Women in the Labor Force*. New York: Seminar Press.

Theil, Henri. 1967. *Economics and Information Theory*. Chicago: Rand McNally.

————. 1972. *Statistical Decomposition Analysis*. Amsterdam: North Holland.

Torda, T. 1972. "The Impact of Inflation on the Elderly." *Federal Reserve Bank Cleveland Economic Review* (October/November):3-19.

Treas, J., and Walther, R.J. 1978. "Family Structure and the Distribution of Family Income." *Social Forces* 56:845-865.

Troll, L.E. 1973. "The Family of Later Life: A Decade Review." *Journal of Marriage and the Family* 33:263-290.

Uhlenberg, P. 1977. "Changing Structure of the Older Population of the USA during the Twentieth Century." *The Gerontologist* 17:197-202.

U.S. Bureau of the Census. 1967. *Trends in Income of Families and Persons in the U.S. 1947-1964*. Technical Paper no. 17. Washington, D.C.: U.S. Government Printing Office.

————. 1972. *Public Use Samples of Basic Records of the 1970 Census: Description and Technical Documentation*. Washington, D.C.: U.S. Government Printing Office.

————. 1976. *Statistical Abstract*. Washington, D.C.: U.S. Government Printing Office.

U.S. Department of Health, Education, and Welfare. 1969. *Toward a Social Report*. Washington, D.C.: U.S. Government Printing Office.

Vaughan, D.R., and Lancaster, C.G. 1979. "Income Levels and Their Impact on Two Subjective Measures of Well-Being: Some Early Speculations from Working Progress." In *Statistical Uses of Administrative Records with Emphasis on Mortality and Disability Research*, edited by Linda DelBene and Fritz Schevren, pp. 169-174. Washington, D.C.: Social Security Administration.

Walker, J.W. 1976. "Will Early Retirement Retire Early?" *Personnel* 53:33-39.

Wolf, W.C., and Fligstein, N.D. 1979. "Sex and Authority in the Workplace." *American Sociological Review* 44:235-252.

Index

Index

About the Author

Fred C. Pampel is an assistant professor of sociology at the University of Iowa. He received the B.A., M.A., and Ph.D. from the University of Illinois, Urbana-Champaign. Dr. Pampel has published articles on stratification, ecology, and aging in such journals as *American Sociological Review, Social Forces*, and *Social Problems* and has presented papers at the meetings of the American Sociological Association and the Midwest Sociological Society. He is currently doing research on cross-national changes in social-security systems and labor-force participation of the aged.